GOVERNING RISK IN GM AGRICULTURE

This book addresses the issues and methods involved in governing risks posed by genetically modified (GM) agriculture. It examines the evolution of policies intended to ensure the safety of GM crops and food products in the United States and Europe, and the regulatory approaches and other social controls employed to protect human health, the environment, conventional farming and foods, and the interests and rights of consumers.

Discussion encompasses the cultural, political, and economic forces that shape the design and application of the methods of risk governance, as well as other contextual features such as the influence of multinational companies seeking acceptance of their GM ventures. This discussion also examines the influence of the dynamic public discourse fostered by progressive concepts of risk governance and the approaches taken to meet its demands for transparency, public participation, and appropriate consideration of public perceptions and values despite conflicting views of experts.

Michael Baram is Professor Emeritus at Boston University School of Law. He is the author of seven books and more than 110 articles on the social control of hazardous technologies in the United States and Europe. His research, publications, and legal and advisory activities have dealt with regulation, liability, and industrial management of risks to public and worker health and safety and the environment in several technological sectors.

Mathilde Bourrier is Professor of Sociology at the University of Geneva, Switzerland. She is the author of three books and has published numerous articles in international journals. Her research, publications, and advisory activities deal with the social construction of safety, safety management, and organizational reliability in medical, nuclear, and other technological risk sectors.

Governing Risk in GM Agriculture

Editors

Michael Baram

Boston University, School of Law

Mathilde Bourrier

University of Geneva

CAMBRIDGE UNIVERSITY PRESS
Cambridge, New York, Melbourne, Madrid, Cape Town, Singapore,
São Paulo, Delhi, Dubai, Tokyo, Mexico City

Cambridge University Press
32 Avenue of the Americas, New York, NY 10013-2473, USA

www.cambridge.org
Information on this title: www.cambridge.org/9781107001473

First published 2011

Printed in the United States of America

A catalog record for this publication is available from the British Library.

Library of Congress Cataloging in Publication data

Governing risk in GM agriculture / edited by Michael Baram, Mathilde
Bourrier.
   p. cm.
Includes bibliographical references and index.
ISBN 978-1-107-00147-3 (hardback)
1. Genetically modified foods – Law and legislation.   2. Genetically modified
foods – Safety measures.   3. Risk.   I. Baram, Michael S.   II. Bourrier, Mathilde,
1966–   III. Title: Governing risk in genetically modified agriculture.
K3927.G68   2010
344.04′232 – dc22   2010031498

ISBN 978-1-107-00147-3 Hardback

Contents

Part II: Future Challenges

Preface

New technologies may provide a vast array of societal benefits but may also threaten established interests and values, and human and environmental well-being. Thus, modern democratic societies strive to address their potential, reduce uncertainties, exploit their benefits, and minimize risks by a variety of means. Such is the case with the introduction of perhaps the most challenging technology of all, biotechnology, which provides methods of genetic manipulation that are being introduced into the agricultural and food systems of nations across the globe.

This book aims to illuminate the issues and methods involved in addressing the uncertainties and risks of genetically modified (GM) agriculture. It therefore deals with the evolution of policies intended to ensure the safety of GM crops and food products, and the diverse regulatory approaches and other social controls they employ to protect human health, the environment, conventional farming and foods, and the interests and rights of consumers.

Discussion of the policies encompasses cultural, political, and economic forces that shape their design and application, as well as other contextual features such as the influence of multinational companies seeking acceptance of their GM ventures. This discussion also examines the influence of the dynamic public discourse that is fostered by progressive concepts of risk governance, and approaches taken to meet its demands for transparency, public participation, and appropriate consideration of public perceptions and values despite conflicting views of experts.

The contributors to this book were brought together and encouraged to undertake this multidisciplinary effort by the late Professor Bernhard Wilpert of the Technical University of Berlin. Our efforts were carried out under the aegis of NeTWork, an international consortium of faculty and professionals from various organizations and disciplines that he conceived and directed for twenty-six years. Over this period, NeTWork activities have led to many workshops and publications on issues arising from the introduction of new technologies and methods of analysis and social control, including the publication of fourteen books, six special issues of professional journals, and numerous papers by the many participants inspired by their involvement in NeTWork. Further NeTWork activities are under the direction of Professor Gudela Grote, Swiss Federal Institute of Technology (ETH-Zurich); Professor Mathilde Bourrier, University of Geneva; Dr. Babette Fahlbruch, TUV Nord (Berlin); and Dr. Gilles Motet of the Fondation pour une Culture de Securite Industrielle (Toulouse).

The coeditors wish to gratefully acknowledge the support of Professor Wilpert and his staff at the Technical University of Berlin, and the several organizations that provided the resources needed to sustain NeTWork over the years: the Werner Reimers Foundation (Bad Homburg), the Maison des Sciences de l'Homme (Paris), Eindhoven University, the Technical University of Berlin, the Netherlands Ministry of Social Affairs and Employment, and now the Fondation pour une Culture de Securite Industrielle (Toulouse).

Finally, we dedicate this book to the memory of our distinguished colleague and humanistic mentor, Bernhard Wilpert.

Professors Michael Baram and Mathilde Bourrier

Contributors

Juliana Mezzomo Allain is a social psychologist at the Federal University do Santa Catarina, Brazil. Her articles and research focus on social representations of science, technology, and environment.

Michael Baram is Professor Emeritus, Boston University School of Law. His research, publications, legal, and advisory activities have dealt with regulation, liability, and industrial management of risks to public and worker health and safety and the environment in several technological sectors, including chemical and biotechnological processes and products, and nuclear and other energy-related activities.

Mathilde Bourrier is Professor of Sociology, University of Geneva, Switzerland. Her research, publications, and advisory activities deal with the social construction of safety, safety management, and organizational reliability in medical, nuclear, and other technological risk sectors.

Halina Szejnwald Brown is Professor of Environmental Science and Policy at Clark University, Worcester, Massachusetts, and was previously a chief toxicologist for state government. Her research and publications deal with the corporate role in sustainability transition, sociotechnical innovation, and environmental policy.

Paulo José Leite Farias is a public prosecutor in the Department for the Protection of Environmental and Urban Interests of the Federal District and Territories of Brazil (MPDFT) and Law Professor (IDP and IESB).

He is the author of works on constitutional, environmental, water, and urban law.

Tobias Hirzinger holds a Ph.D. in Economics and has conducted research on the organization and costs of GMO-related traceability measures in the food industry.

Klaus Menrad is Professor of Marketing and Management at the Straubing Center of Science, which involves five German universities. His research and publications deal with innovations in the agro-food chain and the coexistence of GM and non-GM crops in agriculture and food processing.

Hubert P. J. M. Noteborn is Deputy Director, Office for Risk Assessment of the Food and Consumer Product Safety Authority (VWA) in the Netherlands. He develops strategies for addressing risks in the food and feed chains through proactive risk management and stakeholder engagement, and has published on plant genetic breeding, food safety, and risk analysis.

Daniela Reitmeier of the German Biogas Association has conducted research on coexistence between GM and non-GM crops at the Straubing Center.

Marianna Schauzu, Department of Food Safety, Federal Institute for Risk Assessment in Berlin, is responsible for coordinating safety assessments of GMO and derived food and feed. She is a member of German delegations to the OECD Task Force for the Safety of Novel Foods and Feeds and to the CODEX Task Force on Foods Derived from Biotechnology.

Armin Spök is head of the biotechnology research unit at IFZ – Inter-University Research Centre for Technology, Work, and Culture in Graz, Austria. A member of expert groups at EFSA and OECD, and a lecturer at several universities, he specializes in technology assessment of biotechnology and risk governance.

Freija H. van Duijne holds a Ph.D. on Risk Perception in Consumer Product Use and is a member of the Office for Risk Assessment of the Food and Consumer Product Safety Authority (VWA) in the Netherlands. Her work addresses consumer behavior and risk perception with regard to innovative products.

Philip J. Vergragt is a Professor Emeritus of Technology Assessment at Delft University of Technology, Senior Associate at Tellus Institute, and a Research Professor at Clark University. His research interests are technological innovation for sustainability, sustainable consumption and system innovation, and small-scale experimentation and learning. He has published more than seventy academic papers and book chapters, and coauthored two books.

1 Governing Risk in GM Agriculture

An Introduction

Michael Baram and Mathilde Bourrier

Biotechnology and the Transformation of Agriculture

Biotechnology is generating the knowledge and skills for modifying all forms of life – plant, animal, human, and microbial. It is enabling researchers to map the genetic composition of organisms and identify the functions of their genes, and to determine the roles that selected genes play in creating proteins that, in turn, establish the physical and biological traits of the organisms. With this knowledge, researchers are then able to conceptualize modified versions of selected organisms that would be endowed with new traits, such as various species of plants, and undertake a process that subsequently involves splicing new genetic material into the genomes of the plants to modify their genetic composition and proteins. If successful, the redesigned plants will have the new intended characteristics. Thus, the scientific approach to agriculture pioneered by Mendel and others in the nineteenth century is dramatically amplified by biotechnology.

Over the past decade, commercial interests have promoted genetic modification (GM) of basic commodity food crops such as corn, soy, and rice, and important nonfood crops such as cotton, to endow these species with traits that will enhance agricultural productivity. Notable achievements include modified versions of selected crops with superior ability to withstand the chemical herbicides used in agriculture to eradicate weeds and to withstand various insect pests, crop diseases, frost, and drought. In

1

addition, crops have been modified to improve their commercial quality and nutritional value to make them more desirable to the manufacturers of processed foods and attractive to consumers.

These remarkable achievements far surpass what can be done by the traditional agricultural practice of modifying crops through cross-breeding, a trial-and-error process carried out over generations of experimentation that can be successful only within a very narrow range of related species. In contrast, the biotechnological approach enables the splicing of genes from totally unrelated species for the rapid production of modified crops with traits that could not be imparted by natural processes or by the artisans of cross-breeding. Well-known examples involve the splicing of selected genes from fish into tomatoes to create tomato crops that withstand frost and the splicing of bacteria genes into corn and cotton to create versions of these crops that repel and destroy insect pests.

The ability to incorporate genetic material from unrelated species into traditional crops makes GM agriculture a disturbing development to persons whose values and beliefs hew to a religion or tradition that rejects the unnatural, and to others who have cultural or economic commitments to conventional agriculture. It is also worrisome to many others because the long-term consequences of growing and consuming GM crops are uncertain and could be harmful to ecosystems and their biodiversity, lead to inadvertent modification of wild plants and conventional crops, and cause harm to the health of the people and animals that consume genetically modified (GM) crops and derivative food products. For these and other reasons, GM agriculture has fueled a global public discourse, and the process of developing policies and regulations for governing GM agriculture has been contentious and has sparked intense conflicts in many countries.

Another cause of widespread concern is the prospect of biocolonialism. A small group of very large multinational corporations (MNCs) based in the United States and European chemical industry sectors have led this new agricultural enterprise and could eventually gain control of global food systems. These MNCs have been acquiring biotech research firms and seed marketing companies, doing the research and producing the test results needed for official approval of their GM crops, patenting their innovations, and suing customers for patent infringement if they attempt to save the seeds of GM crops for subsequent use. They also aggressively market their GM crop seed to farmers in developed and developing nations. As a result, acreage dedicated to growing GM versions of corn and soy now far exceeds that used for growing conventional corn and soy in the United States, Brazil, Canada, and several other major agricultural nations. A similar trend is anticipated for GM versions of rice, alfalfa, potatoes, and other major crops that are essential to the food and feed systems of many nations.

MNC activities also encompass a broader range of plants, animals, and bacteria to create GM versions of these organisms that will serve as sources of nonfood products for industrial and consumer use, such as vaccines, drugs, fuels, pesticides, fertilizers, plastics, building materials, and organic agents for treating and destroying industrial wastes. Growing, harvesting, distributing, and using these nonfood GM crops and organisms in a manner that ensures their total containment so they do not mix with or contaminate conventional food crops, or GM food crops, and wild plants, is considered essential for safeguarding human and animal health, wildlife, and ecosystems. This presents a major challenge for risk governance because of the technical and managerial difficulties and costs involved in ensuring complete containment of the nonfood crops by physical or biological means.

The Risk Discourse

Perhaps no other technology has prompted a public discourse about its uncertainties and risks as extensively and intensely as the discourse fueled by GM agriculture. This may be due to the intersection of several factors, such as the aggressive promotional activities and ambitions of powerful corporate proponents, public mistrust of risk regulators and risk analysts, the high value assigned to conventional agriculture by defenders of national culture and national autonomy, the extremely precautionary mindset of consumers in Europe and Japan after "mad cow disease" and other food safety incidents, exploitation of public concerns about food safety by the media, the persistence of interest groups dedicated to opposing corporate-driven technologies and "Frankenfoods" in particular, and the democratization of risk regulation, which makes it more transparent and attentive to public opinion.

According to the corporate proponents of GM agriculture, it is inevitable that their increasing capability to design and produce new crops containing genetic material from diverse life forms will progressively transform agriculture, the livestock and fish farming sectors of the food system, forestry, and the downstream industries that use plants and animals as raw materials for making a universe of processed foods, medications, building materials, and many other products. GM proponents' optimistic view, presented with supportive scientific studies and test data, holds that the risks posed by GM crops are minimal; that managing any residual risks will be economically and technically feasible (e.g., by maintaining buffer zones around GM crop planting areas); and that GM crops and foods will provide health, environmental, and economic benefits for developed nations.

Proponents promise even greater benefits and humanitarian outcomes for less developed and poor countries, namely the ability to ensure reliable and sufficient food supplies to meet the needs of their growing populations by planting high-yield GM crops designed to withstand drought, pests, and other naturally occurring agricultural adversities. They also promise that consuming GM rice and other GM crops with nutritional enhancements will overcome dietary deficiencies in certain cultures and thereby eliminate the chronic illnesses caused by the traditional reliance on a single conventional crop. Proponents further claim that more efficient production of GM crops will enable such countries to sell surpluses in the lucrative international markets created by free-trade treaties. Finally, they point out that growing hardy varieties of GM crops that are intrinsically pest-resistant, instead of conventional crops that require the broad-scale application of toxic chemical pesticides and other agrochemicals, can provide a cascade of health and environmental benefits, such as avoid exposing farmers and their families to toxic chemicals, prevent toxic contamination of public water supplies and fishing areas, and make agricultural activities more environmentally sustainable.

Opponents contest these claims and present many arguments for resisting GM agriculture, including that growing and consuming a food crop containing genes from unrelated species violates nature, confounds adherence to dietary regimes ordained by religion or by personal choice, and could pose new risks to human and animal health over the long term. They warn that the new genetic content of GM crops will be released and flow into, pollinate, or otherwise cause contamination of related wild plants and conventional crops; eliminate insect and plant species; destabilize ecosystems and food systems; and cause loss of biodiversity and other irreversible ecological harms. Some of these risk claims have been evaluated by industry and government and found to be plausible, such as that pest-killing GM crops will eradicate certain insect species that are necessary for the survival of birds and other wildlife, and that the few insects of such species that survive because of their superior resistance will have progeny that are similarly resistant, thereby accelerating the evolution of super-resistant insects. Studies prompted by these and other concerns have, in some instances, led to more stringent requirements on the siting and configuration of GM crop-growing.

Opponents have also sought to refute claims that GM agriculture will benefit poor countries, arguing that it will instead cause social dislocation in agrarian regions by displacing small-scale subsistence farming with large-scale agribusiness owned and controlled by large companies remotely based in developed nations, and that consumers of the new foods will be exposed to allergenic risks and dietary disorders. Finally, there are deep fears in the poorer nations that they will be used as subjects of experimentation with new GM crops by the multinational firms that dominate GM agriculture. Although opponents lack conclusive factual support for most of these contentions, several incidents indicate that some of their arguments have merit, and that has kept many others from accepting industry claims.

Public discourse on the uncertainties, benefits, and risks of GM agriculture has been robust, but its influence on the development of regulatory programs and other aspects of risk governance has varied. This is made clear in several chapters that follow. In the United States and other major commodity crop growing countries such as Argentina, Australia, and Canada, the discourse has been overwhelmed by well-established commercial and governmental interests in exports, with the result that residual issues are channeled into formal regulatory proceedings wherein industry views and scientific studies dominate decision making. In large rapidly developing nations such as India and China, the risk discourse continues but has been subsumed to official policies designed to meet the urgent food needs of their rapidly growing populations. As a result, early doubts and exclusionary policies have been replaced by policies that accept GM agriculture as a societal necessity. Brazil and Spain have similarly changed course and come to accept GM agriculture because of the opportunities it provides for boosting their exports under global free-trade regimes. However, the discourse remains vibrant and has brought about precautionary and exclusionary policies in Japan and the majority of the twenty-six member-states of the European Union (EU), including Austria, France, Germany, Greece, Italy, and Poland. Indeed, several have rejected EU directives that would slowly open the door to GM crops and have established GM-free zones.

New developments continuously arise that recharge the discourse and, in some instances, cause reexamination of policies. Perhaps most notable are several incidents of contamination of conventional crops by GM crops in the United States that have caused business losses as orders for the conventional crops were cancelled. Such contamination, which can arise from gene flow or the inadvertent mixing of both types of crops, presents a problem that is considered unacceptable by farmers, food retailers, and consumers but that persists despite containment efforts of regulators and GM seed makers and their customers. Also entering the discourse is the growing preference by elite consumers for organic foods and conventional crops from local farms, a preference that is spreading to a much broader sector of consumers in highly developed nations.

Another emergent consideration is the application of nanotechnology to a growing number of consumer products despite the risks it poses to workers and others heavily exposed to nano-scale materials. It is foreseeable that nano-scale substances will be applied to conventional food products to enhance nutrition, flavor, shelf life, and other qualities, in lieu of genetic modification, and this awaits the reactions of the food industry and consumers. Another topic entering the discourse involves the growing of GM crops for producing vaccines, drugs, and other non-food items. Given the proven difficulties of segregating GM crops to prevent contamination of conventional food crops, this development poses new threats to food safety that will intensify concerns and cause more stringent regulation of GM agriculture.

The practice of genetically modifying food crops is entering its second decade, accompanied by many issues and conflicts. Is it morally wrong to mix disparate species? To what extent should cultural traditions, attitudes, and perceptions shape public policy, or should these be subordinated to expert judgments about safety and the assurances provided by companies and regulators? Is it irresponsible or dangerous to proceed given current uncertainty about health and environmental risks and the limitations of risk assessment and short-term field testing as means of reducing this uncertainty and avoiding worst-case scenarios? Will commercial experience produce learning about risks that will enable GM agriculture to be more safely managed over time by the companies, regulators, and growers involved in GM agriculture? Can the promised benefits for human well-being be achieved without destabilizing agrarian societies or bringing about biocolonialism by multinational firms? Are existing corporate practices, legal and regulatory safeguards, and international treaties sufficient to provide biosafety and protect biodiversity or should more precautionary principles be followed? These are some of the critical issues confronting nations as this powerful technology advances.

Governing the Risks

Many countries have developed systems for governing GM agriculture and food products. Although they differ in their institutions, procedures, and criteria for decision making, each governance system is premised on the need to prevent unacceptable risks to human and animal health, natural resources, and ecosystems. Some countries also strive to contain GM agriculture so that it does not harm biodiversity, interfere with conventional agricultural activities, or impair the availability of non-GM foods to consumers. In countries with democratic and transparent processes for policy making and regulation, the types of risks being addressed and the decision criteria used to determine when a risk is unacceptable are derived from the processing of scientific and economic information and cultural and political considerations. These matters are discussed in several chapters that follow.

The activities subject to risk governance systems may encompass the import, distribution, field testing, sale, and planting of GM crop seed, and the import, testing, and marketing of GM crops, their derivative by-products, and GM food and feed products for consumption by humans and livestock. Thus, governing GM risk involves several important sectors of commercial activity, the agricultural, food production, and food retailing sectors, each of which has been subjected for many years to numerous requirements for conventional seeds, crop growing, and food products. Governance also involves protecting environmental quality and consumer rights.

As a result, the threshold question for many countries has been whether these previously existing frameworks and institutions are suitable for governing the risks posed by GM crops and foods, or whether new approaches and expertise are needed. In sharp contrast to the threshold policy determination in the United States that the same regulatory requirements and procedures are sufficient and must be applied, the EU has created new requirements and an elaborate procedural framework for the GM enterprise.

A system for governing the risks may involve the application of several types of social controls, as discussed in the ensuing chapters. These may include reliance on self-regulation by corporate seed producers and the agricultural, food producing, and retailing entities and trade associations involved in the GM enterprise, and the application of information disclosure requirements to inform the marketplace and respect consumer rights. In common law countries, such as the United States and Britain, there is also reliance on the judicial system to impose liability on companies or individuals when their activities involving GM crops or foods fail to meet prevailing standards of care and cause harm to persons or property. However, in all countries, the most favored social control is some form of risk regulation by one or more public agencies that have been empowered by national legislation, a development usually accompanied by the creation of a scientific advisory apparatus.

Regulatory approaches differ, with some agencies enacting and enforcing detailed prescriptive rules and permit procedures, and others applying more flexible performance-based requirements to the entities subject to their authority. Common features include field testing and risk assessment requirements, permit procedures for agency review and approval of new GM crops before commercial planting, and additional procedures for review of food products with GM content before commercial marketing. In addition, various means of eliciting, listening to, and responding to public opinion have been implemented by progressive agencies in democratic nations, and in the EU, regulations impose special labeling requirements for marketing foods with GM content. A more detailed account is presented in subsequent chapters, including discussion of the criteria and assumptions applied in agency decision-making processes, such as use of cost-benefit analysis to determine whether a risk is reasonable, application of the "precautionary principle" when coping with scientific uncertainty and reliance on templates for approving GM foods that are shown to be "substantially equivalent" to conventional food products.

Corporate proponents of GM crops and foods must therefore comply with numerous requirements to gain regulatory approvals. However, the requirements and their stringency differ between countries because regulatory activities, although directed by official policies, are nevertheless subject to the influence of many factors, political, economic, and cultural, as well as the ongoing risk discourse and the occurrence of harmful incidents, or the lack thereof. As a result, regulators in the United States, for example, have relaxed many requirements, deferred to corporate studies and findings, and disregarded petitions by consumer groups for the labeling of GM foods. In contrast, regulators in the EU domain are attentive to Eurobarometer and other public opinion polls in pursuing their mandates and have been extremely precautionary and stringent, indeed to some observers as being obstructionist.

Despite such differences, each governance system ultimately creates a responsibility for safety management by GM proponents in the conduct of their activities. Fulfilling this responsibility requires their compliance with risk regulations and meeting other standards of acceptable behavior. However, when such requirements are ambiguous, incomplete or otherwise inadequate, or nonexistent as in poor countries, safety management is confronted by ethical challenges. In developed nations, companies are expected to meet these challenges by developing a safety culture that promotes deep organizational commitment to identifying and minimizing risks and voluntary adoption of appropriate safety practices. As discussed in Chapter 9, GM agriculture may benefit from safety management knowledge gained in other, more mature technological sectors.

Reflections on Risk and Responsibility

For decades, progressive countries have sought to gain the benefits and minimize the risks of technological advance, and devised policies for these purposes. Policies for risk governance have regulation as their main feature, and regulators have relied on scientific and technological expertise for analytic methods, studies, facts, and informed opinions to develop rules and other requirements for addressing risks.

Given commercial and other pressures to exploit the benefits of a new technology despite its uncertainties and risks, the usual governmental resolution is to allow regulated introduction of the technology into society on what is essentially an experimental basis, on the assumption that the risks will be acceptable and that learning gained from actually using the technology will reduce uncertainties, enable experts to better clarify its risks, and bring about changes in regulation that will be more effective in preventing the risks over time.

Yet for some technologies, such as GM agriculture, experimental introduction and the risks to health and the environment it poses may also cause disruption of activities essential to societal well-being, such as conventional agriculture and food production, and attempts to apply the learning gained from experimentation for corrective purposes may be futile. In addition, the issue of when such risks and potential disruptions should be considered acceptable for experimental purposes and borne by the public clearly calls for more than the quantitative analysis and judgments of technical experts used by regulators, especially in the context of democratic society in which public values and beliefs are supposed to be heard and respected.

As the public has become more informed and aware of the implications of technological advance and the values that influence expert advice, it has become less willing to entrust decision making to regulators and technicians and more demanding about its informed involvement in the regulatory process. As a result, traditional modes of expert-driven regulation have become less acceptable, and are confronted by demands to make decision processes more transparent and open to the diversity of values and views of society.

Experience with GM agriculture and foods reveals the struggle to develop regulatory approaches that hear, respect, and fairly consider conflicting values and views of experts and the nonexpert citizenry. The same can be said for other new technologies now being introduced. Thus, a new apparatus for risk governance may be in the making in this age of doubt and skepticism about experts, regulators, and the corporate sector.

Part I RISK GOVERNANCE AND PUBLIC DISCOURSE

2 Governance of GM Crop and Food Safety in the United States

Michael Baram

Introduction

The safety of GM crops and foods is an issue that causes great public concern and stringent regulation in European nations and several other countries. In stark contrast, it receives little public attention in the United States, where GM crops and foods rapidly advance through permissive regulatory reviews into the marketplace.

This chapter discusses the American approach to governing GM crop and food safety, and the cultural and political factors that shape this governance system. It then describes and evaluates the major federal regulatory programs and common law liability doctrines as they apply to safety issues and uncertainties in the development and marketing of GM crop seed; the growing of GM crops and their harvest, distribution, and sale to the manufacturers of processed food products; and the subsequent production and marketing of GM food products.

Throughout the chapter, the fourfold concept of GM safety that was identified earlier in this book is addressed, namely whether the GM enterprise poses unacceptable risks to public health, natural resources, and conventional crops, and whether it reduces the consumer's ability to choose and acquire non-GM food products.

The U.S. Context for GM Crops and Foods

Among developed nations, the United States is the leading proponent and most permissive regulator of GM crops and foods. Congress has generously supported scientific research on crop genetics and applications of genetic engineering to agriculture, but refrained from legislating new requirements to deal with adverse consequences. The executive branch, led by the President's Office, has promoted the commercialization and export of GM seeds, crops, and foods, and discouraged regulation that would treat these products differently than their conventional, non-GM counterparts. The regulatory agencies, which are subject to presidential direction, have acted accordingly by lessening test requirements, creating regulatory exemptions, and approving commercialization despite scientific uncertainties about risks to public health and the environment. They have steadfastly resisted petitions for more stringent safety reviews and precautionary policies, and rejected proposals for labeling GM products that would enable informed choice by consumers.

Federal courts of the judicial branch of government, which are authorized to review the factual and legal bases for regulatory decisions that have been challenged, have upheld agency decisions that favor the advance of GM agriculture. Other units of government have also contributed to the advance of GM agriculture, such as the Patent Office, which has expansively interpreted its rules and granted patents for an endless variety of GM crops, and trade negotiators who have sought to eliminate any barriers in other countries to the importation of American-made GM products.

As a result, the United States provides a very fertile context for the advance of GM agriculture and foods. Its MNCs, led by Monsanto, DuPont, Dow, and other giants of the chemical industry, have acquired biotechnology research firms and all major seed companies in the United States to expedite development and distribution of new varieties of GM seed, and use their substantial resources to aggressively sell these products at home and abroad. Large, industrial-scale agricultural enterprises eagerly plant, harvest, and sell GM crops, particularly GM versions of major commodity crops such as corn, canola, cotton, rice, soy, and alfalfa, which have been engineered for herbicide tolerance, pest resistance, and other features that promise increased productivity and profit.

Firms also produce and market numerous products derived from GM crops, such as high value oils and ubiquitous food additives such as the sweetening agent, corn syrup. Companies that produce animal feed and human food products have increasingly purchased GM crops and derivative products, and the feed and food industries now sell an extensive range of products with GM content. Completing the commercial cycle are food retailers, ranging from supermarkets to food service firms, which sell GM foods to the public, which purchases and consumes the products with few reservations.

Dedicated opponents have failed to slow this rapid transformation of the American farming and food systems. Environmental and consumer safety organizations closely monitor and sound alarms, petition agencies and challenge regulatory decisions in the courts, and use the media to project their views, but have failed to stimulate public resistance and gain more stringent regulations. Although public concerns about food safety, nutritional quality, and environmental protection are widespread, they have had no discernible effect on the expanding GM agricultural enterprise. In addition, the cadre of small farmers who are committed to growing conventional and organic crops have far less political influence than the large, industrial-scale firms that are committed to GM agriculture.

However, the GM enterprise is troubled by several developments. Claims that GM crops pose environmental risks and contaminate non-GM crops are increasingly supported by scientific evidence and field observations. For example, it is now established that "gene flow" from certain GM crops occurs and infects conventional crops and related species of wild plants with genetic material that has pesticidal and herbicide resistance functions. In addition, there is scientific consensus that

GM crops engineered to kill insect pests actually accelerate the reproduction of highly resistant insects, and also harm nontarget species that
play vital roles in the functioning of ecosystems.

GM seed companies, crop growers, and regulators, confronted with
accumulating evidence of environmental impacts and property damage,
have come to recognize the need for constraints on the location and configuration of GM crop plantings and for buffer zones around the selected
planting sites. In addition, there is the need for additional measures to
ensure that equipment and facilities used in farming, harvesting, storing,
and shipping GM crops are not used for conventional or organic crops,
for the adoption of special planting practices, and for improved versions
of GM seed that will reduce gene flow. The gradual accumulation of
these safety measures, which involve physical and well as biological containment approaches, may impact productivity and profit and thereby
moderate enthusiasm for GM agriculture. These issues and practices are
discussed further in Chapters 6, 7, and 9.

Another challenge for GM agriculture is posed by the rapid growth of
elite consumerism that is expressed in the preferences of more educated
and higher income sectors of the public for natural and organic foods
from small, local farms, and the inevitable diffusion of these preferences
across a much broader range of consumers. Farmers and food retailers
who wish to capitalize on this trend dedicate more acreage and supermarket shelf space to non-GM and certified organic food products. In
addition to these developments in the domestic marketplace, the European and Japanese markets for GM crops and foods virtually remain
closed despite a decade of American pressures, a discouraging situation
for larger American growers of GM crops who depend on exports for
significant financial return.

Finally, there are prospects of liability and business loss for the proponents and practitioners of GM agriculture. GM seed companies and
downstream farmers, distributors, and sellers who are implicated in incidents of GM "contamination" of conventional crops and foods face lawsuits that can result in substantial damage awards by the courts, or the

need to negotiate costly settlements of these lawsuits out of court. In addition, they will incur the substantial legal fees and other transaction costs of defending or negotiating, regulatory penalties, and other business losses that can include the recall of products from the marketplace and their destruction, and loss of reputation and customers. Several of these scenarios are discussed later in this chapter, based on lawsuits arising from incidents in which conventional crops were rejected by domestic and foreign customers because of actual or suspected GM contamination.

Nevertheless, the American context for GM agriculture and food remains favorable because the public remains acquiescent and regulators and the large domestic market continue to be accommodating. This is due, in part, to the values, attitudes, and behaviors at play in American culture.

Cultural Influence

American culture is a complex brew of romantic beliefs, utilitarian values, and pragmatic behaviors. With regard to agriculture, there is reverence for the "natural" but rapid acceptance of the technologically manipulated, admiration for the small, local family farm and its struggle to maintain traditional agrarian practices but unquestioned purchase of foods shipped across the nation from remote corporate enterprises employing migrant labor and new technologies. Preference for familiar local foods is easily displaced by new fast foods. And despite dedication to the work ethic, consumers increasingly demand convenience products, many of which abuse the normal concept of food. Although such disparities between beliefs and behaviors exist in other nations, in the United States, they have provided the opportunity for aggressive proponents of GM agriculture to establish substantial markets.

The disparities between espoused principles and beliefs and actual behaviors is striking, as shown by the ease with which principles and beliefs are abandoned when consumers make purchasing decisions.

Explanations ranging from changes in family structure and intensifying time and economic pressures felt by consumers, to seductive marketing strategies of the food industry, and the distancing of modern urban consumers from nature and tradition, are all plausible. However, perhaps the most fundamental explanation is that American culture is pervaded by utilitarian values, which makes it accommodating to technological change when the promised benefits of such change exceed the dislocations and other impacts it may cause. Such is the case with technological manipulation of the agricultural and food sectors.

In 1964, J. I. Rodale catalogued a multitude of technological modifications by the food industry in his campaign to enlighten consumers about the latent hazards of processed food products and to stimulate their return to consumption of natural, unmodified foods. Even now, half a century later, his catalog is enlightening about the growth of the processed food industry and consumer acceptance of its technological manipulations, often in the form of chemical additives with hazardous attributes, such as:

- flavoring agents (artificial sweeteners and numerous other flavor, taste, and sensory enhancers),
- preservatives (chemicals that function as antioxidants, antibiotics, coatings, mold inhibitors, bactericides, germicides, fungicides),
- conditioning agents to facilitate industrial production and standardization (emulsifiers, stabilizers, thickeners, dispersants, texturizers, bleaches, pH adjustors, enzymes, binders, anti-sticking and anti-caking agents),
- nutrients (synthesized protein and vitamin supplements, minerals, hormones),
- colorants (dyes, bleaches), and
- special packaging-related treatments (casings, coatings, dehydration).[1]

---

[1] J. I. Rodale et al., *Our Poisoned Earth and Sky* (Rodale Books, 1964).

A catalog of current manipulations, such as use of genetic modification, nano-scale materials, inert gases, and food irradiation, would be far more extensive. However, the point is made that American consumers have accepted an endless parade of technical manipulations of their foods over the last half century, have grown accustomed to such changes, are comforted by the assumption that the federal Food and Drug Administration (FDA) assures the safety of new additives and foods, lack time and interest for looking into the content of their foods or weighing competing scientific studies, and therefore express few reservations about the stream of new food products.

This experience indicates a cultural predisposition for acceptance of further technological manipulations, including genetic modification, by American consumers. Indeed, public complacency has set in over the past decade of GM food consumption because no outbreaks of illness have occurred and no clearly convincing evidence of risk to consumers from GM foods has been produced. An additional explanation for this complacency is that the GM content of processed foods is largely comprised of commodity crops, such as GM soy, corn, and wheat, and their derivatives such as corn oil and syrup. These ubiquitous components of a multitude of processed food products, ranging from bread and pizza to ice cream, yogurt, and soups, are not readily distinguishable or identifiable, enabling them to fall below the sensory screening capacity of most consumers. As a result, consumer attention to the safety of processed foods, whether GM or not, remains focused on traditional concerns about the end product, such as its sanitary quality, the presence of toxic pesticide residues, mold, bacteria, and other features capable of causing illness.

Perhaps the most fundamental explanation of American acceptance of GM agriculture and food, previously mentioned, is the utilitarian ethos that prevails among consumers. Simply put, there is acceptance of GM foods because they have not been proven unsafe, may be more safe than conventional foods in certain respects (e.g., less pesticide residue), are often nutritionally enhanced, have equivalent texture and other sensory features, meet the same sanitary standards as their conventional food counterparts, and are often less costly. Thus, the utilitarian calculus involves weighing benefits that are tangible and proven versus risks that are presumably prevented by regulators and that have thus far been speculative about harm arising from the genetic engineering involved in making the product.

Other safety issues raised by GM agriculture, such as threats to wildlife, ecosystems, and conventional crops, do not enter or are given much less weight in the consumer calculus. Given that most consumers do not know where their food comes from, have not been confronted with any accounts of serious or irreparable environmental harms caused by the planting of GM crops, and have become somewhat accustomed and immune to a decade of warnings of impending disasters by environmentalists, such concerns remain as remote, theoretical issues that do not influence daily decision making in the supermarket by most consumers.

Thus, American culture has presented few obstacles to corporate introduction of new products such as GM seed, crops, and foods, a situation that has led to an extraordinary increase in the acreage devoted to growing GM versions of commodity crops in the United States since 1996. Data from the federal Department of Agriculture indicates that the GM share of soy acreage rose from less than 10 percent in 1996 to more than 90 percent in 2007; for GM cotton acreage, from zero to near 70 percent; and for GM corn, from near zero to more than 50 percent.[2] According to another report in 2006, since Monsanto created the first GM crops in the early 1990s, the percentage of all agricultural land in the United States devoted to GM crop growing has risen steadily to almost a third, and that a major increase is anticipated now that GM varieties of

---

[2] United States Department of Agriculture Economic Research Service, Adoption of Genetically Engineered Crops in the U.S., U.S. Dept. Agriculture, www.ers.usda.gov/data/BiotechCrops/ExtentofAdoptionTable1.htm.

rice, beets, and other species have been approved for introduction into commerce.[3] More recent but less definitive reports indicate much higher rates for GM crops.

Nevertheless, as noted earlier, the cultural context that shapes the market for GM products is not immutable. The consumer's utilitarian calculus can be influenced by objective factors, such as verifiable evidence of risk or a harmful incident that impugns the safety of a GM food, hard data about price increases, and subjective factors such as the views of elites about lifestyle and fashion, which can have a cascade effect on the beliefs and behaviors of other consumers. Although no evidence has convincingly shown a GM food to be unsafe for human health, and claims about immediate threats to the environment have been blunted somewhat by new GM crop management practices that try to minimize their occurrence, there are indications that assumptions about the lower cost of GM foods and their desirability due to less toxic pesticide use and the reduced presence of pesticide residues, are in flux. In addition, as discussed in Chapter 7, the advent of engineering and growing GM crops to produce pharmaceuticals and other industrial products may raise public concerns about contamination of human food and animal feed by genetic material intended for these other purposes.

GM agriculture also faces the prospect that it may be displaced by competing technologies. Forthcoming uses of nanotechnology to endow food products with increased nutritional value and shelf life, and other appealing features are being planned, and may prove to be less costly for the food industry and more acceptable to the public than GM options. Despite considerable concern about the occupational hazards and environmental impacts arising from use of nano-scale materials, regulatory agencies and the public seem to be more comfortable with nanotechnology than genetic engineering.

---

[3] Clive James, International Service for the Acquisition of Agri-biotech Applications, Global Status of Commercialized Biotech/GM Crop (*ISAAA Brief* No. 35. 2006).

Potential liability for GM contamination of conventional crops, the costs of new management practices to prevent gene flow and harm to nontarget species of pests, surging demand for acreage to grow organic foods and biofuel crops, increased use of toxic herbicides, and continuing European resistance to GM crops and foods amplified by costly verification and labeling requirements are among the factors that have caused some American agricultural enterprises to return a portion of their GM acreage to growing non-GM crops. These factors can make GM crops and derivative food products more costly. To the extent these developments and their economic consequences enter the consumer calculus, the advance of GM agriculture may be slowed. Thus, despite the bullish data on GM acreage, other forces are at work that may make the cultural context and market for GM crops and foods less favorable.

Governance

Governance of new technological developments in the United States, such as GM crops and foods, and the risks they pose is usually accomplished by three independent but interactive systems of social control: government regulation, common law, and private self-regulation. For more than a century, a series of public laws have been enacted to empower federal and state regulators to prevent agricultural activities and foods from harming public health, natural resources, and property such as privately owned land, crops, and livestock. For more than two centuries, tort liability and other common law doctrines derived from England have been adjusted and applied by state courts to hold companies accountable for harms caused by their activities and products, including diverse agricultural practices and foods. And voluntary self-regulation by companies and industry standards developed by their trade associations have usually been encouraged by government as a commonsense alternative or supplement to government regulation of risks in most business sectors, including agriculture and the processed food industry.

Each of these social controls is responsive to changes in the cultural context. For example, an outbreak of illnesses caused by a particular food product draws national media attention, alarms the public, causes retailer and consumer avoidance of the product, and subsequently leads to recall of the product from the marketplace, lawsuits by victims seeking compensation, investigations and interventions by regulators, and congressional hearings that can lead to new legal requirements for food safety. This chain of events causes economic and reputational loss to the product manufacturer, widespread criticism of the company and its regulators, and lawsuits.

As a result, each of the three systems of social control is impacted and will likely be adapted accordingly. The rational manufacturer and its trade association will take steps to improve self-regulatory practices to prevent future loss-causing incidents of a similar nature, restore public trust, and demonstrate that new laws and regulation are unnecessary. Under public scrutiny and pressure, the regulator will be invigorated and do more vigilant oversight and may enact new rules to restore public trust, and judges may adapt common law liability doctrines to do "compensatory justice."

This scenario briefly indicates how the social controls involved in governing food safety typically respond and function in the United States when a conventional food product causes an outbreak of food poisoning. The Starlink Corn episode, discussed later in this chapter, indicates that a similar scenario will arise when a GM crop or food is implicated, even if the harm is limited to economic loss from actual or suspected GM contamination of conventional food and there is no evidence of harm to human health.

The governance system is also affected by political and economic forces. For example, the deregulation movement launched by the Reagan administration in the 1980s, and the "new federalist" movement that favors shifting governance responsibilities from the federal level to the fifty states, have gained political support and reduced the role of federal regulation as a social control over many industrial and commercial activities. In addition, the globalization of commerce movement, promoted by treaties to eliminate national barriers to free trade, has had the effect of suppressing domestic regulation when it would make U.S. firms less competitive, or conflict with treaty obligations.

Thus, governance of the safety of GM crops and foods at any point in time in the United States is the result of the interactive functioning of these three social control mechanisms and their responsiveness to incidents and to changes in the cultural context. This approach to governance lacks the clarity and certainties of governance in EU nations where regulation is the dominant system of social control, private litigation is disfavored, and corporations have cooperative working relationships with regulators in contrast to the adversarial relationships that prevail in the United States.

Federal Regulation

A "Coordinated Framework"[4] for federal regulation of "biotechnology products" was announced by the President's Office of Science and Technology Policy (OSTP) in 1986, and was followed by an amplified version in 1992. It stands as the only policy guidance on federal oversight and regulation of genetically engineered products, including GM crops and foods. It assigns oversight roles to four federal agencies, asserts that previously enacted laws that empower these agencies are sufficient for regulating GM product risks, and warns the agencies that any GM product regulations they enact should be based solely on end product risks without consideration of the biotechnological processes involved in making the products. Because Congress has not acted to amend or override this presidential policy, it has been dutifully followed by the designated agencies, including those assigned to GM crops and foods, the Department of

---

[4] Coordinated Framework for Regulation of Biotechnology, 51 Fed. Reg. 23302 (Jun. 26, 1986); Exercise of Federal Authority within Scope of Statutory Authority: Planned Introductions of Biotechnology Products into the Environment, 27 Fed. Reg. 6753 (Feb. 27, 1992).

Agriculture (DA), the Food and Drug Administration (FDA), and the Environmental Protection Agency (EPA).

This bold presidential action represents a notable departure from the usual federal approach to new technologies in which Congress would hold public hearings, consider the views of various interested parties, slowly deliberate and reach consensus, enact new law to empower agencies with specially designed authorizations to regulate the distinctive features and hazardous attributes of the new technology, provide funding, and oversee agency implementation.

The Coordinated Framework clearly promotes Reagan-era political themes such as minimizing federal constraints on the advance of commercially advantageous technology and preventing growth of the federal bureaucracy. Therefore, it limits the powers of the designated regulators to statutory authorizations enacted long before the advent of biotechnology and thereby restrains them from fully addressing unique features and uncertainties posed by biotechnological methods for making the products. Although Congress could have enacted laws that would override or displace the presidential policy, it has failed to do so because public concern and political pressure have been insufficient.

In addition to restricting regulation to the ill-fitting mandates of earlier existing laws and to risks posed by a final product "in the context of its intended use," the agencies are directed to employ risk analysis to determine if there is a sufficient factual basis for regulatory action, and apply cost-benefit analysis to determine on economic grounds the extent to which a risk is "unreasonable" and worthy of regulation, that is, "when the value of the reduction in risk obtained by additional oversight is greater than the cost thereby imposed." Regulators are further directed to minimize regulatory burdens on product developers, accommodate rapid advances in product development and commercialization, and use flexible performance-based standards rather than rigid prescriptive or design standards to deal with end product risks.

Various assumptions are expressed in the policy to support these directives: "that by the time a product is ready for commercialization, it will have undergone substantial review and testing" and "information regarding its safety should be available"; that "agency resources are scarce, and cannot be applied to every possible problem"; that "determining the scope of oversight on grounds other than risk would also tend to discourage useful innovations"; and that a new GM product "should be subject to no greater degree of oversight than was a comparable organism or product previously used in a past safe introduction in a comparable target environment."

The designated regulators have adhered to these guidances because they are part of the executive branch of government and therefore subject to presidential management, and Congress has not used its authority to intervene. The guidances and assumptions also explain why the designated regulators have shown disregard for public concerns about moral or ethical aspects of making or using biotech products, relied heavily on company-provided safety studies and self-certifications, and used "substantial equivalence" templates to exempt many products from their regulatory control. A detailed review of implementation by the three regulatory agencies follows.

Department of Agriculture

The Department of Agriculture (DA) is directed by several laws to enhance American agriculture and forestry and protect these sectors from harmful organisms and products. Within this vast federal department, the Animal and Plant Health Inspection Service (APHIS) implements the Plant Protection Act (PPA),[5] which calls for restricting the introduction of any plant that is a "plant pest," the PPA term for an organism that can harm other plants and plant products. Pursuant to the PPA, APHIS has authority to restrict the import, shipment, field testing, and commercial planting of GM seed and crops, but has used its discretion to create a permissive regulatory program in keeping with presidential policy.

---

[5] Plant Protection Act, 7 U.S.C. §§ 7701–7772 (2000).

APHIS regulations[6] provide that a company that plans to import or field test or sell a new GM plant must first obtain a permit, and that a permit will be granted if the company provides field test data and other technical information that convinces the agency that the new GM plant is not likely to be a plant pest. Yet after finding that many GM plants it had permitted on this basis did not subsequently exhibit plant pest qualities, APHIS created a simple "notification" option[7] for companies with any GM versions of several plant species (e.g., corn, soybean, cotton, tomato, potato, etc.). Under this option, such a company is authorized to field test after merely notifying the agency that its GM plant meets APHIS criteria and promising that the company will adhere to APHIS performance standards. The criteria relate to the new genetic material spliced into the plant genome, such as its stability, and its inability to cause disease in other plants, harm nontarget organisms, and create a new plant virus. The performance standards involve controls that confine the new GM crop to the field test site.

The notification option expedited the field testing of thousands of new GM plants on the basis of self-certifications and promises about containment by companies, a situation that has aroused much concern and criticism of the agency by public interest groups. Because the notifications are supported by information that companies claim as proprietary, even if the information is provided to APHIS on its request, it is not generally available to others who want to evaluate it for its scientific quality. This lack of transparency frustrates and antagonizes the critics despite the agency's claim that it deserves trust because of its expertise.

To further facilitate rapid introduction of new GM crops, APHIS has also provided companies with the opportunity to obtain a "nonregulated" status for its GM plant if the agency accepts the company's claim that the plant is similar to another plant that APHIS had earlier determined was not a plant pest. In similar fashion, it also applies

---

[6] 7 C.F.R. § 340.
[7] 7 C.F.R. §340.3(a).

a "familiarity principle" when reviewing risk and safety studies, based on its view that safety issues do not differ between GM plants and conventional plants when similar traits are being conferred.

Although these developments have made the agency extremely accommodating to companies promoting GM plants, Congress has not intervened. Indeed, in 2000, a congressional committee reported favorably on the agency's program, stating that:

> Since 1987, APHIS has processed more than 5,000 permits and notifications for field testing at more than 22,000 sites and nearly 50 petitions for deregulation. Of the 44 different types of plants modified using rDNA techniques, field testing has occurred for varieties altered for herbicide resistance (28%), insect resistance (24%), product quality (19%), virus resistance (10%), agronomic properties (6%), fungal resistance (5%), and other properties, including bacterial resistance (8%). In no instance has any biotech plant approved for field testing by USDA created an environmental hazard or exhibited unpredictable or unusual behavior compared to similar crops modified using conventional breeding methods.[8]

However, APHIS has taken some steps to make its regulatory program more robust. Concerned about incidents of contamination of conventional crops, and fearing that contamination of both conventional and GM human food crops by new GM crops encoding compounds for pharmaceutical and other industrial products would lead to far more serious incidents that endanger public health and disrupt the food system, the agency in 2005 revised its regulation on notification to provide that such non-food GM crops may only be introduced under a permit, making them ineligible for the notification procedure.[9] In addition, the agency has had to make its procedures compliant with environmental laws. For example, federal courts have determined that APHIS failed to comply

---

[8] Committee on Science, US House of Representatives, Seeds of Opportunity, Report 106B (2000).

[9] 7 C.F.R. 340.4 on the Introduction of Plants Genetically Engineered to Produce Industrial Compounds.

with the National Environmental Policy Act's command for environmental review before it permitted Monsanto and other companies to plant GM corn and sugarcane that had been modified to produce pharmaceutical products, and that it also failed to address implications for endangered species as required by the Endangered Species Act.[10]

In December 2005, by which time APHIS had approved more than 10,600 applications for some 50,000 field tests, the Department of Agriculture's Inspector General released an audit critical of APHIS oversight of field testing activities at a sample of 91 test sites in 22 states. Many deficiencies were found. According to the audit, APHIS was not aware of the precise locations of many test sites, and did not review company protocols for containing test crops and preventing their persistence and escape into the environment after completion of field tests. Of particular concern, it had not required planters of drug-producing GM plants to report and verify appropriate disposition of their harvests, did not prevent passersby from taking the experimental GM plants for possible consumption, and did not require that the companies involved prove their financial ability to do site cleanup and proper disposition of their products.[11]

These findings of deficiencies in APHIS safety management of experimental field testing and its apparent disregard for the special risks posed by drug-producing GM crops led the Inspector General to make twenty-eight recommendations, some of which the agency quickly rejected on dubious grounds. For example, in rejecting the recommendation that it require companies to report on the actual disposition of pharmaceutical plants after harvest to ensure they would not be mixed with or otherwise contaminate conventional food crops, the agency said that such reports

---

[10] *See* Center for Food Safety v. Johanns, 451 F.Supp.2d 1165 (D. Hawaii 2006). *See also* Geertson Seed Farms v. Johanns, 2007 WL 518624 (N.D. Cal. 2007) and International Center for Technology Assessment v. Johanns, 473 F.Supp.2d 9 (D.C. 2007).

[11] Office of Inspector General, S.W. Division, U.S. Dep't of Agriculture, Audit Report 50601–8-Te, APHIS Controls Over Issuance of Genetically Engineered Organism Release Permits (2005). *See also USDA Finds Deficiencies in Regulation of Field Tests*, 25 (2) Biotechnology L. Rep. 148 (2006).

are "not necessary to ensure confinement measures are met because the information is already captured in permit conditions and pre-harvest reports."[12]

The Audit Report identified deeper problems in the agency's regulatory culture that undermine its credibility. These range from the failure of APHIS biotechnologists to document their reviews and scientific analyses for approving field test applications, to the agency's failing to seek information from companies that is missing from their reports, completing its site inspections, and not fully recording reported violations nor providing instructions for destroying GM test crops after their harvest.[13]

The National Research Council (NRC), a prominent scientific organization that frequently advises federal agencies, also evaluated APHIS performance and found a broader range of problems, including lack of scientific rigor and transparency in evaluating risks, failure to fully consider all available scientific information and develop new gap-filling data, and disregard for potential impacts on nontarget organisms.[14] NRC also identified other problems that it attributed, in part, to congressional failure to amplify the agency's regulatory powers, such as APHIS' lack of authority to carry out postmarket monitoring to identify and address unforeseen downstream impacts, and its disregard for allergenic risk in approving GM plants under the notification process.[15]

Although APHIS has not been moved by these critiques to improve its performance, it has been responsive to business losses. Following several loss-causing incidents involving "low level presence of regulated genetically engineered plant materials in conventional seeds or grains," the agency has announced it will evaluate its program for possible changes it may make within the scope of its regulatory

---

[12] Audit Report *supra.* at 43.

[13] Audit Report, *supra.* at 4.

[14] Gregory Mandel, *Gaps, Inexperience, Inconsistencies, and Overlaps: Crisis in the Regulation of Genetically Modified Foods and Animals,* 45 WMLR 2167, 2232; and Nat'l Research Council, Environmental Effects of Transgenic Plants 37 (2002) at 148.

[15] *See* Mandel, *supra,* at 2234, 2235 & n.372; *See also* Nat'l Research Council, Environmental Effects of Transgenic Plants 37 (2002) at 111, 233.

authority.[16] However, its performance as GM risk regulator, manager of safety at GM test sites, and protector of conventional agriculture from contamination by GM plants and particularly from GM drug-producing plants, remains a source of great concern to informed observers in the United States.[17]

Environmental Protection Agency

Under its statutory authority, EPA's responsibilities are mainly limited to evaluating and regulating those crops, GM and conventional, that have pesticidal features to determine if they may be safely sold and used in the United States.[18] It must also determine whether any such product it approves for consumption would bear pesticide residues, and if so, it must then determine if safe levels (tolerances) can be set for the residues, or whether the residues qualify for exemption.[19]

Because of the limitations of its statutory mandate, EPA's regulatory program does not encompass the much broader range of GM crops, such as those with herbicide resistance or drug-producing attributes, nor does it apply to pesticidal GM crops made in the United States for sale and use in other nations only. Like APHIS, it adheres to the guidelines for minimal regulation provided by the Coordinated Framework and implements a relaxed regulatory approach.

Its governing statute defines a pesticide as "any substance or mixture...intended for preventing, destroying, repelling, or mitigating a pest," and defines a pest as "any insect, rodent...virus, bacteria...."[20] It also provides a criteria for decision-making that is similar to that put

---

[16] APHIS Policy on Responding to the Low-Level Presence of Regulated Genetically Engineered Plant Materials, 7 C.F.R. § 340.

[17] Rebecca Bratspies, Some Thoughts on the American Approach to Regulating Genetically Modified Organisms, 16-SPG Kan. J.L. & Pub. Pol'y 393, 421–422.

[18] Federal Insecticide, Fungicide, and Rodenticide Act, 7 U.S.C.§136 (1988) [hereinafter FIFRA]. For EPA regulations, see 40 C.F.R. parts 150–189.

[19] Federal Food, Drug, and Cosmetic Act, 21 U.S.C. §§ 346(a) [hereinafter FFDCA].

[20] For the full definitions of "pesticide" and "pest," see FIFRA, *supra*, at 136(u),(t).

forth by the Coordinated Framework, namely that sale and use of the product is to be permitted by EPA unless it finds that the product poses an "unreasonable risk to man or the environment, taking into account the economic, social, and environmental costs and benefits of the use of the pesticide."[21]

For GM crops with pesticidal features, the agency has narrowed its regulatory focus to those crops containing bacterial genes that have been incorporated in a plant, or other genetic material that has been spliced into a plant's genome to produce pesticidal substances. By these and other determinations, EPA has exempted genetic material that is derived from another plant that is sexually compatible with the receiving plant.[22]

The developer of a GM crop that falls within EPA's narrowed range of regulatory responsibility must submit an application and supporting technical information to the agency and secure EPA approval before selling or using the product in the United States. The agency may require additional information or studies, and in approving the product, must ensure that it bears a label that specifies the parameters for its safe use, parameters that EPA has determined are necessary to prevent unreasonable risk to health and environment.[23] Noncompliance with any of these requirements is subject to EPA sanctions.

EPA's review of an application for approval ("registration") involves its evaluation of the product's active ingredients, the intended crop planting circumstances and sites, and data on the effects of such plantings on human health, nontarget species, and environmental features such as groundwater and surface water. Following registration of the new product and its sale, the developer is thereafter required to report adverse effects arising from its use, and provide additional information that EPA may request to determine if the registration should be maintained, suspended, or cancelled.

[21] FIFRA, *supra*, at §136(z)(bb).
[22] For details about these and other exemptions, see William L. Anderson et al., Environmental Law Institute, Biotechnology Deskbook 36–39 (2001).
[23] 40 C.F.R. 156.

The application is usually preceded by experimental field testing. The agency allows a developer to carry out confined, small-scale field tests to gain data it needs to support an application, but requires a developer to apply for an experimental use permit (EUP) for larger scale field tests. An EUP will be granted if the applicant provides sufficient data for risk assessment by the agency and the assessment indicates that the field test will not cause unreasonable risk. The data needed for an EUP is less substantial than what is required for final approval (registration) of the pesticidal crop, but the agency may require inspection and crop destruction, and also set a food residue tolerance if the experiment involves food production.[24]

The limited scope of EPA's program has been a continuing concern to critics of GM crops and foods, and environmentalists. A report by the Pew Foundation, as part of its "Initiative on Food and Biotechnology" program, questions whether EPA and APHIS provide effective postmarket oversight of such products to ensure their safety, address the stability of commodity crop and food product markets, and maintain public trust.[25]

These concerns have been heightened by highly publicized incidents involving contamination of conventional crops and foods for human consumption. These include the previously noted StarLink Corn incident in which a pesticidal GM corn, approved by EPA as a product for animal feed, was found at low levels in crops destined for human food as well as in human food products, and the Prodigene incident in which a vaccine-producing corn, unapproved for any food or feed use, had become mixed with soybeans intended for human consumption.[26]

The Pew report also points to EPA's failure to directly regulate the farmers who plant, harvest, and sell such pesticidal GM crops, and not taking enforcement action against them when they fail to comply with restrictions the agency has set for crop planting and distribution. The

---

[24] 40 C.F.R. 172.

[25] Michael Taylor & Jody Tick, Pew Foundation, Post-Market Oversight of Biotech Foods-Is the System Prepared? (2003).

[26] Id.

agency claims that its legal authority is limited to imposing such restrictions only on the developers and sellers of pesticidal crop seed, and requiring that they include the restrictions in their contracts of sale to their farming customers ("grower agreements"). This indirect arrangement for transferring EPA restrictions downstream to crop growers and sellers has proven ineffective, with surveys showing that many farmers disregard the restrictions and that the companies selling GM seed lack motivation to police their customers. Congress has not acted to provide EPA with the additional authority it would need to directly regulate downstream activities.

Many have accused the agency of misusing its regulatory authority and facilitating the introduction of pesticidal GM crops. According to Friends of the Earth, EPA accepts substandard testing data from product developers, disregards conflicting studies from independent researchers, ignores allergenic and other risks to health, and raised the maximum permissible levels of herbicide residues on food crops to provide incentives for the marketing of new herbicide-tolerant GM crops.[27] According to Gregory Mandel, "EPA is not evaluating the potential impact of transgenic pharmaceutical producing, industrial compound producing, herbicide-tolerant, drought-resistant, salinity-tolerant, virus-resistant, temperature-tolerant, or disease-resistant plants on the environment."[28]

These charges have prompted the agency to sponsor research on methods for assessing the potential allergenicity of GM crop proteins and human allergenic susceptibility, the impacts of such crops on nontarget species, the evolution of more resistant insect pests, and the development of crop planting and management strategies to slow such evolution in target pest populations.[29]

---

[27] Press Release, Friends of the Earth, GM Crop Safety Tests Flawed (Nov. 16, 2004). (on file with author).

[28] G. Mandel, *Gaps, Inexperience, Inconsistencies, and Overlaps: Crisis in the Regulation of Genetically Modified Foods and Animals*, 45 WMLR 2167, 2231.

[29] Environmental Protection Agency, Ecological Exposure Research, http://www.epa.gov/eerd (last visited June 18, 2008).

Finally, as noted earlier, EPA is also mandated to ensure that any pesticide residues in foods do not cause "unreasonable adverse effects."[30] It implements this responsibility by determining safe dietary levels and tolerances for the residues, unless it finds this unnecessary to protect consumer health, in which case it exempts the pesticide residue. Thus, if the pesticidal residue of a GM crop has not been exempted or approved by EPA as falling within a tolerance level, the crops sold that bear such residues will be considered "adulterated" food products by the FDA and subject to enforcement action and sanctions by the FDA to prevent their further sale.[31] Obviously, this is another complex and contentious aspect of EPA's regulation of pesticidal GM crops.

Food and Drug Administration

The FDA is authorized by the Food, Drug, and Cosmetic Act to protect public health by ensuring that foods are safe, sanitary, and properly described to consumers.[32] It is also directed by the Coordinated Framework to encompass GM food products within its regulatory program. Although the main features of its regulatory program were designed long before the advent of biotechnology, Congress and the agency have made few modifications to deal with the special characteristics and uncertainties of GM food products and have essentially ignored controversies that have arisen about their safety and desirability. Thus, the agency's oversight of both GM and non-GM foods alike is mainly focused on whether the food product is "adulterated" by an unapproved additive or pesticide residue, and "misbranded" by a misleading product label or other promotional material used by its manufacturer.

According to its statutory mandate, FDA is not empowered to conduct pre-market review of a new food product unless the product contains an additive that has not been previously evaluated and approved

---

[30] FFDCA, 21 U.S.C. 346a.
[31] Id.
[32] 21 U.S.C. 301–397.

or exempted, by the agency,[33] or bears a pesticide residue that exceeds its EPA-set tolerance level, as discussed earlier. Thus, FDA rules provide that a food containing an additive may not be sold unless the agency has either exempted the additive on grounds that its long-standing use or safety studies indicates it is "generally recognized as safe" (GRAS), or the agency has determined on the basis of safety studies that the additive can be safely used under certain specified conditions.[34] The safety studies involve consideration of the properties of the additive and data regarding its probable consumption, cumulative effects, and other matters regarding its safety for the uses intended. Most of this information is provided by the company applying for approval to sell the food product. FDA may determine that a non-GRAS additive can only be safely used in certain quantities or within other parameters. Yet if it accords GRAS status to the additive, no restrictions are imposed and food containing the additive is no longer subject to FDA regulation because of its additive content.

Following announcement of the Coordinated Framework, FDA issued a policy statement that it would treat GM and non-GM food products in the same manner and not differentiate because of the biotechnological methods used to make GM food, and regulate only when it finds that end product attributes pose unreasonable risk to human health.[35] Thus, GM and conventional foods are subject to the same FDA approach for regulating additives. The policy also states that FDA assumes that the genetic material used to make a GM product "will likely be the same or substantially similar to substances commonly found in foods, such as proteins, fats and oils, and carbohydrates." This assumption signaled that it would, in general, accord GRAS status to the genetic material incorporated in a GM food, and that it would therefore not subject GM food to

---

[33] FFDCA, 21 U.S.C. 402,409.

[34] FFDCA, *supra,* at 201(s) and 321(s). See also 21 C.F.R. 170.3.

[35] Statement of Policy: Foods Derived From New Plant Varieties, 57 Fed. Reg. 22984 (May 29, 1992). fda.gov/Food/Biotechnology (June 23, 2009).

pre-market review because inclusion of new genetic material would not cause the food to be adulterated.

By this action, FDA created a large hole in its pre-market review program that is extremely accommodating to GM foods, in keeping with the Coordinated Framework. Although details are not available, critics believe that FDA applies this assumption in most instances, relies mainly on information provided by GM food developers, and rarely calls on them to do additional scientific studies.[36] The policy also states that FDA expects companies to voluntarily consult with it prior to marketing new GM foods, especially with regard to genetic content that may have toxic or allergenic characteristics, to minimize subsequent regulatory problems. A guidance for companies about the consultation process, as well as a description of FDA's power to impose sanctions, are included in the policy statement. In its 1992 Policy Statement, FDA claimed that the voluntary consultation process was being followed by virtually all companies.[37] It has not discussed the prevalence of consultations since that time.

Friends of the Earth, a long-standing opponent of GM food, claims that the consultation process is flawed because it does not require testing, companies routinely ignore FDA requests for additional information, and that at most, the agency merely reviews company-provided summaries of data rather than the full content of the studies from which the data were derived.[38] In addition, there is no transparency. The data submitted by companies, on which the agency bases its determinations, is usually claimed to be proprietary, kept confidential by FDA, and withheld from the public. According to a notable agricultural policy expert, "I know of not a single independent scientist in the U.S. that has gained

---

[36] G. Mandel, *Gaps, Inexperience, Inconsistencies, and Overlaps: Crisis in the Regulation of Genetically Modified Foods and Animals*, 45 WMLR 2167, 2219.

[37] Statement of Policy: Foods Derived from New Plant Varieties, 57 Fed. Reg. 22984, 22991 (May 29, 1992).

[38] Press Release, Friends of the Earth, GM Crop Safety Tests Flawed (Nov 16, 2004) (on file with author).

access to such data on any current GM crop or food." He further charges that independent scientists have not received funding or technical cooperation from FDA that would enable them to carry out independent assessments of the GM food safety claims made by companies.[39]

Thus, there is no mandatory pre-market review at FDA for most GM food products, and those that are reviewed arise from company initiative and are permissively treated because of FDA's reliance on company-submitted summaries of alleged proprietary studies that are not available to other scientists or the public. Most GM foods with pesticide residues are treated in similar fashion. As noted earlier, they will not be considered adulterated by the FDA and therefore not subject to pre-market approval by FDA if EPA has previously exempted the residue or the residue conforms to EPA's tolerance level. Because EPA relies on information submitted by companies that claim the information is proprietary, independent scientific review and meaningful public involvement are lacking in its proceedings as well.[40]

The second major feature of FDA's regulatory program for GM food products is its authority to prevent "misbranding" to ensure that labeling and promotional materials accompanying a product in commerce are not fraudulent or misleading. Here, the major issue confronting FDA has been the demand by opponents of GM food and proponents of consumer rights that FDA require that GM foods be labeled as such. Despite persistent pressure, the agency has refused to impose a mandatory GM food labeling requirement, claiming that there is no factual basis for it to conclude that bioengineered foods differ from other foods in any meaningful or uniform manner, and that GM foods as a category of food products do not present any different or greater safety concern than foods developed by traditional plant breeding.[41]

---

[39] Charles M. Benbrook, GMOs, Pesticide Use, and Alternatives: Lessons from the U.S. Experience at 15, available at http://www.biotech-info.net/lessons_learned.pdf.

[40] Id.

[41] Statement of Policy: Foods Derived From New Plant Varieties, 57 Fed. Reg. 22984 (May 29, 1992).

The FDA policy statement asserting this "substantial equivalence" assumption nevertheless indicates that the agency retains authority to require that a specific type of GM food be labeled under certain circumstances, such as if using the common name of its non-GM food counterpart would mislead consumers in that it would not adequately indicate GM-imparted characteristics of the food such as a change in its texture or taste, or fail to indicate GM-created safety issues such as a new and unsuspected allergenic hazard. FDA has issued a Guidance for Industry that outlines how food producers may voluntarily label their products to indicate its GM content, or conversely to indicate its lack of GM content. In carefully considered language, the Guidance provides examples of label wording it would find appropriate for such purposes, wording that would not mislead consumers or conflict with the agency's assumption about the equivalence of GM and non-GM foods.[42] This contrasts with the mandatory labeling and traceability requirements for GM foods in the EU, as discussed in Chapter 3.

FDA has resisted critics who oppose its policies and assumptions with regard to the GRAS status of GM foods, and the absence of pre-market review and mandatory labeling. A federal court, petitioned by a consumer interest group to review and invalidate these agency determinations and policies, denied the group's claims that the FDA had not followed appropriate regulatory procedures, made arbitrary determinations, and had violated the rights of persons to be able to choose non-GM foods for religious or other personal reasons. Reinforced by this judicial affirmation of its policies and practices, FDA has continued to refuse to modify its regulatory program.[43]

As an aside, it should be noted that FDA's regulatory responsibilities also encompass pre-market review of new pharmaceuticals to determine if they are safe and effective, and that their production process can

---

[42] *FDA, Guidance for Industry: Voluntary Labeling Indicating Whether Foods Have or Have Not Been Developed Using Bioengineering 2, 4 (2001).*

[43] Alliance for Bio-Integrity v. Dept. Health and Human Services, 116 F.Supp.2d 166 (D.D.C. 2000).

ensure quality control. Thus, the drug evaluation branch of the agency must review new vaccines and other drugs derived in whole or part from GM crops designed for this nonfood purpose. Food product companies and food retailers have expressed great anxiety that GM drug-producing crops could contaminate both GM and non-GM food crops intended for human consumption, as in the Prodigene incident previously mentioned, and threaten consumer health and the food system. Although medicinal or industrial GM crops do not fall under the authority of the agency's food review branch, the seriousness of the threats they pose have caused the agency to work more closely with APHIS and EPA on how to identify, prevent, and respond to such contamination.

To return to GM foods, FDA claims it lacks authority to carry out postmarket examination of food company records for evidence of food-caused harms, or to order recalls of unsafe foods. Thus, it has not carried out systematic postmarket oversight of GM foods and looks to APHIS for addressing postmarket contamination issues.[44] However, the StarLink Corn incident illustrates how postmarket contamination has implications for FDA. The pesticidal corn had been found in taco shells, a consumer food product. Because EPA had approved the corn for use as animal feed but not for human food because of its suspected human allergenic potential, EPA enforcement and sanctions followed in due course. In addition, the presence of the corn in human food caused the food to be "adulterated" and prompted enforcement action by FDA as well.

The StarLink case is discussed again later in this chapter for its liability implications. Briefly here, the incident was followed by lawsuits brought by growers of conventional crops against Aventis, the maker and seller of the StarLink seed. These growers claimed that prices for their crops had fallen and contracts for their crops had been cancelled because customers suspected that the conventional crops they had ordered were contaminated. Aventis eventually negotiated an out-of-court settlement

---

[44] Michael Taylor & Jody Tick, Pew Foundation, Post-Market Oversight of Biotech Foods-Is the System Prepared? (2003).

of grower claims of economic damage for an amount that exceeded $100 million. Although no evidence of human health impact was ever produced, StarLink and other contamination cases have made FDA aware of the need to work more closely with EPA and APHIS on means of preventing and responding to "low-level contamination" incidents. The need for such collaboration has become more urgent and important because of the arrival of GM crops intended for the development of medicinal and industrial products, as discussed in Chapter 7.[45]

Another challenge for the agency has been posed by food products from clones of livestock. After a decade of deliberation and peer review of its studies, the agency has concluded that meat and milk from clones of cattle, swine, and goats, and from offspring of such animals "are as safe to eat as food from conventionally bred animals," and announced that the Department of Agriculture will work with stakeholders to provide "an orderly market transition." Noting further that an animal clone is a genetic copy of the donor animal, and its reproduction does not involve altering, adding, or deleting DN, FDA decided that it "is not requiring labeling or any other additional measures for food" from these species of cloned animals and their offspring.[46]

Thus, FDA has exempted from regulatory oversight a broad range of food products derived from clones who are the offspring of animals that may have been genetically modified. Those who have opposed the FDA action on the basis of their values have been ignored by the FDA because they lack a factual basis for refuting the agency's findings. In a somewhat more precautionary approach, the European Food Safety Authority (EFSA) is advancing toward a similar outcome. According to EFSA, disease and death rates of animal clones are significantly higher than

---

[45] Press Release, USDA, USDA Clarifies Policy on Low-level Presence of Genetically Engineered Material, available at http://www.aphis.usda.gov/newsroom/content/2007/03/llppolicy.shtml.

[46] Center for Veterinary Medicine, FDA, Animal Cloning: Risk Management Plan for Clones and their Progeny, (Jan. 15, 2008) available at http://www.fda.gov/cvm/cloning.htm.

what has been recorded for conventionally bred livestock, but it anticipates that these rates are likely to decrease as the technology improves.
It also expects that human food products from both sources will have
similar nutritional value. However, EFSA cautions that food safety will
depend in part on removing unhealthy clones from the food chain as is
done with unhealthy conventional animals, and that there may be environmental impacts. EFSA has also recognized concerns based on personal values and sought ethical guidance from the European Group on
Ethics in Science and New Technologies to aid its deliberations.[47]

To sum up, FDA, EPA, and APHIS comprise a complex but relaxed
federal system for regulating the safety of GM crops and foods. Because
of their limited statutory mandates and eagerness to adhere to the free-
market, anti-regulation themes of the Coordinated Framework, these
agencies provide a loosely connected network of permissive regulators
with each acting in a manner that expedites the advance of GM crops
and foods and minimizes any obstacles created by uncertainties about
safety.

Common Law Liability

In most nations, the legal framework for governing technological risks is
dominated by regulatory programs that do risk assessments, enact rules
and standards, issue permits and licenses, and monitor and take enforcement or other actions when needed to ensure compliance. However, the
governance framework in the United States and the United Kingdom
also includes an additional feature, a robust common law system that
functions independently of the regulatory programs with few exceptions.

---

[47] *See* Opinion of the European Group on Ethics for Science and New Technologies on
a request from the European Commission, available at http://ec.europa.eu/european_
group_ethics/activities/docs/opinion23_en.pdf. *See also* Scientific Opinion of the Scientific Committee on a request from the European Commission on Food Safety, Animal
Health and Welfare and Environmental Impact of Animals derived from Cloning by
Somatic Cell Nucleus Transfer (SCNT) and their Offspring and Products Obtained
from those Animals, The EFSA Journal (2008) 767, 1–49.

Common law can be simplistically described as a system comprised of general principles for fairly adjudicating certain types of civil disputes, and of courts that provide a forum and special rules for hearing the disputes, clarifying their factual content, and applying the general principles to resolve the disputes. In the United States, each of the fifty states has its own common law system, and over time, each state's courts have developed their own variations on the principles, with some state courts being notably flexible in modifying or adapting the principles to address new factual circumstances or when presiding judges feel it necessary to "do justice" in resolving the disputes.

Because disputes are brought to these courts by an aggrieved person (the plaintiff) who claims that a personal injury or economic harm has been caused by the wrongful action of a named party (the defendant), the remedy sought is usually a court judgment that would impose an obligation on the defendant to compensate the plaintiff for the harm suffered, that is, to impose legal liability for compensatory damages. The plaintiff may also seek additional remedies such as the award of punitive damages to punish the defendant more severely if the court finds that the defendant acted recklessly or in willful disregard of the plaintiff. The plaintiff may also seek a court order to enjoin a continuing activity that is allegedly wrongful, or to enjoin a defendant from commencing an activity on grounds that it is highly likely to create imminent, significant, and irreversible harm. At any point prior to a court decision in such cases, the parties may settle the dispute out of court and terminate the lawsuit.

Procedural requirements and rules of evidence regarding use of expert witnesses and testimony, and the ability of the parties to bear the transactional costs involved, such as fees for attorneys and expert witnesses, are among the many factors that influence the progress and outcomes of the lawsuits. In recent years, courts have often consolidated into a single "class action," the many similar lawsuits that may follow a major accident at an industrial facility or the widespread sale of a harmful product.

The principles, so-called theories of liability, that have proven over decades to be most appropriate for plaintiffs to rely on in cases involving harms caused by a process or a product are those known as Negligence, Strict Liability, and Nuisance.[48] In the few lawsuits brought in recent years for harms allegedly caused by the sale of GM seed and its use in growing a GM crop, discussed subsequently, plaintiffs have relied on one or more of these three principles. Lengthy treatises are needed to describe these principles in their full complexity and differentiation across the fifty states. What is provided here are some brief working definitions, as follows.

The Negligence theory of liability requires that the plaintiff establish that the defendant owed him or her a duty to exercise reasonable care in conducting its activity, or in making or selling its product; failed to meet that duty of care; and that this failure was the proximate cause of the harm suffered by the plaintiff. An example would be a case in which harm was caused by a defendant's production process (e.g., crop growing) because the defendant had failed to use customary or standard practices or comply with government regulations to ensure its safety. Another example would be a case in which harm was caused by a defendant's product because the defendant had failed to correct a manufacturing defect, a design defect, or had failed to warn and provide safe use instructions to its customers or other downstream users about a non-obvious hazard in using the product for its intended purpose.

Strict Liability theory requires that the plaintiff prove that the defendant's allegedly harmful activity was ultra-hazardous, unreasonably dangerous and contextually inappropriate, or that the defendant's product was defective in its design, manufacture, or warning, and that the intrinsic defect was the proximate cause of the harm incurred by the plaintiff. Thus, unlike the requisite for negligence, the plaintiff need not prove that the defendant's behavior fell below a standard of care, which is usually a more difficult burden. Strict liability has been applied in cases that involved, for example, harms arising from the manufacture or storage of

---

[48] M. Baram, *Liability and its Influence on Designing for Product and Process Safety*, 45 Safety Science 11–30 (2007).

explosives in a populated area, or from sale and use of a product with a defective component or erroneous instruction for its safe use.

Nuisance theory requires that the plaintiff prove that the defendant conducted an unreasonable activity on its property that has interfered with the plaintiff's use and enjoyment of his or her property or damaged the property. This is a particularly troublesome theory for a court to apply because of the potential breadth of its application. Thus, courts often balance various factors such as the likelihood and severity of the harm, the societal value of the activity, and specific contextual considerations. Cases have involved, for example, keeping livestock on one's property in an urban environment, or operating a facility that discharges noxious odors or pollutants into the community.

Plaintiffs have recently sought to have courts extend Nuisance theory to hold a product manufacturer liable for the damages arising from use of the product by the manufacturer's customers, as in cases against the makers of lead paint products and GM seed, with some courts holding that Nuisance is an appropriate theory where it can be shown that the manufacturer was substantially involved in the downstream, harm-causing use of their product by another party. This illustrates the extraordinary flexibility of common law principles when interpreted and applied by activist judges.

As this brief survey indicates, common law provides a plaintiff with several options for securing remedies that can be costly and even financially ruinous for a defendant company, especially when the company causes a major accident or sells a product that harms many persons. The defendant's losses often extend far beyond the liability for damages that may be imposed by the courts, and include injunctions against its further conduct of the activity or sale of the product, recalls of the product, restoration of the area contaminated by the incident, adverse publicity, loss of customers and investors, and the prompting of regulatory interventions and penalties, for example.

Common law therefore has the clear potential to make companies more attentive to the safety of their activities and products, and to thereby prevent many harms that would not have been prevented by regulation, because it creates fears about liability and additional adverse impacts that rational managers and directors of companies should take into consideration in their decision making. This "deterrent function" of the common law can thereby fill regulatory gaps and essentially create a precautionary principle in the governance of technological risks.

However, this optimistic appraisal is moderated by other considerations. Common law is unreliable and unpredictable because of the many variables involved, such as the attitude and values of the presiding judge, the effectiveness of the attorneys representing the parties, the attitudes and capabilities of the judge and jury in dealing with complex factual issues, laws, and regulations that in some instances explicitly or implicitly preempt common law remedies, and the basic issue of having a plaintiff willing and able to bear the emotional and economic costs of bringing and sustaining a lawsuit against a well-endowed corporate defendant. As for its deterrent effect, obviously much will depend on the willingness of corporate officials to heed the prospect of loss and the need for improving safety despite the economic gain from continuing to do business as usual.[49]

GM Liability Scenarios

The potential of the common law for promoting the safety of GM agriculture and foods by imposing economic losses and deterring unsafe practices and products can be estimated by evaluating three prototypical scenarios. In these scenarios, the vulnerability of GM seed producers, crop growers, and the makers and sellers of GM food products is considered.

The first scenario involves the making and selling of a GM food product in compliance with the regulations and exemptions discussed earlier, but that is later shown to cause harm to consumer health. Although no such incident has been proven in court, its possible occurrence is a

---

[49] *Id.* Also see M. Baram, et al., Alternatives to Regulation (Lexington Books, 1982).

continuing concern as more GM food products enter the marketplace without rigorous scientific appraisal and pre-market review by FDA. If such an incident occurs, there is a considerable body of prior court decisions involving allergenic reactions and other harms to consumers caused by conventional food products that would be applicable and persuasive. In those prior cases, judicial application of Negligence and Strict Liability (for defective products) theories has enabled injured consumers to secure awards of compensatory and punitive damages against the product makers and sellers, and been followed by product recalls and sanctions by FDA and state agencies against the defendants. It seems reasonable to assume that harms caused by GM foods would not be treated differently by the courts, provided the plaintiffs are able to establish causation.

The second scenario involves the growing of a GM crop from which gene flow or pollen drift occurs and causes "GM contamination" of a neighbor's conventional crop, and subsequently leads to cancellation of orders for the conventional crop by customers in the United States or abroad who have zero-tolerance for GM content in the crops they purchase. In most states, the property damage and business loss incurred by the neighbor provides the basis for a lawsuit against the GM grower that could be based on liability theories such as Negligence for growing the GM crop without a sufficient buffer zone or other means of containment, and Nuisance for intentionally carrying out an activity that interferes with the neighbor's use and enjoyment of his property or harms his property interests in the conventional crop.

In addition, in many states the neighbor may also seek damages under several theories of liability from the maker of the GM seed that was used. Under Negligence theory, the neighbor would have to establish that the maker was negligent in designing or producing the seed product or selling it without appropriate warnings and instructions for its safe use, that this negligence breached the standard of care the maker owed the neighbor as a bystander, and that the breach was the proximate cause of the harm that ensued. Under Strict Liability, the neighbor would focus not

on the maker's negligent conduct, but on the product's hazardous characteristics, and have to establish that the product itself was intrinsically
defective for its intended use because of a design or production defect or
because it lacked sufficient warnings and safe use instructions, and that
such defectiveness of the product was the proximate cause of the harm.
As noted earlier, a few courts have also accepted the Nuisance claim
that the maker of a product is liable when it is substantially involved
in another's use of its product that creates the nuisance that harms the
neighbor's property interests. Thus, the neighbor may also recover damages under Nuisance theory in such courts.

The third scenario involves the inadvertent mixing of GM and conventional crops by downstream parties who play important roles in the
food supply system, such as those who store, distribute, transport, and
sell crops to the makers of processed food products. As in the second scenario, customers who contracted for conventional crops without any GM
content are likely to cancel orders, and the consequent business losses
would accrue to all parties within the food system. Once again, Negligence and Strict Liability theories could provide a basis for imposing
liability on the parties implicated in the "contamination" incident and
possibly on the makers of the GM seed as well, except in those states
that do not allow these liability theories to be applied in cases involving
claims of purely economic loss. In such states, these theories are limited
to cases involving personal injury, and other law must be relied on by
the plaintiff to secure damages for economic loss, such as contract and
warranty law.

In each of these briefly described scenarios, other factors will also
play an important role. The plaintiff must prove causation by a prepon-
derance of the evidence. This poses a major challenge in the first scenario
involving a personal injury claim because of scientific uncertainty about
GM food. The defendant will also have the opportunity to refute the
plaintiff's evidence of causation and other aspects of the plaintiff's case,
and may raise potentially conclusive defenses such as federal preemption
of common law, expiration of the time in which the case can be brought

because of the state's statute of limitations, and by arguing that the harmful features of the product or activity were not known to, nor knowable by, the defendant. In addition, a case may hinge upon state law regarding the defendant's compliance with all applicable regulations. For example, state courts differ with regard to whether full regulatory compliance may be accepted by the court as a repudiation of the claim that the defendant acted negligently.

Several cases involving GM crops have arisen that resemble the second and third scenarios. These have been briefly summarized by Jane Early for the leading professional association of attorneys.[50] The most prominent case, *In re Starlink Corn Products Liability Litigation*, discussed previously, was a third scenario case that grew into a nationwide "class action," consolidating claims of economic loss by numerous growers against the seed maker.[51]

According to Early,

The Starlink case arose from the U.S. release of a biotech variety approved only for use in animal feed (because of its potential allergenicity) into the human food system. EPA's approval to commercially plant the Starlink corn for animal feed was conditioned on the existence of an effective identity-preservation system. Nevertheless, Starlink was found in taco shells and a range of other foods. After Starlink was found in the human food chain, U.S. EPA required that it be completely eliminated (zero tolerance) in the recall. In addition to paying many hundreds of millions of dollars to actually recall corn and corn-containing food products, Aventis, the parent company that now owns Starlink proprietor Aventis Crop Sciences USA, Inc., agreed to pay $110 million to settle a class action with farmers who claimed the contamination caused a decrease in commodity corn prices. Thousands of farmers shared in the Starlink class action

[50] J. Early, *Potential Grower Liability for Biotech Crops in a Zero-Tolerance World*, Agricultural Management Committee Newsletter, American Bar Association, v.9, n.1 (2005).

[51] Starlink Corn Products Liability Litigation, 212 F.Supp.2d 828 (N.D. Ill. 2002).

settlement without having to prove any actual harm other than depressed corn prices.

A second scenario-type case that followed StarLink had a different outcome, however. In *Sample v. Monsanto*,[52] the occurrence of pollen drift from plantings of GM corn and soybean seeds made by Monsanto caused a decline in prices of conventional crops, leading growers of such crops to seek damages under Nuisance and Negligence theories. A federal court, applying the common law of the relevant state, dismissed the case because that state's law bars use of these liability theories when the only harm claimed is economic loss.

Thus, common law is complex and unpredictable because many legal and factual variables influence outcomes, particularly when early cases involving a new technology and new factual circumstances are being brought to different courts. As a result, there is uncertainty about liability, which may cause some GM proponents to disregard precautionary measures. However, it may cause others who are more risk-averse or who have high name recognition in the volatile food marketplace, to take the extra steps needed to minimize potential harm to avoid severe business losses, tougher regulatory scrutiny of its future scientific studies, and loss of confidence among consumers, firms it does business with, and investors. Thus, it would seem that uncertainty about common law liability and other business losses is more likely to promote safety rather than lessen it.

Conclusion

The United States relies on a relaxed regulatory scheme and a potentially potent common law liability system to govern the safety of GM agriculture and food. Under this approach, innovation and commerce involving GM seeds, crops, and foods have flourished without causing harm to public health or serious environmental impact. The most troublesome

---

[52] Sample v. Monsanto Co., 283 F.Supp.2d 1088 (E.D. MO 2003).

consequence has been the recurring incidents of inadvertent, low-level contamination of conventional crops and foods that incur business losses.

Several factors may have contributed to this good fortune. Despite fears, there may be natural limits on the capacity of GM crops and foods to harm health and the environment. Another may be that regulatory expertise at FDA and the other agencies may have been sufficient to effectively employ relaxed methods of oversight and regulation, and to have exercised sound judgment on the quality of industry-provided studies, despite the critics who have argued that safety requires more stringent and detailed prescriptive rules, prolonged testing, independent studies, postmarket vigilance, transparency, and public involvement in proceedings. More likely is that the foreseeable and rapid economic impacts on crop and food markets and the lawsuits that would follow any reports about suspected or actual harms to human health and the environment have caused GM seed companies and food producers to be precautionary in advancing their new products.

Yet this approach to ensuring the safety of the GM enterprise has limitations that should be cause for several concerns and improvements. Relaxed regulation that depends on industry-developed studies and neglects robust postmarket surveillance fails to inspire confidence that hazards will be eliminated from the forthcoming multitude of new products and that existing products will not have serious adverse and irreversible effects over the long term. This is especially important because GM crops and foods are being introduced in developing nations that lack the regulatory apparatus and expertise to protect their interests and look to the U.S. system for assurances of safety.

Another concern is that the recurring incidents of contamination of conventional crops indicate that the U.S. system is currently incapable of ensuring coexistence between GM and conventional farming and thereby preserving consumer access to non-GM food. Clearly, there is a need for improvement in this regard, particularly because a new generation of GM crops with traits for producing medical and other industrial products are being introduced and if this leads to contamination of conventional or GM food crops, it will cause turmoil in agriculture and food systems, destroy consumer confidence in food safety, and endanger public health. Thus, finding means for ensuring coexistence between food crops and non-food GM crops must be a priority.

Finally, the isolation of the regulatory apparatus from human concerns needs to be addressed. GM regulators at the FDA, APHIS, and EPA operate in closed systems without transparency, and without respecting and considering personal values and consumer concerns in their deliberative processes, as if technical expertise and satisfying the claims of corporate entrepreneurs will be sufficient for dealing with the deep social consequences of genetic agriculture. These have become essential features of risk regulation in progressive democracies and been embraced by other regulatory programs in the United States. Their absence from GM regulation is a cause for mistrust and the likelihood that lawsuits involving narrow private interests would proliferate, creating a situation in which diverse court decisions and ad hoc settlements across fifty states would play a major role in shaping the future of the GM enterprise to the detriment of the public interest.

A new Congress could focus on these issues and provide the agencies with a more enlightened and effective mandate than that provided by the "coordinated framework" enacted almost two decades ago. It would expand agency authority for dealing with safety issues, direct regulators to provide transparency and engage with the public, and oversee agency implementation. And it could address expanding markets for GM crops and foods and the vulnerability of developing nations by working toward creation of a coordinated international regulatory system.

There also remains the hope that GM agriculture, led by the large firms producing GM seed and BIO, the industry's leading trade association, will evolve into a more mature industry with socially responsible self-regulation. This transformative process has been taking place in the global chemical industry and reflected in its Responsible Care program,[53]

---

[53] M. Baram, "Multinational Corporations, Private Codes, and Technology Transfer for Sustainable Development," 24 *Environmental Law Journal* 33 (1994).

a work in progress by an industry that also dominates GM agriculture. New movements for corporate social responsibility and sustainable technology are growing, as discussed in the chapter by Vergragt and Brown, and promoting ethical consciousness and transparency among leading multinational firms. Thus, higher standards of care and social responsibility may infect GM agriculture and make self-regulation a more useful part of the system for governing its safety.

3 The European Union's Regulatory Framework

Developments in Legislation, Safety Assessment, and Public Perception

Marianna Schauzu

Introduction

Over the first fourteen years of commercialization of genetically modified (GM) crops, the acreage of GM crops has consistently grown each year, with the number of countries increasing from 6 in 1996 to 25 and a global area of 134 million hectares in 2009. Herbicide-tolerant soybean continued to be the principal GM crop, followed by insect and/or herbicide tolerant maize, cotton, and rapeseed. The United States, Brazil, Argentina, India, Canada, China, Paraguay, and South Africa are the major growers with 64 to 2.1 million hectares of GM crops, followed by Uruguay, Bolivia, the Philippines, Australia, Burkina Faso, Spain, and Mexico with 0.8 to 0.1 million hectares of GM crops. Among the ten countries that grew less than 50.000 hectares are the European Union (EU) member-states[1] Czech Republic, Portugal, Romania, Poland, and Slovakia.[2]

Many countries have established regulatory frameworks with regard to the deliberate release of genetically modified organisms (GMO) and

---

[1] In Germany, the GM maize variety MON810 was cultivated until 2008. Invoking of a safeguard clause under Directive 2001/18/EC by the German Competent Authority suspends the approval of this GM crop as of April 2009.

[2] James, C. 2010. Executive Summary: Global Status of Commercialized Biotech/GM Crops: 2009. ISAAA Brief 41–2010. ISAAA: Ithaca, NY.

derived products in the early 1990s.[3] Two types of regulatory systems can be distinguished. Whereas some countries, such as the United States and Canada, have enacted "product-based" legislations, the EU's regulatory system for GMO and derived foods and feeds is "process based."

Directives on the Deliberate Release of GMO

The EU began to govern the deliberate release of GMO into the environment in 1990 when Directive 90/220/EEC entered into force. The scope of this Directive covered experimental releases as well as the placing on the market of GMO for cultivation, import, and/or processing.[4]

Authorization Procedure for the Placing on the Market of GMO

The authorization requires a case-by-case assessment of the potential risks to human and animal health of each GMO to be placed on the market. Applications are forwarded to the EU member-state where the GMO or derived product is to be placed on the market for the first time. The application must be accompanied by data and results obtained from laboratory and greenhouse research, as well as from developmental releases, concerning the ecosystems that could be affected by the use of the product, and by an assessment of any risks to human health and the environment related to the GMO.

The risk assessment is performed by the Competent Authority (CA) of the EU member-state that receives the application. The other member-states are invited to provide comments. If the CA confirms in its opinion that the information provided by the applicant establishes that the placing on the market of the GMO would not pose a risk to human health and the environment, and if no objections are raised by

[3] OECD. 2003. Biotechnology Regulatory Developments in OECD Member Countries. OECD. Paris.

[4] Directive 90/220/EEC. Official Journal of the European Communities L 117: 15–27, 8.5.1990.

other member-states, consent is given to the placing on the EU market by the CA of the member state that had received the application.

If any of the member-states raises an objection, the European Commission submits to a Regulatory Committee, composed of government representatives of the member states, a proposal for a Commission decision. If the Regulatory Committee fails to deliver an opinion, the Commission forwards its proposal to the EU Council of Ministers. If the Council does not deliver an opinion within three months, the Commission is authorized to adopt its proposed decision. The Commission may also ask its Scientific Committees for their scientific opinion.

Authorizations under Directive 90/220/EEC

The first permits for the placing on the EU market of GM plants to be used in food and feed production were granted to Monsanto for its herbicide-tolerant soybean in April 1996 and to Syngenta (then: Ciba-Geigy) for its insect-tolerant maize Bt176 in January 1997. Further authorizations in accordance with Directive 90/220/EEC for cultivation or import of three GM rapeseed and three other GM maize lines followed during 1997 and 1998 (see Table 1).

In all cases the CA's initial assessment reports and the consulted Scientific Committees came to the conclusion that the GM plant is as safe as the conventional counterpart, but objections to the placing on the market were raised by other member-states. In the case of Bt176 maize, the Commission adopted its proposed decision after both the Regulatory Committee and the Council had failed to provide an opinion. All other authorizations granted in accordance with Directive 90/220/EEC were based on Commission decisions in accordance with the opinions of its Scientific Committee on Plants.

National Safeguard Measures

Directive 90/220/EEC contained a so-called safeguard clause providing that where any member-state has justifiable reasons to consider that a

Table 1. *Authorizations (A)/Notifications (N) of Genetically Modified Plants for Food and/or Feed Use* (last update: June 2010)*[5]

Product	Directive 90/220/EEC	Regulation (EC) 258/97	Directive 2001/18/EC	Regulation (EC) 1829/2003
HR Soybean 40-3-2	Import, Food Feed, A: 04/1996			Renewal ongoing
IR Maize Bt176**	Cultivation, Food, Feed, A: 01/1997			
HR Rapeseed MS1 X RF1**	Cultivation, Feed A: 06/1997	Food (Oil) N: 06/1997		
HR Rapeseed MS1 X RF2**	Cultivation, Feed A: 06/1997	Food (Oil) N: 06/1997		
HR Rapeseed Topas 19/2**	Import, Feed A:04/1998	Food (Oil) N: 06/1997		
HR Maize NK603		Food A: 03/2005	Import, Feed A: 07/2004	
HR Rapeseed GT73		Food (Oil) N:11/1997	Import, Feed A: 08/2005	Renewal ongoing
IR Maize MON810	Cultivation, Feed A: 04/1998	Food N: 02/1998	Renewal ongoing	Renewal ongoing
HR Maize T25	Cultivation, Feed, A: 04/1998***	Food N: 02/1998		Renewal ongoing
IR Maize Bt11	Import, Feed A: 04/1998	Food N: 02/1998		Renewal ongoing
IR+HR Maize MON809****		Food N: 10/1998		
IR Sweet Maize Bt 11		Food A: 05/2004		
HR Rapeseed MS8 X RF3		Food (Oil) N: 04/2000	Feed A: 03/2007	Renewal ongoing
HR Rapeseed Liberator L62****		Food (Oil) N: 11/1999		
HR Rapeseed Falcon GS40/90****		Food (Oil) N: 11/1999		
IR Cottonseed IPC531		Food (Oil) N: 12/2002		
HR Cottonseed RR1445		Food (Oil) N: 12/2002		
IR Maize MON863		Food A: 01/2006	Import, Feed A: 08/2005	
HR Maize GA21		Food A: 01/2006		Food + Feed A: 03/2008
HR+IR Maize 1507			Import, Feed A: 11/2005	Food + Feed A: 03/2006

[5] http://ec.europa.eu/food/dyna/gm_register/index_en.cfm

Product	Directive 90/220/EEC	Regulation (EC) 258/97	Directive 2001/18/EC	Regulation (EC) 1829/2003
HR+IR Maize NK603 X MON810			Import, Feed A: 01/2006	Food + Feed A: 10/2007
HR+IR Maize DAS 59122–7				Food + Feed A: 10/2007
HR+IR Maize 1507 X NK603				Food + Feed A: 10/2007
HR Sugarbeet H7–1				Food + Feed A: 10/2007
HR Soybean A2704–12				Food + Feed A: 09/2008
HR Cotton LL Cotton 25				Food + Feed A: 10/2008
HR Soybean MON89788				Food + Feed A: 12/2008
HR Rapeseed T45				Food + Feed A: 03/2009
IR+HR Maize 59122 X NK603				Food + Feed A: 10/2009
IR+HR Maize MON88017				Food + Feed A: 10/2009
IR Maize MON89034				Food + Feed A: 10/2009
IR Maize MIR604				Food + Feed A: 11/2009
IR Maize MON863 X MON810				Food + Feed A : 03/2010
IR+HR Maize MON863 X NK603				Food + Feed A : 03/2010
IR+HR Maize MON863 X MON810 X NK603				Food + Feed A : 03/2010
Amylopectine EH92-527-1			Cultivation A : 03/2010	Feed***** A : 03/2010

HR = herbicide resistant, IR = insect resistant.

* Nonfood and nonfeed GMO (e.g., carnation) are excluded from this list.

** Approval for marketing withdrawn by the European Commission Decision of April 25, 2007.

*** Authorization for cultivation of T25 maize expired on April 18, 2007.

**** Have not been marketed.

***** Authorization for feed use and the adventitious or technically unavoidable presence in food.

GM plant, which has received consent for placing on the market, constitutes a risk to human health or the environment, it may provisionally restrict or prohibit the use and/or sale of that product on its territory.

The safeguard clause was invoked on nine separate occasions under Directive 90/220/EEC during the late 1990s and in 2001, three times by Austria, twice by France, and once each by Germany, Greece, Luxembourg, and the United Kingdom. The scientific evidence provided by these member-states as justification for their measures concerning GM maize varieties Bt176, T25, MON810, rapeseed varieties MS1XRF1 and Topas19/2, respectively, was submitted to the Commission's Scientific Committee(s) for opinion. In all of these cases, the Committee(s) came to the conclusion that there was no evidence that would justify overturning the original authorization decision.[6]

After October 1998,[7] the Commission had ceased authorizing the placing on the market of further GM crops under Directive 90/220/EC due to lack of support of the majority of EU member-states.[8] This created a *de facto* moratorium and started a revision of the EU's regulatory regime to better address the challenges posed by GMOs.

Revision of the Deliberate Release Directive

The revision of Directive 90/220/EEC in 2001 was a first step to overcome the so-called moratorium. The new Directive 2001/18/EC[9] introduced mandatory labeling and traceability requirements for GMO to be placed on the market. Approvals are now limited to a period of 10 years and applicants are requested to provide postmarket monitoring

---

6 http://europa.eu/rapid/pressReleasesAction.do?reference=MEMO/03/221&
   format=HTML&aged=0&language=EN&guiLanguage=en.
[7] In October 1998 the Commission authorized two GM carnation varieties with modified flower color. Table 1 contains only GM plants authorized for food and/or feed use.
[8] France, Greece, Italy, Denmark, and Luxembourg, later joined by Belgium and Austria, usually vote against further proposals for approval of GMOs.
[9] Directive 2001/18/EC. Official Journal of the European Communities L106: 1–39. 17.4.2001.

plans for some categories of products. The consultation of the Scientific Committee(s) is obligatory. Applicants are requested to provide information and reference material to enable the identification and detection of GMO to facilitate postmarket inspection and control.

According to Directive 2001/18/EC, member-states may take appropriate measures to avoid the unintended presence of GMOs in other products. To help member-states in developing national approaches to coexistence, the Commission adopted, on July 23, 2003, a recommendation on guidelines for the development of national strategies and best practices to ensure the coexistence of genetically modified crops with conventional and organic farming.[10] By February 2009, fifteen of the twenty-seven EU members states had adopted specific legislation on coexistence (Austria, Belgium, Czech Republic, Denmark, France, Germany, Hungary, Lithuania, Luxembourg, Latvia, the Netherlands, Portugal, Romania, Sweden, and Slovakia).[11]

Authorizations under Directive 2001/18/EC

The first GM plant to be authorized in accordance with Directive 2001/18/EC was the herbicide-resistant maize line NK603. Although there was still no majority in the Regulatory Committee as well as in the Council to either accept or reject the approval for import and processing, the Commission decided to grant the authorization in July 2004, based on the positive opinion adopted by the newly established European Food Safety Authority (EFSA)[12] in November 2003. Further authorizations for the import of another three GM maize and two GM rapeseed varieties, and recently for the cultivation of a GM potato have been granted since (see Table 1).

---

[10] http://europa.eu.int/comm/agriculture/publi/reports/coexistence2/guide_en.pdf.

[11] http://ec.europa.eu/agriculture/coexistence/index_en.htm.

[12] EFSA was established in January 2002 to be an independent provider for scientific assessments ensuring food safety across the EU member states and across the food and feed sectors. It replaced the Commission's Scientific Committees.

Renewal of National Safeguard Provisions

In spite of the revision of Directive 90/220/EEC, eight of the nine bans remained in place and were renewed under the safeguard provision of the new Directive 2001/18/EC. Only the UK withdrew its ban. In view of the new Directive, the Commission examined the additional information provided by those member-states that had invoked the safeguard clause and submitted it to the newly established EFSA[13] for evaluation. In July 2004, EFSA provided its opinions concluding that the additional information and arguments provided by the member-states did not invalidate the original risk assessments for the GMOs in question. Consequently, the Commission proposed decisions, initially to the Regulatory Committee, requesting member-states concerned to lift their national safeguard measures. The Regulatory Committee, however, on November 29, 2004, failed to reach a qualified majority either in favor or against these proposals. The proposals were therefore transmitted to the Council, which rejected the Commission's proposals on June 24, 2005.

The Commission was required to either submit amended proposals to the Council, or to re-submit its original proposals or to present legislative proposals. Taking account of the Council decision, prior to any further action, the Commission again requested EFSA to provide a scientific opinion taking specific questions into account for the individual GMOs. In its opinion of March 2006, EFSA again judged that the information provided did not constitute new scientific evidence that would invalidate the previous risk assessments.[14] In the light of the EFSA opinion, the Commission proposed draft Council decisions requesting Austria to repeal its measures concerning MON810 and T25 maize.[15] In December 2006, the Council rejected the Commission's proposals. In March 2009,

---

[13] Regulation (EC) No 178/2002. Official Journal of the European Communities L31: 1–24. 1.2.2002.

[14] http://www.efsa.europa.eu/en/scdocs/scdoc/338.htm.

[15] The other three GMO (Bt 176 maize, MS1xRF1 and Topas 19/2 rapeseed) prohibited by the national safeguard clauses have no longer been commercialized by the companies concerned.

another attempt of the Commission to lift the Austrian bans failed when the Council again rejected another Commission's draft decision based on EFSA's scientific opinion of December 2008.[16]

In January 2005, Hungary had joined the member-states that have banned MON810 maize[17] on their territories, followed by Greece in March 2006 and by France in February 2008. This caused the European Commission again to request reviews by EFSA. Following investigation of the evidences presented by Hungary, Greece, and France, EFSA in July and October 2008, respectively, once again reaffirmed the safety of the banned product, stating that, in terms of risk to human and animal health and the environment, no new scientific evidence was presented that would invalidate the previous risk assessments of genetically modified maize MON810.[18]

In March and April 2009, Luxembourg and Germany also postulated cultivation bans on MON810 maize. Moreover, Austria, Luxembourg, and Hungary have prohibited the cultivation of the most recently authorized amylopectine potato, known as "Amflora" potato.[19]

As a response to the existing national bans on cultivation of GM crops and with the aim to enable the authorization system for GMOs to function more effectively, the Commission proposed on July 13, 2010, a new regulation that amends Directive 2001/18/EC. This amendment shall provide member-states with the freedom to allow, restrict, or ban the cultivation, not the import, of GMOs on part or all of their territory on grounds other than those based on a scientific assessment of health and environmental risks.[20] The decision needs approval from the member-states and the European Parliament. It is criticized by both supporters and opponents of GMOs.

---

[16] http://www.efsa.europa.eu/en/scdocs/scdoc/891.htm.

[17] The authorization for the cultivation of T25 maize expired on April 18, 2007.

[18] http://www.efsa.europa.eu/cs/Satellite.

[19] http://europa.eu/rapid/pressReleasesAction.do?reference=MEMO/10/325&format=HTML&aged=0&language=EN&.

[20] http://europa.eu/rapid/pressReleasesAction.do?reference=IP/10/921&type=HTML.

WTO panel dispute on biotech products

In May 2003, Argentina, Canada, and the United States requested the Dispute Settlement Body (DSB) of the World Trade Organization (WTO) to constitute a Panel in pursuance of their complaints concerning the EU's authorization system for GMO. In its reports circulated to Members in September 2006, the WTO Panel found that the European Commission applied a general *de facto* moratorium on the approval of biotech products as of June 1999 that led to undue delays in the completion of the approval procedures. Further, the national safeguard measures introduced by six member-states before the establishment of the Panel were considered as violation of the EC's obligations under the Agreement on Sanitary and Phytosanitary Measures (SPS Agreement). The Panel found that the Commission acted inconsistently with its obligations with regard to all of the safeguard measures at issue, because these measures were not based on risk assessments satisfying the definition of the SPS Agreement[21] and hence could be presumed to be maintained without sufficient evidence. The Panel reports were adopted by the DSB in November 2006. At the DSB meeting on December 10, 2006, the European Commission announced its intention to implement adequate measures to comply with its WTO obligations within a reasonable period of time, given the complexity and sensitivity of the issues involved.[22]

A first step to resolve the trade dispute was taken with the attempts of the European Commission ordering Austria to lift its safeguard clauses it had placed on GM maize. With the proposed amendment of Directive 2001/18/EC the Commission expects that EU member states now

---

[21] Article 5.1 of The WTO Agreement on the Application of Sanitary and Phytosanitary Measures (SPS Agreement) of April 15, 1994, demands "an assessment of risks to human, animal or plant life or health, taking into account risk assessment techniques developed by the relevant international organizations" (http://www.wto.org/english/tratop_e/sps_e/spsagr_e.htm).

[22] Summary of the Dispute: http://www.wto.org/english/tratop_e/dispu_e/cases_e/ds293_e.htm.

reconsider their safeguard measures on GMO cultivation, and rather adopt suitable co-existence measures to avoid the unintended presence of GMOs in conventional or organic crops.

On July 15, 2009, Canada, acknowledging that the EC regulatory procedures on GMO are working, as evidenced by twenty-one authorizations since the date of establishment of the WTO panel, and the EU agreed to end the six-year WTO dispute.[23] EU and Argentina settled their WTO case in March 19, 2010, while the dispute with the United States is still ongoing.[24]

Regulation Concerning Novel Foods

Because the EU Directives on the deliberate release of GMO focused mainly on environmental aspects, a new Regulation providing for food safety assessment was established in 1997.[25] Regulation (EC) No 258/97 concerning novel foods and novel food ingredients (Novel Foods Regulation) introduced both an approval and a notification procedure. The scope of the Regulation covers GMO-derived foods as well as other foods considered novel because they had not hitherto been used for human consumption to a significant degree within the EU. The Regulation also provided specific labeling requirements for GMO-derived food with the intention to enable consumers to make an informed choice. An additional Regulation entered into force in 2000, specifying that only GMO-derived foods that contain new proteins or recombinant DNA (rDNA) would be subject to the GMO labeling requirements. A threshold of 1 percent of adventitiously present GMO-derived material in foods was established.[26]

---

[23] http://europa.eu/rapid/pressReleasesAction.do?reference=IP/09/1142&type=.

[24] http://europa.eu/rapid/pressReleasesAction.do?reference=IP/10/325&format= HTML&aged=0&language=EN&guiLanguage=en.

[25] Regulation (EC) No 258/97. Official Journal of the European Communities L 43: 1–7. 14.2.1997.

[26] Regulation (EC) No 49/2000. Official Journal of the European Communities L 6: 13–14, 11.1.2000.

In contrast to EC Directives that have to be implemented by national laws, EC Regulations are binding and directly applicable in all EU member-states.

Authorization Procedure

The authorization procedure under the Novel Foods Regulation is comparable to that introduced with Directives 90/220/EEC and 2001/18/EC for the commercialization of GMO. It requires the CA of the EU member-states that receives the application to perform a risk assessment, and the European Commission to draft a decision based on this risk assessment after considering the comments provided by other member-states. If there are no objections, the member-state that performed the assessment can authorize the product for marketing in the entire EU. If reasoned objections are raised, these are considered by the Commission who provides a Standing Committee composed of representatives of the national CAs and, if necessary, the Council with a draft decision. If neither the Standing Committee nor the Council can make a decision, it is up to the Commission to adopt the measures proposed in the draft decision.

Notification Procedure

Because foods in general (except, e.g., food additives) had so far not been subject to authorizations, a simplified notification procedure was introduced for GMO derived and other novel foods that were considered substantially equivalent to existing products as regards their composition, nutritional value, metabolism, intended use, and level of undesirable substances contained therein. The notification procedure did, however, not apply to foods containing, or consisting of, GMO, such as yogurt with living GM microorganisms or kernels of GM sweet maize.

The person responsible for the placing on the market can either provide the European Commission with generally recognized scientific evidence or ask a member-state's CA for an opinion on the substantial equivalence of the respective novel food.

The notification procedure was used to legalize processed foods and food ingredients produced from several varieties of GM maize, as well as refined oil produced from GM rapeseed and GM cotton during 1997 to 2002 (see Table 1). In all cases, the applicants had asked the CAs of member-states to confirm the substantial equivalence of the product.

The term substantial equivalence was first defined by the OECD Group of National Experts on Safety in Biotechnology as a tool for determining the safety of GMO-derived foods (see "Safety Assessment" section of this chapter). Both the term substantial equivalence and the underlying approach were "borrowed from the U.S. Food and Drug Administration's (FDA) definition of a class of new medical devices that do not differ materially from their predecessors and thus, do not raise new regulatory concerns."[27]

Because the purpose of a genetic modification is to change a plant's characteristics, the result will always be a difference in the plant's chemical composition. Thus, the most reasonable interpretation is that a food derived from a GMO is considered substantially equivalent to its conventional counterpart if the genetic modification has not resulted in intended or unintended alterations in the composition of relevant nutrients and inherent toxicants, and that the newly introduced genes and expressed proteins have no adverse effect on the dietary value of the food and do not pose any harm to consumers or to the environment.[28]

This definition was the guiding concept for the EU member-states who issued opinions on the substantial equivalence of processed foods derived from GM maize and GM rapeseed. Without questioning the assessments performed by these member-states, several member-states were of the opinion that the notification procedure should no longer be

[27] Miller, H. I. 1999. Substantial equivalence: Its uses and abuses. Nature Biotechnology 17: 1042–1043.

[28] Schauzu, M. 2000. The concept of substantial equivalence in safety assessment of foods derived from genetically modified organisms. AgBiotechNet 44.

applied to GMO-derived foods. Another criticism was the reliance of the notification procedure on the opinion of only one member-state without involving the others.

The so-called moratorium was overturned by the first marketing approval that was granted in accordance with the Novel Foods Regulation for Bt11 sweet maize in May 2004 (see Table 1). This was, however, not due to a change in member-states' voting behavior but to a decision taken by the European Commission after neither the Standing Committee nor the Council had reached a qualified majority. In its decision the Commission referred to the opinion of its Scientific Committee on Food (SCF) that considered Bt11 maize as safe for human food as its conventional counterparts, and stated that the methodology used for the safety assessment was in line with recent guidelines prepared by the Scientific Steering Committee (SSC)[29] and with Codex Principles and Guidelines on Foods Derived from Biotechnology.[30]

Regulations on GM Food and Feed

The new regulations concerning GMO-derived foods and feeds, effective as of April 2004, represented another attempt to respond to criticism. Regulation (EC) No 1829/2003 on genetically modified food and feed[31] replaced the GM food related part of the Novel Foods Regulation. Thus, it also dismissed the simplified notification procedure provided for in the Novel Foods Regulation and requires an authorization procedure (see Figure 1) for all GMO-derived products instead. The old system has been replaced by a "one door – one key" procedure for the scientific assessment and the authorization of GMO and derived food and feed. A single

---

[29] The SSC Guidance Document for the risk assessment of genetically modified plants and derived food and feed of March 6–7, 2003, was the basis for the EFSA Guidance Document that as a requirement of Regulation (EC) No 1829/2003 was to be published before entering into force of the Regulation in April 2004.

[30] Codex Alimentarius. 2004. Principles for Risk Analysis and Guidelines for Safety Assessment of Foods Derived from Modern Biotechnology. FAO and WHO. Rome.

[31] Regulation (EC) No 1829/2003. Official Journal of the European Union L268: 1–23. 18.10.2003.

Figure 1. Authorization procedure for GM food and feed in the European Union.

risk assessment is conducted, and a single authorization is granted, for a GMO and its possible uses. GMOs likely to be used as food and feed can only be authorized for both uses, or not at all. However, cultivation of GMO or commercialization of GMO for nonfood or nonfeed purposes still needs an authorization in accordance with Directive 2001/18/EC.

Authorizations are limited to a ten-year period but are renewable. Applications for renewals of authorizations for products that have been lawfully placed on the Community market before Regulation (EC) No 1829/2003 entered into force are required within nine years from the date of which the products were first placed on the market.

The assessment of environmental risks as well as the safety assessment of GM food and feed is no longer the responsibility of member-states but of EFSA, whose opinions are made available to the public with the opportunity to make comments. CAs of member-states are also invited to provide comments. Based on an EFSA opinion, the European Commission drafts a proposal for granting or refusing authorization. A Standing Committee of Representatives of member-states (MS Committee) then decides whether to accept the Commission's proposal through a weighted voting system. If the committee's proposal is neither accepted nor rejected by a qualified majority of member-states, it is referred to the Council of Ministers. If the Council takes no decision within three months, or does not reach a qualified majority indicating that it opposes the proposal, the European Commission can adopt it.

In addition, the labeling provisions were extended to cover GM feed as well as foods produced from GMO but not containing any GMO-derived material, such as refined oils produced from GM oilseeds that are not distinguishable from conventional oil. A threshold of 0.9 percent was established for the adventitious or technically unavoidable presence of genetically modified material, that is, new proteins or rDNA, in foods or feed, when the marketing of such material within the EU has been authorized in accordance with the law.

A so-called zero tolerance applies to food and feed containing material from GMOs that are not approved in the EU.[32]

The applicant is further obliged to provide with the application a method to detect the genetic modification as well as reference material that enables the European Commission's Joint Research Center to validate the detection method.

Regulation (EC) No 1830/2003 requires traceability of GMO and derived products and provides a legal basis for case-by-case decisions on postmarket monitoring requirements where deemed necessary.[33] Under the new rules, business organizations must transmit and retain information about products that contain or are produced from GMOs at each stage of the placing on the market.

Regulation (EC) No 1829/2003 also provided for transitional measures allowing applications that were in an advanced stage of the authorization procedure to continue to be considered and authorized under the relevant legislation, however, in accordance with the requirements laid down in Regulation (EC) No 1829/2003. Hence, three decisions

---

[32] Heberer, T. et al. 2007. Zero tolerances in food and animal feed – Are there any scientific alternatives? A European point of view on an international controversy, Toxicology Letters 175: 126–127.

[33] Regulation (EC) No 1830/2003. Official Journal of the European Union L 268: 24–28. 18.10.2003.

authorizing the placing on the market of GM food were adopted under the Novel Foods Regulation, and five decisions authorizing the placing on the market of GM feed were adopted under Directive 2001/18/EC (see Table 1).

Of the eighty applications forwarded to EFSA by June 2010, five have been withdrawn, eighteen authorizations were granted by the Commission during March 2006 and March 2010 for foods and feeds derived from GM varieties of maize, soybean, cotton, rapeseed, sugar beet, and potato, and six applications for renewals of authorization of existing products are pending (see Table 1). Thirteen of the remaining applications have been assessed by EFSA by June 2010.[34]

Safety Assessment

Whereas regulatory frameworks differ across jurisdictions, the approaches to the safety assessment of foods derived from GMO are similar in most countries, as they are based on general principles and guidelines for risk assessment that have been elaborated by international and national organizations with competence in food safety long before the first commercialization of GMO-derived foods.[35]

Skepticism toward GMO in quite a few EU member-states has caused the European Commission to finance a research project to address scientific as well as societal issues related to the introduction of GM crops. The European Network on Safety Assessment of Genetically Modified Food Crops, with the acronym ENTRANSFOOD, began its work in February 2000. One of the objectives of the ENTRANSFOOD project was to evaluate the adequacy of current food safety assessment methods and strategies that had been developed and continuously adapted in accordance with the state of the art by various international and national organizations during the last two decades. As one of the

[34] http://www.efsa.europa.eu/en/gmo/gmoscdocs.htm.

[35] OECD. 2000. Compendium of National Food Safety Systems and Activities. Ad Hoc Group on Food Safety. OECD. Paris.

results, a guidance document for safety assessment was published in 2004 that served as a model for the guidelines later published by EFSA.[36] The results of the ENTRANSFOOD project reassured the adequacy of the comparative safety assessment strategy applied to GMO-derived foods. The authors of the guidance document even argue "that foods from GM crops are better characterized than other nonregulated plant-derived foods, due to the additional rigor in the current regulatory require-ments and testing regime compared to that for conventionally bred crops."[37]

Common to all approaches to safety assessment of GMO is the con-cept of substantial equivalence that was first described in the OECD report that resulted from the work undertaken by a Group of National Experts on Safety in Biotechnology and published in 1993.[38] It is based on the idea that existing products used as foods or food sources can serve as a basis for comparison when assessing the safety and the nutritional value of a GMO-derived food. It implies that if the modified food is found to be substantially equivalent to an existing food or food com-ponent with regard to phenotypic and agronomic characteristics and chemical composition, it can be treated in the same manner with respect to safety. The concept of substantial equivalence is used as a starting point and guiding concept for the safety assessment. It is considered a pragmatic tool for identifying differences between a GMO and its non-modified counterpart. Differences are then subject to further analyses with regards to their impact on human health. The objective of the safety assessment is to determine whether the new food is at least as safe as a comparable food produced from conventional crops.

[36] EFSA. 2004. Guidance Document of the Scientific Panel on GMO for the risk assess-ment of genetically modified plants and derived food and feed. EFSA Journal 99, 1–94 (final, edited version of 28 April 2006, published in May 2006).

[37] König, A. et al. 2004. Assessment of the safety of foods derived from genetically mod-ified (GM) crops. Food and Chemical Toxicology 42 (7): 1047–1088.

[38] OECD. 1993. Safety evaluation of foods derived by modern biotechnology – Concepts and principles. Organisation for Economic Co-operation and Development (OECD), Paris.

In contrast to conventional breeding techniques, genetic engineering allows insertion into the plant genome of single genes coding for new traits such as herbicide or insect resistance. In addition to the introduction of the intended new characteristics, unintended effects may also occur. Similar to traditional breeding techniques, unintended effects could potentially be caused by genetic rearrangements or metabolic perturbations. There is no indication that such unintended effects are more likely to occur in GM crops than in conventionally bred crops.[39] Yet, the introduction of GM crops requires a pre-market safety assessment that includes not only a characterization of the novel genes and gene products but also an array of analyses with regard to any unintended effects that may be evident in the phenotype or the chemical composition of the GM plant when grown under the same conditions as the nonmodified controls.

Molecular Characterization

Genetic engineering does not only provide tools for the construction of GMO but also for the analysis of the inserted DNA sequences and its flanking regions in the plant genome to determine whether rearrangements of the transgene construct or the insertion site have occurred and whether endogenous genes might have been disrupted or open reading frames have been created through the insertion. The amino acid sequences deduced from any open reading frames are to be compared to known sequences of allergens and toxicants. If fusion proteins are expressed, these would undergo the same safety assessment as intentionally introduced new proteins.

Comparative Analyses

Different from conventionally bred crops, GM plants are subjected to thorough analyses not only of their genetic but also phenotypic and

[39] Cellini, F. et al. 2004. Unintended effects and their detection in genetically modified crops. Food and Chemical Toxicology 42(7): 1089–1125.

chemical characteristics. Alterations in the phenotype are identified through a comparative analysis of agronomic characteristics such as growth performance, yield, disease resistance, and others. Comparative analytical studies of the chemical composition of the GM plant or derived food and their conventional counterparts focus on key nutrients, toxins, allergens, anti-nutrients, and biologically active substances that are known to be associated with the crop. OECD member countries are continuing to elaborate Consensus Documents identifying key components that should be analyzed as well as ranges of variation to perform a fully comprehensive compositional analysis of specific food crops.[40] For soybean, the data to be analyzed would cover, for example, the content of proteins, fat, and crude fiber, the composition of amino acids and fatty acids, the levels of endogenous anti-nutrients such as trypsin inhibitors, lectins, phytoestrogens, stachyose, raffinose and phytic acid, and endogenous allergens. Those parameters that fall outside the range of natural variation would be considered further in safety assessment.

Critics rightly point to the restriction of the comparative analyses that can only detect differences of known characteristics or parameters but not any unpredictable modifications. This is, however, also true for conventionally bred plants. The new profiling techniques that are being developed to analyze and compare whole genomes, transcripts, proteins, and metabolites may in the future assist in the safety assessment of GMO. However, in the first place they might be a means of improving our knowledge of plant physiology and metabolisms in general and thus, contribute to optimizing plant breeding.

New Proteins and Metabolites

Intended alterations in the composition of the GM plant such as newly expressed proteins or plant metabolites are analyzed with regard to potential toxicity and allergenicity. The source of the transgene must be

[40] OECD Consensus Documents for the Work on the Series on the Safety of Novel Foods and Feeds: http://www.oecd.org/document/9/0,2340,en_2649_201185_1812041_1_1_1_1,00.html.

considered carefully to make clear whether or not it encodes a toxin or allergen. In case of a new protein with no history of food use, its properties are compared to those of known toxicants and allergens. A comparison of the amino acid sequences will reveal homologies. Food allergens share further specific characteristics, such as stability of digestion by proteolytic enzymes. Digestion studies are among the relevant tests applied to newly expressed proteins.

Further toxicological test requirements, such as animal feeding trials, need to be considered on a case-by-case basis, taking into account the source, familiarity, and characteristics of the protein. For instance, proteins that have not been previously consumed with foods are generally to be subjected to a 28-day toxicity study in rodents, conducted in accordance with the protocol elaborated by the OECD.

Whole GM Foods and Feeds

If the composition of the GM plant is substantially modified, or if there are any indications for the potential occurrence of unintended effects based on the preceding molecular, compositional, or agronomic analyses, the whole GM food or feed should be tested in a 90-day toxicity study in rodents. Special attention must be paid to the selection of doses to avoid nutritional imbalances as well as to an adequate interpretation of statistical analyses. The importance of the latter is highlighted by the controversy caused by a publication of Séralini and colleagues in March 2007.[41] Supported by Greenpeace Germany, Séralini and colleagues reanalyzed the statistical data of a ninety-day feeding study in rats and came to the conclusion that "with the present data it cannot be concluded that GM corn MON863 is a safe product." The EFSA[42] as well as the Agence Française de Securite Sanitaire des Aliments (AFSSA)

---

[41] Séralini G.-E., Cellier, D., Spiroux de Vendomois, J. (2007): New Analysis of a Rat Feeding Study with a Genetically Modified Maize Reveals Signs of Hepatorenal Toxicity. Arch. Environ. Contam. Toxicol., Online-First Ausgabe 13 März 2007 (http://www.springerlink.com/content/02648wu132m07804/fulltext.html).

[42] See http://www.efsa.europa.eu/en/scdocs/doc/GMO_statement_MON863.pdf.

and the Federal Institute for Risk Assessment (BfR), however, are of the opinion that Séralini and colleagues have not provided new evidence that would call in question the results of previous assessments of the rat study considered as one set of data in the comparative safety assessment of the MON863 maize. The BfR concluded that the mostly minor, though statistically significant differences observed between test and control groups showed no consistent pattern but reflect the existing natural range of variation. Therefore, the observed statistically significant differences are not toxicologically relevant.[43]

Supplemental information on the possible occurrence of unintended effects can be obtained from comparative growth studies conducted with young rapidly growing animal species such as broiler chickens.

Advances in molecular biology, toxicology, biochemistry, and nutrition will lead to GM crops with more complex changes in metabolism, such as nutritionally enhanced crops, but will also provide new methodologies that can be developed into new safety assessment tools.

Competent authorities and safety assessment bodies are aware of the need to amend the existing guidelines for safety assessment of GM crops and derived foods and feeds accordingly to make all conceivable efforts to protect consumers from health risks.[44]

Acceptance of GMO and Derived Foods

Starting with the first arrival of GM soybeans at European harbors in 1996, consumer and environmental organizations have voiced their concerns about the safety of GM crops and derived foods, about consumer freedom of choice, and about the impacts the new technology may have

---

[43] http://www.bfr.bund.de/cm/208/90_tage_studie_an_ratten_mit_mon863_mais.pdf; http://www.gmo-safety.eu/news/493.statistically-significant-differences-occur-practically-feeding-studies.html.

[44] EFSA is currently updating its guidance document for the risk assessment of genetically modified plants and derived food and feed.

on society. These concerns have been echoed in opinion poll-type surveys. The most inclusive of these is the Eurobarometer, the official public opinion instrument conducted since 1991 on behalf of the European Commission.[45] When in the first surveys European citizens were asked to indicate which of different technologies they consider positively, they put biotechnology and genetic engineering at the end of the scale. This changed when in 1999 nuclear technology and in 2002 nanotechnology had been added to the list. Both technologies scored below biotechnology and genetic engineering. However, when asked more precisely whether they consider these technologies positive or negative, only 41 percent of the participants had a positive attitude toward biotechnology and genetic engineering in 1999, compared to 50 percent in the 1996 survey. Correspondingly, the negative attitudes increased from 11 percent to 23 percent. In 2002, a slight increase of acceptance (44%) and a decrease of negative attitudes (17%) were observed.

A comparable tendency was observed in the 1996 survey with regard to acceptance of GM food. Of those persons who gave reasons for their opinions such as usefulness, risk, moral acceptance, and whether the technologies should be encouraged, the "decided public," 61 percent had a positive attitude in 1996 whereas only 49 percent were in favor of GM foods in 1999. The relatively positive attitude of Europeans toward GM food observed in 1996 corresponds with the success of the first product that entered the market in the United Kingdom (UK) in February of the same year. Puree produced from GM tomatoes had been authorized in accordance with UK national law and sold very well, although a clearly visible label stated that it was "made with genetically modified tomatoes." Another label informed "that the benefits of using genetically modified tomatoes for this product are less waste and reduced energy in processing." In addition, the launch of the product was accompanied by a leaflet describing the aims and the technology used. A benefit for the

[45] European Commission. 1992–2003. Public Opinion Analysis, Special Eurobarometer Reports (http://europa.eu.int/comm/public_opinion/archives_en.html).

consumer was the slightly lower price compared to conventional tomato puree. However, in July 1999 the GM tomato puree disappeared from the shelves of supermarkets. Not long before, in August 1998, the public was alarmed by a TV interview with Arpad Pusztai, a scientist working at the Rowett Research Institute in Aberdeen, UK, who announced that he had observed toxic effects in rats fed with GM potatoes. The results of the feeding study were assessed by the UK Royal Society, which found the data invalid because of technical limitations of the experiment and the incorrect use of statistical tests. In May 1999, the Royal Society concluded that the results do not provide evidence that GM foods cause risks to human health.[46] However, the results of the 1999 Eurobarometer survey indicated that in the UK, acceptance of GM foods had decreased from 67 percent in 1996 to 47 percent. In 2002, the upward trend observed in the Eurobarometer survey (50% acceptance) was more distinct in the UK, with 63 percent of UK citizens having a positive attitude toward GM foods.

The results of the Eurobarometer surveys may have influenced the votes taken by EU member-states with regard to authorizations of GMOs. In 2002, acceptance of GM foods was rather high in Spain (74%), Finland, and Ireland (70%). The lowest acceptance rates were reported from Greece (24%) followed by France (30%), Luxembourg (35%), Italy (40%), Denmark (45%), Austria (47%), and Germany (48%). Except Germany that usually abstains, the member-states where acceptance is low are the same that voted against the authorization of GM plants and derived foods. Another interesting finding of the Eurobarometer surveys of 1996, 1999, and 2002 is that basic knowledge of genetics is lacking. For instance, 35 percent of participants agreed that only GM but not ordinary tomatoes contain genes, and 20 percent believe that by eating a GM fruit a person's genes could also become modified.

---

[46] The Royal Society. 1999. Review of data on possible toxicity of GM potatoes (http://www.royalsoc.ac.uk).

The outcome of the Eurobarometer survey conducted in 2005[47] show that Europeans are becoming increasingly optimistic about biotechnology in general. However, the acceptance of GM food has taken another downturn. Of the "decided" public, 58 percent oppose and 42 percent support GM food. Only in Spain, Portugal, Ireland, Italy, Malta, Czech Republic, and Lithuania do the supporters outnumber the opponents. In contrast, supporters are few especially in Austria, Greece, Hungary, Germany, and Latvia.

During September and October 2005 a special Eurobarometer was conducted on risk issues.[48] It indicated that GMO is not the major concern Europeans think of. When prompted to respond spontaneously, only 8 percent of the participants considered GMOs a possible problem or risk associated with food. The most frequently cited risk was food poisoning (16%), followed closely by chemicals, pesticides, and toxic substances at 14%, and obesity at 13%. However, when the question was asked more precisely, that is, to what extent they are worried about GM products in food or drinks, 25 percent of participants answered 'very worried' and 37 percent answered 'fairly worried,' which is in the midrange of the 'worry' scale, however, it is rather high compared to the 2002 results. On the other hand, quality (42%) and price (40%) appear to be the key factors influencing the food purchasing behavior, whereas food safety (8%) and production methods (7%) are not primary preoccupations of consumers and do not appear to be the most important issue in guiding their food choices. Greece (81%), Italy (77%), and Cyprus (76%) stand out for the extent of their concern over GM products in food or drinks whereas the Netherlands, Sweden, and Finland ranked lowest for their level of worry (42% to 46% answered 'worried'). From the fourteen items on the list of potential risks, GM products in food or drinks came out as the top concern only in Austria, that is, seven Austrians

---

[47] http://ec.europa.eu/research/press/2006/pdf/pr1906_eb_64_3_final_report-may2006_en .pdf.

[48] http://ec.europa.eu/food/food/resources/special-eurobarometer_riskissues20060206_ en.pdf.

in ten conveyed their concern about the use of GM products in food or drinks.

In the European Commission funded reseach project "Consumer Choice," polls were conducted in ten EU countries during 2006 and 2007. In countries in which GM products were available in shops at the time of the polls (the Czech Republic, the Netherlands, Poland, Spain, and the UK), only 20 percent of buyers actively avoided such products. The checking of data of actual purchases against answers to questions about their preferences and intentions from the purchasers revealed that most of the responses are not a reliable guide to what purchasers do in the shops. The authors of the study therefore regard it as likely that in many European countries GM products would be bought if they were offered for sale.[49]

It is quite reasonable to presume that in the EU public, risk perceptions and attitudes have had negative impacts on the commercialization of GM foods. At least in Germany there are almost no GM plant derived foods on the shelves of supermarkets. According to a 2006 survey, however, 93 percent of cattle and pig feeds and 89 percent of poultry feed in Germany had been found to contain GM maize, soybean, and rapeseed.[50]

Conclusion

Whereas the safety of conventionally bred crops is taken for granted based on a history of safe use, the placing on the market of GMOs requires a pre-market safety assessment. The EU legislation on GMO and derived food and feed provides that only GMO derived products that have been demonstrated to be as safe as their conventional counterparts are authorized and can thus be commercialized. The EU legislation on GMO provides for a transparent safety assessment

---

[49] http://www.kcl.ac.uk/schools/biohealth/research/nutritional/consumerchoice/ downloads.html.

[50] Bendiek, J. and Grohmann, L. 2006. GVO-Kontrolle von Lebensmitteln, Futtermitteln und Saatgut: eine bundesweite Übersicht. J. Verbr. Lebensm. 1: 241–245.

procedure and for extended labeling as a tool for consumers to make informed choices.

The safety assessment of GM crops and derived foods is conducted on a case-by-case basis and can be tailored to all crop-trait concepts, including future GM crops with more complex traits. If differences between the GM crop or derived food and its traditional counterpart are identified, these are examined with respect to possible impacts on human and animal health and the environment. As a result, a relative statement is made on whether the GM crop is as safe as the conventional comparator that is generally accepted as safe.

GM crops are therefore better characterized than conventionally bred crops, including knowledge on the site and nature of the genetic modification. It may be suggested that both GM crops and conventionally bred crops be treated the same in safety assessment, bearing in mind that safety assessments are not required for non-GM crops.

The public debate that was started with the arrival of the first GMO in Europe was mainly caused by nongovernmental organizations (NGOs) with explicit interest in discussing the issues associated with the emerging biosciences. They demanded public participation in the decisions about regulation and scientific assessment, and supported beliefs that there is potential for negative impact and uncertainty associated with unintended human health effects that are hidden by producers or regulators to serve a vested interest.

It was therefore not that much a surprise when the results of the Eurobarometer surveys revealed that there is a lack of public confidence in GM food. Yet recent polls have also shown that in practice, consumers frequently behave different from the way they say they would do and that they are in general not careful to avoid GM products offered for sale.

The European Commission and its scientific body EFSA have reacted to the criticism with amendments of legislation and revisions of guidance documents for safety assessment.

However, the reported poor acceptance of GM food in many of the EU member-states has also caused internal disagreement among member-state authorities. Given the procedure of decision making as laid down in the EU legislation on GMO, the European Commission is facing difficulties in fulfilling its function of balancing diverging national interests with the aim of reaching a common European position. With the recently proposed amendment to the legislation the European Commission aims to send a strong signal to citizens that Europe takes into account their concerns regarding GMOs.

The development of a communication strategy to adequately inform consumers about the real risks and hazards as well as benefits from GM food in relation to traditional foods and techniques might be even more important for the future contribution of genetic engineering to agriculture and food production in Europe.

4 The Dutch Approach to Safety Governance of GM Agriculture

Hubert P. J. M. Noteborn and Freija H. van Duijne

Introduction

The European approach to regulating genetically modified (GM) crops and foods has had unsettling consequences. It demonstrates that industrialists, politicians, scientific experts, and national regulatory authorities have failed to adequately address public concerns. These concerns arise from public awareness of the uncertainties and risks, and from lack of confidence in the studies performed by scientists and regulators.[1] The concerns also reflect differences in perceptions and values, which have been shaped by recent history involving BSE, dioxin pollution, and food irradiation.[2]

The expert committees that drafted European regulations on GM agriculture focused exclusively on potential safety concerns and designed the regulatory system accordingly.[3] The experts targeted scientific issues such as the development of resistant "superbugs" and "superweeds," as

---

[1] G. E. Séraline et al., New Analysis of a Rat Feeding Study with a Genetically Modified Maize Reveals Signs of Hepatorenal Toxicity, *Arch. Environ. Contam. Toxicol* (2007), http://www.springerlink.com/content/02648wu132m07804/fulltext.html.

[2] T. Ten Eyck, Shaping a Food Safety Debate. Control Efforts of Newspaper Reporters and Sources in the Food Irradiation Controversy, 20 *Science Communication* 426–447 (1999).

[3] D. Burke. The Recent Excitement over Genetically Modified Foods, in Mill Hill Essays (1997), http://www.nimr.mrc.ac.uk/millhillessays/1997/food.htm (last visited June 19, 2008).

well as adverse effects on human and animal health. In contrast, the concerns of the public, NGOs, and environmentalists centered on longer-term environmental consequences, consumer choice, impacts on traditional farming, and other societal issues such as the influence of industry in the regulatory process and commercial pressures. In addition, food is a symbolic lifestyle factor, and familiarity with food products is important to European consumers including the Dutch citizens. Thus, the current European regulatory regime, which emphasizes technical expertise and narrowly ranks food safety as its top concern, has proven an inadequate approach to meeting public concerns.

These problems have been apparent in the Netherlands since 1996 when the Dutch government allowed the importation and limited processing of Monsanto's glyphosate-tolerant soybeans on the basis of scientific studies that showed the product to be safe for the environment and human health.[4] Environmentalists and consumer groups violently protested upon arrival of the first shipments from the United States and Canada. In retrospect, it seems that this response may have been due to several factors. The imports would obstruct consumer choice because no labeling of GM products was required at that time, and the products and their derivatives, such as GM soybean oil, would be indistinguishable from conventional, non-GM alternatives. Also the expert evaluation, which led to the approval, was seen as inappropriately narrow and not reflective of societal values, and information on potential benefits was not presented.

Increased transparency and public participation in regulatory procedures are needed to enhance stakeholder and public confidence in food safety governance. Whereas regulators must identify potential harms, other concerns such as long-term outcomes, and information on the potential benefits of GM crops would bring about a more thoughtful and acceptable regulatory approach. Moreover, the regulatory approach must respect both expert and nonexpert values, address safety in

---

[4] Commission Decision (EC) No. 96/281 of 30 April 1996, O.J. (L 107) 10–11.

addition to corporate social responsibility, and promote a dialogue between experts and nonexperts to gain trust and legitimacy. This chapter summarizes the Dutch experience with GM agriculture and suggests ways of filling these gaps.

Agriculture in the Netherlands

In the Netherlands, like elsewhere, plant breeding has been an artistic quest over the centuries, advancing on a trial-and-error basis. Particularly significant events were the introduction by early European explorers of new food plants to Europe from the Americas (maize, potato, and tomato) and Asia (rice, spices, and soybean). After 1884, Dutch agriculture took a more scientific approach, and around 1904 started to inspect field crops to ensure good, consistent seeds and healthy seed potatoes. To this end, they crossed and backcrossed different varieties mainly by the homologous recombination of different genomes, thus mixing thousands of unknown genes.

The government then established a Descriptive List of Varieties of Arable Crops to protect and reward seed breeders' efforts and guide growers in their choice of crop plants. The Breeder's Decree of 1941 and the Seeds and Planting Materials Act of 1967 provided incentives for commercialization with legal protections for developing and marketing new crop varieties. If a farmer's seeds met the criteria for a novel crop variety, such as distinguishability, uniformity, and stability, the farmer could register the seeds with the Dutch Register of Varieties, thus ensuring that no one but the original breeder could commercially reproduce the crop for up to twenty-five years. Because Dutch agriculture emphasized exports, the regulatory system encouraged seed innovation to produce new varieties that would be better than existing plants and result in higher yield crops for export.

As a result, the Register of Varieties shaped plant breeding in the Netherlands over a period of fifty years, and the genetic basis for characteristics such as taste and smell, pest and disease resistance, and edible quality were considered to be of minor importance.[5] Because pests, crop diseases, and weeds were being controlled with synthetic chemicals, there was no pressing need to determine and incorporate genetic resistance features. The Register of Varieties regime also unintentionally contributed to loss of biodiversity and loss of genetic variability.

Until 1990, the Dutch system did not require safety assessments for these crops and derivative foods prior to their entering the market. Although the common practice of selecting favorable varieties and discarding those exhibiting unwanted properties in the course of a breeding program may have included some evaluation of safety, this was not formally required. Even today, Dutch breeders may employ a plethora of non-GM techniques to manipulate genetic characteristics, such as protoplast fusion, embryo rescue, and mutagenesis, without undergoing the rigorous safety assessments required for GM varieties, and do not know precisely which genes they introduce into new crop varieties. Therefore, the Dutch public's perceptions about the safety of conventional crops and foods are grounded more in culture and tradition than in scientific safety testing.

Introduction of GM Crops in the Netherlands

The Dutch government and parliament believe that GM varieties are a very important field of development for the economy and civil society at large. GM crop plants have the potential to resolve problems such as improving the sustainability of agriculture. However, the public considers it necessary to ensure that safety, administrative transparency, and personal freedom of choice are not compromised. The risks posed by GM crops and foods have been debated for the past thirty-five years. In the mid-1970s the focus was primarily on the risks of doing research with

[5] Wiskerke, J. S. C. (1999) Farmers use of diversity case study – Europe – the Netherlands http://members.shaw.ca/oldwheat/Resources/FarmersuseofdiversityNL.pdf.

recombinant DNA, whereas today we are witnessing major controversies about the cultivation and use of GM crop plants. The application of GM technology to plant breeding has forced the Dutch government into a "learning by doing" policy cycle. This started in December 1974 when the Dutch Association for Biochemistry distinguished between two types of risks: the possible dangers of recombined organisms for humans and the environment, and the social risks posed by exceeding species boundaries. The Royal Dutch Academy of Sciences then drafted guidelines intended to confine the risks to man and the environment to an acceptable level. After DNA research was well under way, a DNA Committee for assessing societal implications and ethical aspects was established in 1981 and published an important report in 1983.

This was followed by Dutch implementation of EU Directives 90/219[6] on contained use of GMOs and 2001/18[7] on deliberate release of GMOs into the environment. In 1990, the government added the Decree on Genetically Modified Organisms (GMO Decree) to the Dangerous Substances Act,[8] integrating the EU Directives into the Dutch legal framework. Enacted in 1990, this decree provided the legal basis for regulating the use of GMOs under Dutch law, and created a permit process in which the National Committee on Genetic Modification (COGEM) assesses the health and environmental risks of GMOs, reports its findings to the Minister of Housing, Spatial Planning, and the Environment (VROM), and brings ethical and societal considerations to the attention of other Dutch officials.[9] Subsequently, Genetically Modified Organisms Regulations (GMO Regulations) were enacted to provide detailed rules primarily for ensuring the contained use of GMOs. Finally, the

---

[6] Council Directive 90/219, 1990 O.J. (L106) 1–39 (EC).

[7] Council Directive 2001/18, 2001 O.J. (L106) 1–39 (EC).

[8] Environmentally Hazardous Substances Act: Decree on Genetically Modified Organisms (GMO Decree 1990), 1993, (Staatsblad 435(NL); Genetically Modified Organisms Regulations (GMO Regulations), 1993, Staatscourant 107 (NL).

[9] Netherlands Commission on Genetic Modification (COGEM), 2007, Governance van biotechnologie: de veranderende rol van wetenschappelijke adviescolleges, Deining Maatschappelijke Communicatie, Report No. CGM 2006–01, 1- 48 (NL).

Decree on Disclosure of Information on Disasters and Serious Accidents (Biro) was enacted,[10] requiring permit-holders to provide municipal executives at the local level with information about GMOs that could lead to a disaster or serious accident. The Biro decree also required that laboratories draw up contingency plans for implementation under such circumstances.

National GM Food Safety Policy

In the Netherlands, in addition to the legislation on regulating environmental risk, activities involving GMOs have also been governed by other legislation. With regard to the safety of GM food and feed products, the Dutch government acted before EU rules took effect and issued regulations governing the entry of such foods and feed into the national market. The Food and Commodities Act became the principal framework for regulating food safety, and under Article 15 of the Act, the government issued temporary emergency regulations for GM foods. The Dutch regulatory program also required authorization for products derived from, but not containing, viable GMOs, irrespective of their substantial equivalence to existing, traditionally bred plants.

Authorization of GM food products required development of a dossier containing reports that demonstrate the product's safety for animals, humans, and the environment, and an assessment of the dossier by the Committee on Safety Assessment of Novel Foods. In addition, the Advisory Committee of the Food and Commodities Act (ACWW) was charged with responsibility for labeling provisions to provide Dutch consumers with objective information.

The government renewed these regulations in 1995 with some alterations in anticipation of the EU Novel Food Regulation, including recognition of "substantial equivalence" as a key concept in Dutch product

---

[10] Disclosure of Information on Disasters and Serious Accidents Decree (Biro), 1994, Staatsblad 463 (NL).

assessments. A permanent advisory body on novel foods was also established, with consumer organizations and industry and trade representatives designated as members of this expert group. National safety policy was also adapted to subsequent EU regulations.

EU GM Food Safety Policy

In the EU, GMOs and derivative products can only be placed on the market after having undergone a stringent science-based risk assessment on a case-by-case basis. Since May 1997, the EU's Novel Food Regulation, as amended,[11] has been fully integrated into the Dutch Food and Commodities Act and the Decree on Novel Foods. Now, GM plants are authorized for food and feed under EU procedures, which apply, to all member-states. Whereas, under the Dutch national system, the government could only act on the basis of hard scientific evidence of adverse health effects, under the EU system, it has more flexibility by acting on the basis of the EU's "precautionary principle," a major feature of EU food safety policy that mandates that if scientific uncertainty exists, member states may take extra care to protect citizens from uncertain or unknown effects of a particular food product.[12]

Since February 1999, the Dutch Committee on Safety Assessment of Novel Foods (VNV Committee) has implemented the EU authorization process. It reports risk evaluations, noting whether it concurs with company study findings, and submits a recommendation to Dutch officials for health and agriculture. The reports are available for public viewing on the Health Council's website. Further, the public may inspect a full dossier, on request, at the Health Council's library. Under the European Novel Food Regulations, any member-state can raise objections to the dossier and the first assessment. If a dossier raises a significant number of questions, the European Commission requests an opinion from the

---

[11] Commission Regulations 258/97, 1997 O.J. (L 43) 1–6 (EC); 1829/2003, 2003 O.J. (L 268) 1–23 (EC); and 1830/2003, 2003 O.J. (L 268) 24 (EC).

[12] Food Safety Regulation in Europe 112, (E. Vos & F. Wendler eds., Inersentia 2006).

Scientific Committee for Human Nutrition. If there is still disagreement, then a decision needs to be taken by the European Council of Ministers (see Chapter 3).

After the Netherlands implemented the European Directive of 1990 (EC 90/218), Dutch farmers began to grow GM plants in small to medium sized trials. In contrast, farmers in the United States and several non-EU nations had started cultivating and commercializing GM crops on a larger, industrial scale. Nevertheless, NGOs and environmentalists actively opposed how the EU addressed GM risks. Some of their concerns, such as the societal desirability of GM plants, did not factor into the Dutch approach to risk assessment at all. Moreover, many consumer groups wanted a more absolutist approach to safety regulation, in which decision makers would ensure that GM foods are 100 percent safe before approving commercialization.

A risk analysis has to provide information regarding the extent and nature of the risks to humans, animals, and the environment. To this end, the Dutch Decree on Genetically Modified Organisms intends that risks be calculated and quantified, but this approach has not been implemented when, as frequently happens, there is a lack of quantitative data.[13] If the likelihood of an undesirable event cannot be estimated or no conclusive scientific evidence is available, the analysis should be based on a worst-case scenario, in line with the precautionary principle. Also, it should be noted that even conventional crops may be found unsuitable for human consumption, as in cases where farmers accidentally reintroduced high levels of poisonous substances through conventional breeding techniques, such as, solanine in potatoes, cucurbitacin in squash/zuchini, and furanocoumarin in celery.[14] The Netherlands does not and could not provide a 100 percent safety guarantee for conventional crops or GM crop plants.

---

[13] Environmentally Hazardous Substances Act: Decree on Genetically Modified Organisms (GMO Decree 1990), 1993, Staatsblad 435 (NL); Genetically Modified Organisms Regulations (GMO Regulations), 1993, Staatscourant 107 (NL).

[14] F. Cellini et al., Unintended Effects and their Detection in Genetically Modified Crops, 42 *Food and Chemical Toxicology* 1089–1125 (2004).

EU legislation follows the approach recommended by the World Health Organisation (WHO), Codex Alimentarius, Food and Agriculture Organization (FAO), and the Organisation for Economic Co-operation and Development (OECD). It also adopts the requirements of the Cartagena Protocol on Biosafety,[15] which the United States, Canada, and Argentina have refused to ratify. The EU approach enables each member-state to exercise its sovereign right to make its own decisions on GMOs in accordance with the values prevailing in its society. As a result, ten years after the first commercial release, 95 percent of GMOs remain cultivated in six countries, none of which are EU member-states: the United States (50.6%), Argentina (16.7%), Brazil (13.2%), Canada (6,1%), India (5.4%), and China (3.3%).[16]

The EU has never officially introduced a moratorium, but between 1998 and 2004, no new GMOs were approved for planting or use in the EU by the EU Commission. What caused this de facto moratorium were factors such as the diversity of approaches to safety that exist at national levels, pressure from opposition groups, inability to cope with segregating and labeling GM food and feed, and demand for protecting consumer freedom of choice. Indeed, at the EU's Environment Ministers Council meeting in June 1999, Austria, France, Germany, Greece, Italy, and Luxembourg issued a declaration that they would effectively block approvals pending legislation for traceability and labeling of GM crop plants and derivative products.

To address these concerns of its member-states, the Commission tightened up its regulatory process to pave the way for ending the national bans and safeguard clauses, and established in 2003 a 0.9 percent labeling threshold for the adventitious or technically unavoidable presence of authorized GMOs in food products, and traceability

---

[15] Secretariat of the Convention on Biological Diversity (2000). Cartagena Protocol on Biosafety to the Convention on Biological Diversity: text and annexes. Montreal, Canada. ISBN 92-807-1924-6.

[16] C. James. Global status of commercialized Biotech/GM crops: 2007. ISAAA Brief No. 37. ISAAA Ithaca, NY. ISBN 978-1-892456-42-7.

requirements after their initial release to market.[17,18] Such regulatory oversight is of utmost importance to address, for instance, nonapproved GMOs that could enter the food chain.

As a consequence, the de facto moratorium on GM crop farming in the EU officially ended on May 19, 2004, when the European Commission gave the Swiss firm Syngenta approval to market its BT 11 maize for human consumption. In May 2003, the United States, supported by Canada and Argentina, however, had launched a WTO case against the EU concerning its authorization regime for GMOs. They claimed that the EU's approval process took too long, hurt their exports of GM crops, and was not based on science. The WTO three-judge panel eventually decided to gather the views of independent and highly reputable scientists from different parts of the world, including Europe and the United States. That consultation process confirmed the legitimacy of the health and environmental issues addressed in EU regulations and procedures. The longer times to assess the safety of GMOs in the EU by the European Food Safety Authority (EFSA) are due to the complexity of the science involved, as well as to the reluctance of the biotech industry to provide suitable data demonstrating the safety of GM crops and their derived products. Although it is a country's sovereign right to make its own decisions, there is still a need to develop a sound international legal framework for these products.

Economic and Social Issues

In Europe, the prevailing view is that farmers should be able to grow the crops they choose, be they GM, conventional, or organic, and that policies and practices should not preclude any of these forms of agriculture. However, GM crop plants have failed to gain acceptance in

---

[17] Commission Regulation 1829/2003, 2003 O.J. (L268) 1–23 (EC).
[18] Commission Regulation 1830/2003. 2003 O. J. (L268) 24–28 (EC).

Europe.[19] Despite early expectations, their commercialization is practically nonexistent in most EU nations, in contrast to their rapidly increasing commercialization in the United States, Asian, and South American countries, and other nations.[20] The European situation is mainly due to environmentalists and consumer groups who vigorously question the sustainability and social desirability of agri-biotechnology. This has caused policy makers to neglect weighing GMO benefits and utility against disadvantages and risks.

Many in Europe also strongly object to the monopolistic business practices of major GM seed producers. For example, Monsanto patents its GM seeds for Roundup Ready crops and has brought many lawsuits against farmers who do not follow its dictate that they must purchase new seeds for such crops from Monsanto every year, destroying the traditional farmer's practice of saving seeds from year to year.[21] Activities by other GM seed companies have also sparked widespread criticism in Europe and undercut claims by companies that GM crops will aid farmers in developing countries. Among other objections, some opponents have claimed that although pest-resistant GM plants may be successful against their target pests, they attract secondary pests, which attack the GM crops. Thus, the claim is made that GM pest-resistant crop plants require the same amount of chemical pesticide due to the secondary pest issue.[22] However, other studies have demonstrated that growing such crops leads to reduced pesticide use.[23]

---

[19] G. Gaskell, Science Policy and Society: The British Debate over GM Agriculture, 15 *Current Opinion in Biotechnology* 241–245 (2004).

[20] C. James, Executive Summary of Global Status of Commercialized Biotech/GM Crops: 2005, 2005, (ISAAA 2005).

[21] K. H. Madsen & P. Sandøe, Ethical Reflections on Herbicide-Resistant Crops, 61 *Pest Management Science*, 318–325 (2005).

[22] http://www.news.cornell.edu/stories/July06/Bt.cotton.China.ssl.html (last time accessed August 26, 2008).

[23] M. G. Cattaneo et al., Farm-scale Evaluation of the Impacts of Transgenic Cotton on Biodiversity, Pesticide Use, and Yield, 103 *Proceedings of the National Academy of Science* 7571–7576 (2006).

The next generation of GM crops promises specific health benefits to consumers. GM crop plants designed to combat dietary deficiencies in vitamin A and iron should be available within a few years. Other varieties may lower risk factors for cardiovascular disease and cancer by increasing the presence of carotenoids, tocopherols, and flavonoids.[24] These advances may diminish the European consumer's concerns and distrust about GM crops and foods. In addition, Dutch scientists and plant breeding companies expect that growing knowledge of plant genetics will reduce existing gaps between genotype and phenotype and enable control over environmental factors such as salt, drought, and wetness. In their opinion, GM crop breeding techniques have tangible benefits and such knowledge will also enable more efficient selection procedures, which will enhance plant breeding for conventional, organic, and GM types of crops.[25]

Ongoing Public Concerns

In an additional effort to address public concerns, the Commission published a White Paper on Food Safety in 2000 stating that food safety policy should be based on a comprehensive farm to table approach.[26] The Commission also adopted Regulation 178/2002,[27] which established the European Food Safety Authority (EFSA). EFSA and its GMO panel composed of independent scientific experts, works closely with the Dutch and other national authorities. Under the GM crop approval scheme, the Dutch competent authority conducts the initial safety assessment,

---

[24] H. P. J. M. Noteborn & W. De Wit, Scientific Challenges for Risk Assessment. in: Biological Resource Management in Agriculture – Challenges and Risks of Genetically Engineered Organisms 139–141 (OECD Documents 2004); See also H. A. Kuiper et al., Safety Aspects of Novel Foods, 35 *Food Research International* 267–271 (2002).

[25] J. Borovitz, et al., Plant Genomics: Third Wave, *Annual Review Genomics*, 443–477 (2004).

[26] Commission White Paper on European Governance, COM (2001) 428 final (July 25, 2001).

[27] Commission Regulation 178/2002, 2002 O.J. (L131) 1–24 (EC).

after which other member-states may provide comments. If there are any objections, EFSA's GMO panel carries out an independent safety assessment. Under Regulation 1829/2003[28] on the market introduction of GM foods and feeds, EFSA now has a central role in the risk assessment process.

Despite EFSA's conduct of independent risk assessments, expert advisors and regulators in several member-states have continued to raise safety concerns, and some member-states have voted to continue their national bans on particular GMOs. Contrary to the U.S. claims, the European Commission provides the basis for the assurance of a high level of protection of human health and consumers' interest in relation to food, taking into account in particular the diversity in the supply of food including traditional products, while ensuring the effective functioning of the internal market. It establishes common principles and responsibilities, the means to provide a strong science base, and efficient organizational arrangements and procedures to underpin decision making in matters of food and feed safety. All GMO-related regulations and directives therefore emphasize science as the basis for agri-biotechnology regulation, but differences in values and conflicting interests continue to be translated into quasi-scientific issues and demands for more risk assessment.

Critics charge that risk assessments based on substantial equivalence or comparative safety are too dependent on assumptions and indirect evidence. French scientists favor a multi-year toxicity study with laboratory animals instead of the internationally accepted ninety-day feeding study that EFSA uses to test GMOs.[29] Others contend that each field trial should be designed for a particular region's ecology. Some officials have spearheaded the anti-GMO movement and declared their regions

---

[28] Commission Regulation 1829/2003, 2003 O.J. (L268) 1–23 (EC).
[29] G. E. Séraline et al., New Analysis of a Rat Feeding Study with a Genetically Modified Maize Reveals Signs of Hepatorenal Toxicity, *Arch. Environ. Contam. Toxicol* (2007), http://www.springerlink.com/content/02648wu132m07804/fulltext.html.

to be GM-free zones.[30] Austrian scientists have reported adverse effects on butterflies of pest-resistant BT maize pollen, but a six-year field evaluation of BT maize in Spain did not identify adverse effects on nontarget species.[31] Thus, many types of objections confront corporate proponents and EU and national regulators of GMOs.

Risk assessments for GM plant breeding cannot completely rule out potential risks and uncertainties. The nonexpert European public knows this and therefore doubts the validity of short-term tests and lab studies as accurate indicators of long-term consequences. It also considers food risks and GM technology within a broader social context than the experts, wants to know the benefits of this food technology,[32] and worries about the social and cultural implications of scientific advances. When regulators fail to address the full spectrum of the public's concerns, opponents exploit this void. However, policy makers and scientists still focus on scientific facts about GMO safety and consider public anxieties as irrational. As a result, the public remains skeptical of the government's ability to manage food safety[33] and continues to feel that European institutions fail to fully address their concerns,[34] and NGOs and the media continue to stimulate anxiety about GMOs.

The scientific reasoning emphasized by regulators reflects a different value system and it is difficult for the public to understand when experts characterize findings as "negligible," "biologically relevant," or "within natural variability," for example. It would be more helpful if the results

[30] GMO Free Europe Home Page, www.gmofree-europe.org.

[31] M. Eizaguirre et al., Six Years After the Commercial Introduction of Bt Maize in Spain: Field Evaluation, Impact, and Future Prospects, 15 *Transgenic Research* 1–12 (2006).

[32] E. F. Einsiedel & J. Medlock, A Public Consultation on Plant Molecular Farming, 8 *AgBioForum* 26–32 (2005).

[33] R. Marchant, From the Test Tube to the Table. 2 *EMBO Reports* 354–357 (2001). See also C. Marris, Public Views on GMOs: Deconstructing the Myths, 2 *EMBO Reports* 545–548 (2001).

[34] L. J. Frewer et al., Societal Aspects of Genetically Modified Foods, 42 *Food and Chemical Toxicology* 1191–1193 (2004).

of risk assessments were presented in a comparative risk ranking to clarify the distribution of costs, risks, and benefits. Thus, it is critical for regulators to improve their communications to the public and to build confidence in the assessment process, particularly because future GM crops will contain multigene modifications that will require even more complex testing and assessment methods. Otherwise, NGOs and other groups will highlight these complexities, raising more public concerns.

Ongoing Debates

Substantial Equivalence
The safety of conventional crops and foods prepared and used in traditional ways are generally assumed to be based on their long history of human consumption. Regulators and experts find it therefore useful to screen GM crops by comparing their agronomical and morphological characteristics to similar conventional crops as a "safe" comparator. The Office of Device Evaluation (ODE) of U.S. FDA first coined the "assessment of substantial equivalence" in evaluating medical devices.[35] In GM plant breeding, this strategy is known as the OECD concept of substantial equivalence or comparative safety assessment.[36,37] Its application also requires a comparison of the chemical composition. Significant differences in these parameters are expected to be indicative for any fundamental change in the GM crop that warrants further testing for adverse human health effects. The successful application of the concept largely depends on the availability of an appropriate comparator and the ability to discriminate between differences

---

[35] Miller H. I. (1999) Substantial equivalence: Its uses and abuses. *Nature Biotechnology* 17, 1042–1043.

[36] Kuiper, H. A., Kleter, G. A., Noteborn, H. P. J. M., Kok, E. J. (2002b) Substantial equivalence – an appropriate paradigm for the safety assessment of genetically modified foods? *Toxicology* 181–182: 427–431.

[37] EFSA (2004) Guidance document of the scientific panel on genetically modified organisms for the risk assessment of genetically modified plants and derived food and feed, *EFSA Journal* 99, 1–93.

resulting from the genetic modification and those differences originating from the plant's germplasm. This strategy is still problematic according to its opponents, because looking for such equivalence involves making assumptions and judgments without fully understanding many of the intrinsic qualities of the GM and conventional crops being compared, and the possible relevance of even small differences between them. One of their main concerns is that GM technology with its subtle transformations of DNA using various types of bacterial and viral DNA may trigger health and environmental effects that may take years to manifest themselves.[38]

Scientific Advice

Safety assessments should be comprehensive and incorporate evidence from toxicological, nutritional, and environmental studies. Communicating to the public the careful scientific considerations that go in to GM testing is important for public understanding and regulator credibility. However, Dutch and European citizens alike feel that scientists lack the requisite knowledge to accurately predict long-term consequences for health, the environment, and society.[39] Indeed, many of these studies involve assumptions about the duration of certain tests that are needed to sufficiently estimate long-term consequences. And each of the studies must make an assumption about what is "long term." In addition, assumptions must also be made to fill data gaps and set margins of safety. The public is largely unaware of these careful scientific considerations, which come much closer to objective evaluations of agri-biotechnology. Thus, communications should also illuminate this judgmental aspect of testing. In this regard, it should be emphasized that the EU approach works cooperatively with international organizations such as the OECD Group of National Experts on Safety in Biotechnology, OECD

---

[38] D. Carusso, 2006. *Intervention Confronting the Real Risks of Genetic Engineering and Life on a Biotech Planet.* Hybrid Vigor Press.

[39] K. H. Madsen & P. Sandøe, Ethical Reflections on Herbicide-Resistant Crops, 61 *Pest Management Science* 318–325 (2005).

Task Force on the Safety of Novel Foods and Feed (1998–present), FAO/WHO Expert Consultations (1991–2003), and the CODEX Task Force on Foods derived from Biotechnology (1999–2005).

Among others, it depends on whether the reader can actually follow the steps that a risk assessor, scientific committee, or panel makes. Obviously, this solves the paradox between substantive and procedural transparency: objectification of lay perspectives and objectification of decision making.[40] For the assessment the reader (layman) should be able to think along with the rationalists (scientific expert).

Presumed Health Risks

Although there is no conclusive scientific evidence linking GM foods to adverse health effects, risks to health remain a top public concern. Anti-GMO NGOs and pressure groups always emphasize health risks in their campaigns, and repeatedly call for more research to uncover alleged health risks.[41,42,43] In essence, they argue that risk research leaves open many gaps and they see protocols as for ninety-day testing and the substantial equivalence strategy as misleading arguments to avoid further testing. Thus, even though EFSA publishes its centralized risk assessments, reasoning, and opinions online, the NGOs stimulate public anxiety by continuing to claim that health risks (such as antibiotic resistance and allergies) are currently unacceptable and require more assessment.[44,45] Indeed, the latest results of the 2006 Eurobarometer

[40] Bal, R., Bijker, W. E., Hendriks, R. (2004) Democratisation of scientific advice. *BMJ*, 329, 1339–1341.

[41] Séraline, G.-E., Cellier, D., Spiroux de Vendomois, J. (2007) New analysis of a rat feeding study with a genetically modified maize reveals signs of hepatorenal toxicity, *Arch. Environ. Toxicol.* DOI: 10.1007/s00244–006–0149–5.

[42] www.goedewaar.nl http://www.goedewaar.nl/aansprakelijkheidsrapport.doc (in Dutch).

[43] Ibid.

[44] http://www.civilcoalition.nl/index.php/article/articleview/68/1/4/ WTO Conflict: slecht voor milieu, gezondheid en ontwikkelingslanden.

[45] Milieudefensie.nl: http://www.milieudefensie.nl/landbouw/publicaties/infobladen/ infoblad9.htm/ Genetic Manipulation Information file agriculture and food (in Dutch).

special survey,[46] which measures public opinions on behalf of the European Commission, shows that 8 percent of the respondents spontaneously mention GMOs when asked about risks associated with food. When asked to what extent they are worried about genetically modified products in food or drinks, 25 percent of EU citizens answered "very worried" and 37 percent answered, "fairly worried."

"Unnaturalness" of GM Technology

Persons who express moral concerns about GM agriculture stress the unnaturalness of the technology,[47] and describe genetic modification as "meddling with nature"[48] and "pushing nature beyond its limits."[49] Genetic engineering techniques were described as "pushing nature beyond its limits" and were thought to "upset the equilibrium of nature."[50] Even though conventional crops do not undergo the rigorous testing GM crops are subjected to, these critics universally reject the GM plants where a conventional alternative exists.[51] By its unnaturalness GM food is also seen as undermining to the Western European food culture. When GM seeds replace traditional seeds, the cultural heritage, or crop species, of particular regions disappears.

Sustainability and Coexistence

In addition to concerns about food safety of GM foods, the public also is uneasy and worried about field tests and agricultural production of GM crops. Knowing nature as an unpredictable force and species adapting

---

[46] European Commission 2006 Eurobarometer Special Issue 238 Risk issues http://ec .europa.eu/public_opinion/archives/ebs/ebs_238_en.pdf.

[47] L. J. Frewer, Communicating about the Risks and Benefits of Genetically Modified Foods: Effects of Different Information Strategies. 23 *Risk Analysis* 1117–1133 (2003);

[48] A. Shaw, 'It Just Goes Against the Grain': Public Understanding of Genetically Modified (GM) Food in the UK, 11 *Public Understanding of Science* 273–291 (2002).

[49] See Marris, supra.

[50] See Marris, supra.

[51] European Commission 2006 Eurobarometer: Europeans and Biotechnology in 2005: Patterns and Trends.

continuously, people fear that cross-pollination between GM plants and conventional plants may result in new, unintended adaptations that will enter the food chain and pose unanticipated health and environmental risks.[52] Examples of ecological disasters due to GM agriculture can be observed in Argentina, where a monoculture of Monsanto's glyphosate-tolerant soybeans led to abundant use of the herbicide glyphosate (due to tolerant weeds).[53] This caused harm to other crops, the emergence of super-weeds, and changes in soil microbacteria.[54] This and other examples give rise to the public's fears that propagators of GM agriculture (multinational corporations, scientists, and regulators) fail to consider broader ramifications for ecosystems and societal interests and values.

In opposition to GM foods, many people now advocate for sustainable food production, organic methods of farming, and "ethical consumerism." They believe GM agriculture is not a sustainable development because some GM crops kill nontarget species, speed the evolution of more resistant versions of the target pest species, and rapidly proliferate at the expense of biodiversity. Everywhere in Europe NGOs, together with local and regional politicians, call for GMO-free zones for traditional or organic agriculture.[55] In addition, GM crops challenge the EU concept of coexistence because organic and conventional seeds are vulnerable to cross-pollination and other pathways of contamination from GM seeds.

Recognition of Benefits

If the public recognized tangible benefits in GM agriculture, GM crops and foods would gain wider acceptance. A recent study of various types

---

[52] E. F. Einsiedel & J. Medlock, A Public Consultation on Plant Molecular Farming, 8 *AgBioForum*, 26–32 (2005).

[53] Friends of the Earth. 2008. Agriculture and foods: Who benefits from GM crops? The rise in pesticide use. http://www.foei.org/en/resources/publications/food-sovereignty/2008/gmcrops2008full.pdf.

[54] Argentina's Bitter Harvest Branford, S. (2004) New Scientist, 17 April 2004, pp. 40–43. http://www.grain.org/research/contamination.cfm?id=95.

[55] http://www.gmo-free-regions.org/ and http://www.gmo-free-europe.org/.

of plant molecular farming revealed that crops were rated more favorably when their benefits for human health were shown. In contrast, if the benefits are confined to increased profits for farmers, the crop was rated less favorably. Therefore, without visible health or other benefits, people are more likely to mention perceived risks in evaluating the acceptance of GM foods.[56,57]

Often claims are made about future developments and benefits of GM agriculture. The promise is that GM agriculture will end food scarcity in third world countries, because of its increased crop yields. However, various reports by NGOs studying data from different countries state that crop yields have not accelerated since the introduction of GMOs.[58,59] NGOs communicate this message widely to state that scientists' beliefs of technological optimism are misleading.

Stakeholder Involvement

Lack of public involvement in the decision-making process for GM crops and foods has contributed to the distrust of Dutch and European governance of GM food safety.[60] If the public does not become more involved in the GM policy-making process, distrust of the regulatory scheme will continue. As a result, both the Netherlands and the EU now promote more informed participation.[61] The Dutch initially focused on

[56] Einsiedel, E. F., Jelsøe, E., Breck, T. (2001) Publics at the technology table: the consensus conference in Denmark, Canada, and Australia, *Public Understanding of Science*, 10, 83–98.

[57] E. F. Einsiedel & J. Medlock, A Public Consultation on Plant Molecular Farming, 8 *AgBioForum*, 26–32 (2005).

[58] Friends of the Earth. 2008. Agriculture and foods: Who benefits from GM crops? The rise in pesticide use. http://www.foei.org/en/resources/publications/food-sovereignty/2008/gmcrops2008full.pdf.

[59] Soil Association. 2002. Seeds of doubts. North American Farmers' experience with GMOs. http://orgprints.org/9041/1/Seeds_of_Doubt.pdf.

[60] L. J. Frewer et al., Societal Aspects of Genetically Modified Foods, 42 *Food and Chemical Toxicology*, 1191–1193 (2004).

[61] D. J. Fiorino, D. J., Citizen Participation and Environmental Risk: A Survey of Institutional Mechanisms, 15 *Science, Technology, & Human Values*, 226–243 (1990).

scientific safety assessments, but despite sponsoring many case reports and projects for public consumption,[62] the public retained negative views on GM foods. Unfortunately, the European Commission's White Paper on European Governance[63] does not provide a practical model for stakeholder participation. Other EU policies attempt to build a framework for risk assessment that incorporates public participation, and underscore the importance of risk communication between regulators and the public. An improved framework will need to include ethics, benefits, economics, and other public concerns as part of the assessment.[64] By developing more informed public participation and recognizing public concerns in transparent proceedings, criticism from those who demand a 100 percent safety guarantee would be less effective.[65]

Principles of VWA's Food Safety Governance

The current Dutch system for food safety governance does not include a formal process for public participation and focuses almost exclusively on scientific concerns. Participation at each level of a transparent assessment process would likely alleviate public concerns. For example, public attention during the first phase of defining the objective of a novel GM plant would identify the controversial aspects of that plant and the government could focus on those issues early in the process. Participatory interacting of the key players at the very start of defining the objectives of a novel GM plant allows development of a planning process, which

[62] H. P. J. M. Noteborn, Tackling Food Safety Concerns over GMOs, in *EC Sponsored Study on the Safety of Genetically Modified Organisms* 107–109 (C. Kessler & I. Economidis eds., European Union 2001).

[63] Commission White Paper on European Governance, COM (2001) 428 final (July 25, 2001).

[64] Commission Communication on the Precautionary Principle, http://europa.eu.int/comm/dgs/health_consumer/library/pub/pub07_en.pdf (last visited June 19, 2008).

[65] Safe Foods Corporation Home Page, www.safefoods.nl; Paganini Project Home Page, www.paganini-project.net.

will be sensitive to controversial issues. Dialogue with the public would bring consistency to the policy-making decisions.[66]

In the Netherlands, the Food and Consumer Product Safety authority (VWA) was set up on July 10, 2002. Because of a number of food safety crises and incidents, Parliament and civil society felt the need for a strong organization to protect food and consumer product safety. Developments in the international sphere demanded one national authority, responsible for supervision, risk assessment, and risk communication.

VWA's Office for Risk Assessment identifies early warning signs of troubling aspects of innovations in GM agriculture, screens potential threats to human and animal health, evaluates public perceptions, and commissions necessary research. This Office has become the "front office" for GMO regulation but confines its duties to weighing the risks and benefits of a particular GM crop and does not engage in policy enactment, decision making, or food law enforcement. Thus, it has considerable independence and follows a sequence of steps intended to improve governance of food safety.

A Participatory Framing Step

The Office staff consults with risk managers, scientists, and stakeholders to define the objectives of a regulatory action on a GMO. This also involves identifying decision-making options, evaluation criteria, and major public concerns. In realizing a transparent and more participative approach we use therefore a modification of risk governance escalator of Klinke and colleagues[67] and Hollander and Hanemaaijer.[68] In this way – from mundane via complex to uncertain and ambiguous GM-related risks – a matrix can be created on which the various types of

---

[66] A. E. M. de Hollander & A. H. Hanemaaijer eds., Coping Rationally with Risks, 52 (RIVM rapport 251701047, RIVM, Bilthoven, The Netherlands 2003).

[67] Klinke, A., Dreyer, M., Renn, O., Sterling, A., Zwanenberg, P. van (2006) Precautionary risk regulation in European governance, *Journal of Risk Research*, 4, (9), 373–392.

[68] Hollander, A. E. M. de, Hanemaaijer, A. H. (eds.) (2003) Coping rationally with risks. RIVM rapport 251701047, RIVM, Bilthoven, The Netherlands, 52 p in Dutch.

objectives can be profiled into categories of necessary risk/benefit assessments and rank the policy-making decisions requiring various numbers of participating actors.[69,70] This process is intended to reach consensus on these matters and expedite policy-making by shaping the questions that specialists will be expected to deal with in the risk benefit step that follows. The mechanisms of potential threats in rapidly emerging technologies are often unknown to experts and society, which means that this or another process will contain uncertainty. However, this participatory framing step will contribute to a public understanding of the government's food safety objectives and help to build public confidence in food safety governance.

A Formal and Documented Risk/Benefit Assessment Step
This stage includes a conventional adverse effect assessment performed by Dutch specialists at research institutes or EFSA's GMO panel. As part of the broader EU regulatory scheme, EFSA reviews this assessment and compares the Dutch approach to similar risk assessments by other countries. These independent specialists analyze the impacts of the GMO being considered on human and animal health. Other specialists may be commissioned by the Office staff to perform additional assessments on, for example, consumer attitudes, economic impact analysis, and ethics. Then, the Office of Risk Assessment and interdisciplinary groups of experts study the adverse health effects assessment and provide consultations on economic impact, perceptions, ethical, and political values, risk-benefit distribution, and social benefit distribution. This transparent review allows subjective perceptions and values to enter the science-based risk assessment as performed by EFSA.

[69] Renn, O. (2004). *Deliberative Approaches to Manage Systemic Risks*. ESOF, Stockholm, 24–29 August, Sweden, http://www.esof2004.org/pdf_ppt/session_material/ortwin_renn_2.ppt.

[70] Klinke A, Renn O. (2002). A new approach to risk evaluation and management: risk-based, precaution-based, and discourse-based strategies. *Risk Analysis* 22, 1071–94.

An Evaluation and Recommendation Step

Given the uncertainties of "scientific facts," political decisions on scientific advances are rarely final.[71] In this stage, the "front office" analyzes the strengths, limits, and uncertainties of the risk/benefit assessment. Where ambiguity exists, the process for ranking decision options is jointly done by explicit dialogue between the "front office" members, risk managers, stakeholders, and the public. This step acknowledges that science alone cannot solve uncertain and ambiguous phenomena associated with value disputes in society.[72] The participatory ranking of policy making prevents escalation of the conflict between GMO proponents and opponents.[73] It should be noted that public participation and consultation in the risk analysis cycle is a new concept[74] and requires more development by VWA.[75] Public hearings, round tables, and consultations, such as those organized by VWA in case of the scare of acrylamide in food, or other explicit dialogue might be included.

The Risk Management Measures and Policy Decision Step

This stage is directed toward the outcome of risk evaluation between risk managers, stakeholders, specific groups at risk, and the public at large. The risk managers at the Ministries of Agriculture and Health decide on management options and the actions to take to mitigate any

---

[71] S. Funtovicz et. al., Science and Governance in the European Union: A Contribution to the Debate, 27 *Science and Public Policy* 327–336 (2000).

[72] G. Meyer et. al., The Factualisation of Uncertainty: Risks, Politics, and Genetically Modified Crops – A Case of Rape, 22 *Agriculture and Human Values* 235–242 (2005).

[73] G. Gaskell, Science Policy and Society: The British Debate over GM Agriculture, 15 *Current Opinion in Biotechnology* 241–245 (2004).

[74] Safe Foods Home Page, www.safefoods.nl.

[75] O. Renn, Deliberative Approaches to Manage Systemic Risks. ESOF, Stockholm, 24–29 August, Sweden, http://www.esof2004.org/pdf_ppt/session_material/ortwin_renn_2.ppt; See also Paganini Project Home Page, www.paganini-project.net and Gabriel Abels, Experts, Citizens, and Eurocrats – Towards a Policy Shift in the governance of Biopolitics in the EU, 6 European Integration Online Papers, 19 (2002), http://eiop.or.at/eiop/texte/2002–019a.htm (last visited June 19, 2008).

risks revealed in the risk assessment. Policy makers and risk managers, in interaction with all parties affected by the decision – monitor the impact of those actions.

Effective Risk Communication

Periodic survey studies, such as the Eurobarometer, provide information that contributes to the policy debate.[76] The surveys play an important role in shaping public discussion of GM applications, but are unable to illuminate complex ethical considerations and worldviews.[77] Focus groups on GMOs might produce more nuanced explanations.[78] For example, a Danish method of deliberation, the "consensus conference," provides a forum for dialogue between a panel of scientists and a panel of citizens.[79] Consensus conferences attempt to bridge the gap between experts' knowledge and laypeople's understanding of a risk. However, the group discussion approach can lead both sides to adhere to their original positions, undermining the potential of group discussions.[80] Promising results in negotiation between citizens and (local) political councils have been reached with techniques for stakeholders management. This method could be adapted to the purpose of the decision-making process for GMO crops and foods. If wisely used, the Internet provides a promising new platform that may be part of an approach for public consultation and communication.

---

[76] G. Gaskell, Science Policy and Society: The British debate over GM Agriculture, 15 *Current Opinion in Biotechnology* 241–245 (2004).

[77] H. Dietrich, & R. Schibeci, Beyond Public Perceptions of Gene Technology: Community Participation in Public Policy in Australia, 12 *Public Understanding of Science* 381–401 (2003).

[78] E. F. Einsiedel & J. Medlock, A Public Consultation on Plant Molecular Farming, 8 *AgBioForum*, 26–32 (2005).

[79] E. F. Einsiedel et al., Publics at the Technology Table: The Consensus Conference in Denmark, Canada, and Australia, 10 *Public Understanding of Science* 83–98 (2001).

[80] G. Rowe & L. J. Frewer, Public Participation Methods: A Framework for Evaluation, 25 *Science, Technology and Human Values* 3–29 (2000).

Conclusion

Genetic plant breeding is not a homogeneous technology, and each application must therefore be considered on a case-by-case basis. One of the key challenges facing food safety governance is to improve the implicit and explicit dialogue on GM crop plants and its derived foods with the public. It is proposed that scientific objectives (technical values) and consumer objectives (social and economic or ethical concerns) are best dealt with in parallel, not consecutively. It is incumbent on specialists, industrialists, and regulators to continue to integrate the public in emerging technologies and their respective risk/benefit assessment and ranking of decision options. The participatory process requires a solid knowledge of group interactions and incentives, technical, social, and cultural competence and, memorable practical experience (i.e., anecdotal and systematic evidence). To summarize, food safety governance should cover principles such as:

- Implicit dialogue, for instance, picking up signals of concern from the public debate or a consumer complaint line, for responding to early warning indicators;
- Screening of warnings for identifying an appropriate deliberative and participatory strategy;
- Planning process identifying risks, costs, benefits, and their distribution;
- Science-based facts and cognitive judgments of experts acquainted with risk/benefit assessments of health and environment;
- Apprehension analysis of social, economic, and ethical values from (organized) stakeholders and other experts (not necessarily from academia);
- Balancing and assignment of trade-offs by an explicit dialogue with affected target groups or the public at large (acceptability of distribution of risk, benefits, and costs);

- Explicit dialogue and participatory ranking of risk managerial options and decisions;
- Learn from best practices of stakeholder management from local and regional politics;
- Extension to reviewing the outcome of the decision-making process and legislation and policy in action.

5   Evolution of the Regulatory System for GM Crops in Brazil

Paulo José Leite Farias and Juliana Mezzomo Allain

Introduction

> No one will deny that scientific research also has risks and engenders dangers. Decisions have to be taken on research projects without knowing in advance what the results will be (if it were otherwise there would be no point in starting). The dangers of such an enterprise are also obvious. They arise from the circumstance that in modern society knowledge, once it has found its way into the world, can be neither kept secret nor ignored by other function systems as soon as it becomes relevant in their context. This is particularly true for the economy because of the pressure of competition. It also holds for the political system in the military field, and for the whole area of intervention and protection policy. (...) Finally, there are risks inherent in scientific research itself, where, for example nuclear energy is in play or genetic engineering experiments are carried out.
>
> Niklas Luhman[1]

Commercial cultivation of genetically modified (GM) crops has advanced in developing countries and is now widespread.[2] The largest increase among developing nations has occurred in Brazil, where, until recently, national policies had restricted GM agriculture. However, since enactment of a new law in 2005 setting forth procedures for approving the planting and sale of GM crops, Brazil has become the leading

---

[1] Niklas Luhmann, *Risk: A Sociological Theory, trans.* Rhodes Barrett (New York: Aldine De Gruyter, 1993) 203.

[2] International Service for the Acquisition of Agri-biotech Applications (ISAAA), http://www.ictsd.org/biores/06–01–20/story3.htm.

exporter of GM soybeans, has GM crops growing on 9.4 million hectares, and now produces an estimated 10 percent of global GM crops, at last count.[3]

This chapter reviews the history of Brazilian policies and presents an analysis of the factors that have shaped their evolution. It illuminates how scientific advances and economic opportunities in global crop and food markets have overcome health and environmental concerns and the safeguards espoused by the Cartagena Protocol.[4]

In 1995, when the first Biosafety Statute was approved by Brazil's National Congress, controversies about GM agriculture had captured the attention of political institutions. Foremost among these controversies was whether an Environmental Impact Statement (EIS)[5] should be developed before each cultivation of a GM crop pursuant to national environmental policy. Arguing for the application of EIS requirements, environmental and consumer NGOs opposed in federal courts the production and commercialization of transgenic soybean

---

[3] The figures are in the latest annual report of the International Service for the Acquisition of Agri-biotech Applications (ISAAA), released on January 11, 2006. See International Centre for Trade and Sustainable Development, "ISAAA Report: Developing Country Biotech Plantings Continue to Expand," Trade BioRes Main Page, vol. 6, n.1 (Jan. 2006), at http://www.ictsd.org/biores/06–01–20/story3.htm.

[4] Principle 15 of the Rio Declaration proclaimed: "In order to protect the environment, the precautionary approach shall be widely applied by States according to their capabilities. Where there are threats of serious or irreversible damage, lack of full scientific certainty shall not be used as a reason for postponing cost-effective measures to prevent environmental degradation." The Cartagena Protocol (signed in 2000 and enforced on September 11, 2003) states: "Aware of the rapid expansion of modern biotechnology and the growing public concern over its potential adverse effects on biological diversity, taking also into account risks to human health, recognizing that modern biotechnology has great potential for human well-being if developed and used with adequate safety measures for the environment and human health."

[5] EIS analyzes the impact a proposed development, usually industrial, will have on the natural and social environment. It includes assessment of long- and short-term effects on the physical environment, such as air, water, and noise pollution, as well as effects on employment, living standards, local services, and aesthetics. See Peter Wathern, ed., *Environmental Impact Assessment: Theory and Practice* (London: Routledge, 1992).

products.[6] Part I of this chapter reviews this history and explains why such opposition was subsequently defeated by Brazilian interests that sought to continue the nation's economic tradition of being a crop-exporting country, and that sought to capitalize on the growing international market for food crops.

Other factors also contributed to changes in policy that favor GM agriculture. For example, in 1998 in Rio Grande do Sul, the southern-most state of Brazil, farmers concerned about international competitiveness started to illegally cultivate transgenic soybean with GM seed smuggled from Argentina. The growing and harvest of GM crops in Brazil was thereby undertaken in violation of national law, and its continuation demonstrated the lack of effectiveness and enforcement of Brazilian rules restricting GM agriculture.

Part II discusses the dramatic shift of Brazilian policy in favor of GM crops and reviews some of its promotional features for cultivation of GM crops. It also comments on the lack of public participation in the process of policy change. The scenario indicates that governance of international trade by the World Trade Organization is a major influence on the policies of developing and exporting nations such as Brazil.

Part III deals with the role of the media and the issue of social representation in the policy change process. It outlines a research project and its results with regard to Brazilian media coverage of GM crop issues from January 2000 to June 2005, a critical period that involved the development and approval of the new Biosafety law of 2005, which favors GM agriculture and discusses the main issues involved.

The research data explain the policy change according to the Social Theory framework of Niklas Luhman. According to Luhman, "Communication is coordinated selectivity. It comes about only if ego fixes his own state on the basis of uttered information."[7] Luhman describes

---

[6] TRF1, n. 98.34.00.027681–8/DF, Relator: Antônio de Sousa Prudente, 10/08/1999, D.J.U, 11/11/1999, at 14.

[7] Niklas Luhmann, *Social Systems* (J. Bednarz, Jr. with D. Baecker, Trans.). Stanford: Stanford University Press. (Original work published 1984), (1995), 154.

problems of coordination among economics, health, ecology, and science as a lack of communication among different subsystems or as a different ratio of resonance of one subsystem upon others. The questions that are raised are whether the economic subsystem has more importance than the other subsystems, regarding GM crop policy making? If so, why? And does globalization of trade promote the economic subsystem over that of the political subsystem?

I. Historical Perspective

A. Agricultural Tradition and Interests

The debate on GM crops is very active and highly inflammable due to its inherent political nature. Any analysis of a policy that neglects historical and social factors will result in incomplete conclusions. To understand current Brazilian policy regarding GM crops, it is therefore important to know about preceding Brazilian involvement with biotechnology, the dichotomy between family agriculture (subsistence agriculture) and industrial agriculture (agribusiness), and many other matters including the nation's rapid development and dependence on agriculture and exports.

Over the past decade, Brazil – the world's eleventh largest economy – has been consolidating its position as an important agro-food producer and major supplier to international markets. Production agriculture accounted for 10 percent of the country's gross domestic product (GDP) in 2005, but with the associated supply chain, the agro-food sector (production agriculture, processing, and distribution) accounts for nearly 27 percent of total exports and employs 18 million people, equivalent to 37 percent of the labor force. The agro-food sector, which was valued at US $254 billion in 2005, accounted for 28 percent of the country's GDP.[8]

---

[8] "Factors Affecting Brazilian Growth or Are There Limits to Future Growth of Agriculture in Brazil?" by Ignez Vidigal Lopes, Mauro de Rezende Lopes, Constanza

Brazil has traditionally relied on its own public sector scientific institutions and government officials, rather than domestic or international private corporations, to develop and extend productive new agricultural technologies. Envisioning the potential of biotechnology, the government of Brazil has made consistent investments in agricultural biotechnology since the 1980s.

The mission of the Brazilian Public Agricultural Research Corporation (EMBRAPA) is to provide feasible solutions for the sustainable development of Brazilian agribusiness through knowledge and technology generation and transference. EMBRAPA develops special programs and projects concerning areas such as food safety, family agriculture, natural resources, advanced technology, and agribusiness, and acts as a partner in several other enterprises.[9]

Significant results in the area of GM crop development have been achieved with public investments. Scientists at the EMBRAPA Laboratory of Genetic Resource and Biotechnology (CENARGEN) have developed and patented their own system for crop transformation (applicable to more than one species of crop) and have field tested their own versions of herbicide-resistant soybean, and virus-resistant potatoes. Further progress toward commercialization of these transgenic varieties may be slow, however, as it must await the negotiation of commercial license agreements with international companies holding relevant transgenic patents, and approvals on biosafety grounds by the National Biosafety Technical Commission (CTNBio).

EMBRAPA's expenditures for research activities have been large for a developing country. A significant amount of EMBRAPA's budget was directed to biotechnology through CENARGEN. For most projects, EMBRAPA's contribution tends to be roughly matched by treasury resources from the National Council of Technological and Scientific Development (CNPq), a funding agency in the Department of Science

Valdes, Marilene Silva de Oliveira, Pedro Rangel Bogado, Getulio Vargas Foundation, Rio de Janeiro, Brazil, 2006.

[9] See http://www.embrapa.gov.br/a_embrapa/index_html/mostra_documento.

and Technology. Still other revenues are available through private or bilateral international sources and through the Program for Support in the Development of Science and Technology (PADCT), a World Bank lending facility for research administered by the Department of Science and Technology. The funds are used for genetic engineering and GM projects on a range of crops including soybeans, cotton, maize, potato, papaya, black beans, banana, cassava, and rice.[10]

As agriculture mechanized and subsistence farming declined, agri-business in Brazil has increased considerably. A prominent example is the development of the Brazilian soybean industry. In the 1970s, Brazil became one of the world's leading producers of conventional soybeans and soybean derivatives, and the second largest exporter after the United States. By another measure, Brazil had negligible tonnage before 1960, but by 1980, had achieved an annual output in excess of 15 million metric tons, a substantial achievement.[11] This development has been facilitated by three overriding and interdependent factors: a favorable world market and the consequent price incentives, a readily available technology, and a favorable government policy.[12]

B. Brazilian Competitiveness in the International Trade Market in the 1990s

Brazil's two largest competitors in the soybean export market – Argentina and the United States – began growing GM soybeans in the 1990s, and it seemed at first that Brazil should do the same to remain competitive. Starting in 1998, however, a growing consumer and environmentalist backlash against GM foods in Europe and Japan raised doubts regarding consumer acceptance, and some experts in Brazil argued that a trade advantage would come from remaining GM free.

---

[10] See http://www.embrapa.gov.br/a_embrapa/index_html/mostra_documento.

[11] Anthony B. Soskin, *Non-Traditional Agriculture and Economic Development: The Brazilian Soybean Expansion, 1964–1982* (New York: Praeger, 1988) 59.

[12] Anthony B. Soskin, *Non-Traditional Agriculture and Economic Development: The Brazilian Soybean Expansion, 1964–1982* (New York: Praeger, 1988) 60.

In export markets, Brazil used its nominal GM-free status to seek price premiums. This effort however was undercut when it became clear that many farmers in Rio Grande do Sul had started growing GM soybeans illegally, using seeds smuggled from Argentina. Like other developing countries, Brazil was at a crossroads: should the country adopt a promotional or a preventive policy for GM foods? Different policies and laws were being adopted in some developing countries to respond to opportunities and challenges that GM foods were creating.

At first, rapid scientific advances in genetic engineering and genomics opened new technological options to address some of the developing world's food production aspirations, but uncertainties about risks to human health and environmental quality generated concerns about potential negative impacts. As expectations of benefits and uncertainty about risks increased, policy makers in developing countries were confronted with the challenge of ensuring that their countries shared the benefits of technology while at the same time managed risks, actual and perceived.

In the next stage, growing interest and investment in research and technology occurred in developing countries. During this stage, Brazil sought to enlarge its economic competitiveness. Like other developing countries, it began to anticipate and invest in new technological trajectories, respond to risk concerns, and start to grow and export GM crops.

II. The Shift in Governing GM Crops in Brazil

A. NGOs vs. Monsanto

On January 5, 1995, Brazil's first Biosafety Law was enacted.[13] This law provided the means to control the use of genetic engineering techniques in the construction, cultivation, manipulation, transportation, marketing, consumption, release, and disposal of genetically modified organisms

---

[13] Statute No. 8974, which was enacted by Decrees Nos. 1752, dated December 20, 1995, and 2577, dated April 10, 1998.

(GMOs), with the purpose of protecting the life and health of humans, animals, and plants, as well as the environment. It defined GMOs, genetic engineering, DNA/RNA, and related expressions, regulated the role of the National Biosafety Technical Commission (CNTBio), established limits on genetic manipulation of living organisms and the release and disposal of GMOs, and listed activities that would be illegal and subject to fines and penalties. It also set forth procedures for the review and approval of GM crops.

Brazil had two paradigms to choose from when regulating these issues, namely the approaches being taken in Europe and North America, which are markedly different. In the EU, regulations are focused on the process of making GM crops; in the United States, on the characteristics of GM products. Brazil, as many other countries, considered both approaches in developing its 1995 law and established a system for regulatory oversight of GM crops that also incorporated controls for genetic engineering research (Article 225). The Departments of Health, of the Environment, and of Agriculture were made responsible for overseeing production, harvest, and trading of GM organisms and GM crops. Most observers view the Brazilian model, since its inception, as being closer to the American paradigm, for it is based on the features of each GM product.

This law also created the National Biosafety Technical Commission (CTNBio),[14] a multidisciplinary advisory group that is responsible for

---

[14] The Federal Biosafety Regulatory Agency, CTNBio, is formed by one representative each of the Departments of Science and Technology; Health; the Environment; Education and Sports; Foreign Affairs; two representatives of the Department of Agriculture, Supply and Agrarian Reform; of one representative from a legally established consumer defense agency; of one representative from legally established associations representing the biotechnology business sector, nominated by the Minister of Science and Technology, based out of a list of three names submitted by these associations; and of one representative from a legally established agency for protection of workers' health. These members of CTNBio serve for a term of three years and may be reelected once. The agency is responsible for issuing standards and biosafety quality certificates. Standards and provisions to be issued by CTNBio and pertaining to activities and projects related to GM crops and derivatives will include their making, culture, handling, use, transportation, storage, marketing, consumption, release, and disposal,

the regulation of products of agricultural biotechnology, among others. It evaluates the scientific and technical issues of environmental, health, and agricultural aspects of releasing GM crops and it reviews applications for testing and commercializing GM crops in the country. Different from the American model, it concentrated the screening of GM crops in one single institution.

In accordance with Articles 2 and 3 of Statute n. 8974, combined with Chapter V of Decree n. 1752, dated December 20, 1995, national, foreign, or international entities that develop, or intend to develop, activities and projects related to GMOs and derived substances, must request a CTNBio a Certificate of Quality in Biosafety (CQB). Furthermore, to conduct a GMO field trial, the proponent must follow the steps required by CTNBio's norms. For example, the first step is a proposal by the chief researcher to conduct the field trial. This proposition is analyzed by a Biosafety Committee of the proponent organization, followed by an analysis conducted by CTNBio. The final decision is that of CTNBio, allowing or forbidding the field trial.

After at least one release into the environment has been approved and the safety of the GM crop has been demonstrated, the applicant can apply for a "flexibilization" permit, which allows future releases and the commercialization of the GM crop. A GM crop that was previously approved by the CTNBio for planned release may be exempted from these norms providing that, according to the judgment of the CTNBio, the experience has shown acceptable risk levels. An exemption may be unconditional or subject to conditions. The guidelines of CTNBio are similar to those in the United States, because they are based on the characteristics and risks of end products, not the process.[15]

with special emphasis on safety of the material and protection of living beings and the environment. The Biosafety Quality Certificate is required by domestic or international entities or companies as a prerequisite to the development of activities related to GM crops and derivatives. Among these entities are those dedicated to teaching, scientific research, technological development, and provision of services involving GM crops and derivatives on Brazilian territory.

[15] Article 7, item VII of Statute n. 8974/1995.

In 1998, Monsanto was granted approval for importation of its Roundup Ready soybeans by CTNBio. Following this approval, Greenpeace and the Brazilian Consumer Defense Institute (IDEC), two non-profit organizations representing environmental and health concerns, filed lawsuits in a lower federal court[16] against Monsanto and the government. These entities argued that importing GM crops posed a serious risk to the environment and human health because the impacts of GM crops were unknown. This lawsuit was the start of a "judicial moratorium" on commercial releases in Brazil that has officially kept GM plants off the market between 1998 and 2003.

Later, on September 10, 1998, another lawsuit was filed by IDEC seeking injunctive relief, with the participation of Greenpeace and the Federal Prosecution Service, against the Brazilian government, MONSANTO, and MONSOY. This action sought to prevent CTNBio from issuing any authorization for the cultivation of the transgenic soybean Roundup Ready until the development of further regulations and the completion of pending environmental impact statements (EIS).

In response to the plea by IDEC, the 11th Federal Court granted the preliminary injunction asserting that, according to the Brazilian Federal Constitution, the government has the duty to defend and preserve the environment, particularly for preservation of the diversity and integrity of the genetic legacy of the country, and must control entities engaged in

---

[16] Two federal court decisions were taken regarding GE organisms in Brazil: The first is specifically on the commercial release of RR soybeans. It is an injunction (ação cautelar) issued by a first-level Federal Court in Brasília in 1999, which was upheld by the second-level court of appeals (Regional Federal Court) in Brasília in June 2000. That injunction requires that at least an environmental impact study must be carried out and rules on GE food labeling must be instated before any commercial release can be approved. The second decision is the sentence issued in June 2000 by the same first-level Judge Prudente on the core suit brought by Greenpeace and IDEC against the government's attempt to release RR soybeans. It goes even further than the above-mentioned injunction, by requiring that the National Biosafety Commission (CTNBio) stop issuing any decisions at all on GE crop releases (not just RR soybeans), until the government institutes new rules for assessing human health and environmental impacts, as well as creating rules for labeling.

research and manipulation of genetic material. The Court also ruled that government authorities should demand a prior environmental impact study of activities that may potentially cause significant degradation of the environment, such as those involving GM crops.

The reasons for these decisions are based in the Brazilian Federal Constitution[17] and other laws that address environmental and health concerns arising from the manipulation of genetic material, and protect biodiversity and consumers. As a result, these entities managed to secure several court orders and injunctions that prohibited the import and cultivation of GM crops and that recognized the "precautionary principle" established by the United Nations Biosafety Protocol and treaties such as the Cartagena Protocol.

B. The Political Shift from Preventive to Promotional Policy

Soon after its election, the Lula administration in 2002 gave permission for the commercial use of GM soybeans in food products and allowed Monsanto's GM soybeans to be grown on a temporary basis.

In early 2003, just before the soybean harvest, finding a solution for the illegally grown GM soybeans in Rio Grande do Sul became one of the central issues for government officials. The GM soybean seed smuggled from Argentina had been grown primarily in Rio Grande do Sul, a state that had established a local regulatory system that favored GM crops activities. Monsanto, the State Government of Rio Grande do Sul, and

---

[17] The Brazilian Federal Constitution of 1988 states the following, in Article 225:

> Art. 225. All have the right to an ecologically balanced environment, which is an asset of common use and essential to healthy quality of life, and both the Government and the community shall have the duty to defend and preserve it for present and future generations.
>
> Paragraph 1 – To ensure the effectiveness of this right, it is incumbent upon the Government to:
>
> (...) II. preserve the diversity and integrity of the genetic legacy of the country and to control entities engaged in research and manipulation of genetic material.

farmers who had illegally planted the GM soybean lobbied for President
Lula to address the issue. In March 2003, the Federal Government issued
Executive Orders n. 113 and 131 that allowed the commercial use of the
illegally grown GM soybeans for the domestic and international markets
until January 2004.

These presidential orders, which have legal effect, stated that the provisions of the 1995 Biosafety Law did not apply to the 2003 crop. They
also conflicted with the court decision in the Monsanto case, which had
prohibited CTNBio from authorizing the cultivation and commercialization of GM soybeans in Brazil until proper regulation pursuant to the
Biosafety Law had been developed. The Government thus ignored the
strong opposition expressed by many consumers, environmental groups,
and the majority of Brazilian farmers who had not planted GM soybeans.

In June 2003 the federal government prepared a new Bill on
Biosafety, for the purpose of modifying prior standards and procedures
for the use and release of GM crops in Brazil. An interministerial work
group was created and, after five months of controversial discussion, the
Executive branch proposed a new law. The main feature of this new proposed law was to require evaluation of environmental and health issues
separate from the evaluation of the Biosafety Commission.

The new government also issued a Labeling Decree (Decreto n.
4.680, de April 24, 2003) to ensure consumer rights to information about
GM foods and GM ingredients destined for human and animal consumption. The Decree provides that all products that contain more than 1
percent of GM raw material must be packaged and sold with a specific
label that displays the transgenic symbol prominently, along with one of
the following phrases: "transgenic (product)," "produced with transgenic
(raw material)" or "with transgenic (raw material)." However, the government has had difficulties in implementing a system of traceability that
would allow full enforcement of the Decree, especially with regard to the
labeling of oil and margarine.

Following a series of modifications by the House of Representatives
and the Senate, the new Biosafety Statute (Statute n. 1105/2005) was

approved in March 2005. The new law provides that risk assessment for research (field trials) be done by CTNBio, and that risk assessment for commercial releases continues to be a CTNBio responsibility. It also mandates inspection of GM crops by the Departments of Health, Agriculture, and Environment.[18] Finally, it allowed the planting and use of Monsanto's GM soya for another year without the need for environmental and health impact assessments.[19]

C. The Importance of Economic Interests in the New Biosafety Law

Examining closely the new Biosafety statute in effect today, one can understand the delicate relationship between the parties that are benefited and those that are not. Because Brazil's economy has a strong exporting component, the likely winners include the industrial-scale farmers that grow, harvest, and export GM crops such as GM soybeans to other countries, and the biotechnology companies, such as Monsanto and DuPont, who develop and sell GM crop seed. The benefits to these two business sectors are enhanced by growing consumer acceptance of GM crops and foods in importing nations, with the exception of EU nations.[20]

From a national perspective, the economic benefits that accrue to Brazil from adopting GM crops are already apparent and likely to become more substantial. EU restrictions on imports from GM-adopting countries have been a major concern, but these are likely to be mitigated in the aftermath of the World Trade Organization ruling that the EU had violated its trade treaty obligations by creating a de facto moratorium against GM crops.

---

[18] Article 16 of Statute n. 11105/2005.

[19] Article 34 of Statute n. 11105/2005.

[20] "Governments as well as consumers must accept GM crop technology if a Gene Revolution is to occur. Otherwise, there is serious doubt about how far the GM crop movement can spread worldwide." (Felica Wu, and William P. Butz, *The Future of Genetically Modified Crops: Lessons from the Green Revolution* (Santa Monica, CA: Rand, 2004) at 64.

Safety is not one of the main purposes of the new law, but encouragement of innovation and economic development is. Thus, the law creates the National Biosafety Commission (CNBS) for formulating and implementing a National Biosafety Policy to expand the use of biotechnology in production of crops.[21] Additional emphasis on economic benefit is provided by Decree n. 6.041, which empowers a CNBS and assigns the Minister of Development, Industry, and Foreign Trade to lead the Committee to qualify for funding of biotechnology research in Brazil over the next ten years.

CTNBio, on the other hand, is continued as the regulatory authority responsible for the approval of GM crops. CTNBio, which is part of the federal Department of Science and Technology, is now comprised of twenty-seven experts from different fields (biosafety, biotechnology, biology, human and animal health, and the environment).[22] Finally, it should be noted that more than three hundred biotechnical corporations in Brazil are carrying out research activities on applications of biotechnology to human health (diagnostics, pharmaceuticals, and vaccines) as well as agriculture. Thus, there is little doubt that Brazil has decided to promote the advancing of biotechnology in the medical and agricultural domains for purposes of economic gain and treats safety as a secondary matter.

III. Media and Social Representations of GM Crops

Some authors assert that GM crops mark the beginning of "the subpoliti-zation of politics"[23] or even "the coming of age of public participation."[24] In many countries, mainly in the European Union, consumers are still worried by the BSE[25] experience and do not trust institutional control of

---

[21] Article 8 of Statute n. 11105/2005.

[22] Article 5 of Decreto n. 6041/2007.

[23] Beck, U. *World Risk Society*. Cambridge: Polity Press, 1999.

[24] Einsiedel, E. & Kamara, W. The Coming of Age of Public Participation. In: G. Gaskel & M. Bauer (Eds.), *Genomics and Society: Legal, Ethical, and Social Dimensions* (95–112). Londres: Earthscan, 2006.

[25] Bovine Spongiform Encephalopathy.

food safety decision making. EU consumers have therefore demanded more public participation in the policy-making process for GM crops and food products. To regain trust by the citizens, several EU and national level strategies have been created. Among these strategies is the use of surveys of public perception and opinion about GM crops and foods as part of the policy-making process (see Chapters 3 and 4).

Studies about the public perception of science are seen as fundamental to define policies for the development of future technological innovations that will be publicly acceptable. In the EU context, this research aims to map public opinion on new technologies, especially biotechnology and its applications in agriculture and food systems.[26] However, in Brazil, this approach is lacking. According to Guivant,[27] the absence of such research results in debates about GM crops that involve a limited set of actors who are not truly representative of the public, and does not amount to public participation.

In the several fields of study that investigate public perception of science and technology, the theory of Social Representations plays an important role. This theory deals with how new scientific knowledge spreads and is appropriated by different social groups, and is derived from research on the popularization of science.[28] According to the theory, social representations are a set of concepts, affirmations, and explanations that originate from communications between individuals and groups.[29] In this sense, they help to master the environment in

---

[26] See: Gaskell, G.; Allum, N., & Stares, S. (2002). Europeans and biotechnology in 2002. Eurobarometer 58.0. *Report to the EC Directorate General for Research from the Project 'Life Sciences in European Society'* QLG7-CT-1999–00286. London School of Economics: Londres.

[27] Guivant, J. (2006). Transgênicos e percepção publica da ciência no Brasil. Ambiente & Sociedade – Vol. IX, n. 1 Jan./Jun. 2006.

[28] Bauer, M. A popularização da ciência como imunização cultural: a função de resistência das representações sociais. In: P.A, Guareschi & S. Jovchelovitch (Orgs.), *Textos em representações sociais* (pp. 229–257). Petrópolis: Vozes, 1994.

[29] Moscovici, S. The phenomenon of social representations. In: S. Moscovici & G. Duveen (Orgs.), *Social representations: Explorations in social psychology* (18–77). Cambridge: Polity, 2000.

comprehending and explaining the facts and ideas that fulfill our universe, and to know what discoveries from science and history mean.[30]

The role that the media plays in the construction of social representation is discussed very eloquently by social theorists. Beck affirms that "mass media coverage is of key importance considering the fact that hazards are generally imperceptible in everyday life."[31] Thus, because "the public can construct an image of the 'biotechnology reality' only on the basis of what the media themselves decide to convey,"[32] a great extension of public opinion research also analyzes what the media displays on GM crops in several different countries.[33] Indeed, some of the more in-depth investigations have come to the conclusion that media coverage has led to a "social amplification of risks"[34] within the population.

However, Guivant affirms that in Brazil, cases of food-related fears within the population are rare and that the Brazilian population "has an attitude of resignation or indifference towards risks as a result of unknowing its dimension."[35] In this section a documented analysis is presented of the contents displayed by the Brazilian media about GM crops from January 2000 to June 2005 (period that includes the creation and approval of the Biosafety law). By analyzing the Brazilian media and the images it conveys, we may have an idea of the issues concerning GM crops in Brazil, and have a clear idea of that arguments prevail: scientific facts, economic interests, environmental values, or health concerns.

---

[30] Jodelet, D. La representación social: fenómenos, concepto e teoría. In: S. Moscovici (Org.), *Psicología social II*. Barcelona: Ediciones Paidós, 1986.

[31] (Beck, 1999, p. 64)

[32] Gutteling, J. et al. (2002). Media coverage 1973–1996: trends and dynamics. In: M. Bauer & G. Gaskel (Eds.), *Biotechnology: The Making of a Global Controversy*. Cambridge: University Press.

[33] Op. cit.

[34] See Frewer, L.; Miles, S. & Marsh, R. (2002). The media and genetically modified foods: evidence in support of social amplification of risk. *Risk Analysis*. 22 (4) 701–711.

[35] (Guivant, 2001, p. 107) Guivant, J. (2001). A teoria da sociedade de risco de Ulrich Beck: entre o diagnóstico e a profecia. *Estudos Sociedade e Agricultura*. n. 16. pp. 95–112.

Table 1. *Number of articles about "transgenic" published per year and per newspaper.*

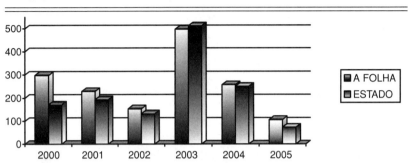

All the articles on GM crops published by two nationwide daily newspapers (*A Folha de São Paulo* and *O Estado de São Paulo*), from January 2000 to June 2005, were analyzed through the newspapers' websites. In collecting the data, the main keyword used was "transgenic."[36] Therefore, every single article (reports, editorials, notes, readers' letters, etc.) was related to this topic as a main theme or not. Data were also analyzed with the aid of the program ALCESTE (*Analyse Lexicale par Contexte d'un Ensemble de Segments de Texte*).[37] This software allows lexicographical analysis of the textual material and offers contextual information characterized by its vocabulary as well as by segments of texts that share this vocabulary. The data collected are divided into classes of words that indicate social representations or at least the construction of images about a given object.[38]

The results are shown below. Table 1 displays an intense media coverage in Brazil on GM crops, with a total of 2,869 articles published during the six years considered. This is a quite high number compared to the amount of articles published on the same topic in other countries.

[36] We used the word "transgenic" instead of "GM crops" because it is the term most used by the Brazilian media.

[37] Reinert, M. *Alceste: Analyse de données textuelles*. Manuel d'utilisateur. Toulouse: IMAGE, 1998.

[38] Nascimento-Schulze, C. M. & Camargo, B. V. Psicologia social, representações sociais e métodos. *Temas em Psicologia da SBP*, 08 (03), pp. 287–299, 2000.

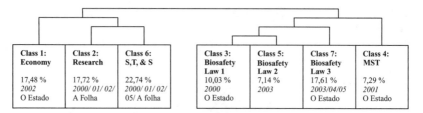

Figure 1. Transgenic *corpus* classes' distribution.

This table demonstrates that in 2001 and 2002 there was a decrease of media interest on this topic, and that 2003 was the year with the most publications. In 2004 and 2005, once again, there was a decrease of interest (although in 2005, only articles published from January to June were gathered). Later it can be seen how the fluctuation of the number of articles relates to their content. In Figure 1, the classes obtained through the lexicographical analysis are described, as well as how the subject of biosafety was presented throughout the time considered.

Figure 1 shows that the articles' contents were divided into seven classes created according to the articles' lexical and semantic closeness. Each class was named after its specific content. First, the *corpus* was divided into two *sub corpuses*. The first one contains the classes: "Economy," "Research," and "Science, Technology, and Society" and is defined by the diffusion of information that is related to the economic aspect or by the popularization of research published by scientific magazines, in a total of 52.92 percent of the entire *corpus*. The second *sub corpus* comprehends the classes: "Bio-Safety Law 1"; "Bio-Safety Law 2"; "Bio-Safety Law 3"; and "Landless Workers Movement – MST" and is related to the diffusion of information on the transgenic policy-making process, as well as to the social factors involved in this matter, in a total of 42.07 percent of the entire *corpus*.

The class "Economy" focuses on the use of transgenic techniques mainly in agriculture, by presenting national and worldwide market situations, but without presenting a favorable or contrary opinion to its use.

The class "Research" presents results of research published by scientific magazines informing the public on what transgenics are, their history and use in several fields, including agriculture, chemistry and, above all, health. Many of these articles present views of defenders and detractors on this technology. A negative discourse was noticed when the possible effects for the environment were discussed, and a very positive discourse when transgenic benefits for health were presented, as well as when they were considered as an advance of scientific and technological knowledge.

The class "Science, Technology, and Society" is related to the class "Research." Although its content does not put the GM crops matter in debate, this theme raises a greater discussion about the general advances of science and technology and its impacts upon society. This class of articles is divided into favorable and contrary opinions toward such advances. Other articles try to explore public understanding of science and technology, frequently considering peoples' fear of new technology as irrational.

The classes "Bio-Safety Law 1, 2, and 3" are closely related and portray the judicial battle that involved a series of decrees and appeals until approval of the new Biosafety Law in March 2005. Together, the three classes correspond to 34.78 percent of the entire *corpus*.

Class "Bio-Safety Law 1" (the Cardoso Law) shows a period marked by the absence of clear rules on the planting and commercialization of GM crops, and CTNBio's role and power. This class content followed the civil action filed by IDEC (Consumer Rights Association) and Greenpeace against CTNbio's approval of commercial plantation of Monsanto soya, in June 1998.

Class "Bio-Safety Law 2" describes some problems created by the Executive Order that authorized the planting of genetically modified soya for the years 2003–2004. By this Executive Order, the government acknowledged that GM soya seeds had been planted in violation of the 1995 Biosafety Law, but nevertheless allowed the growers to commercialize their GM crops.

Class "Bio-Safety Law 3" portrays the disagreements inside the government in 2003 between the Ministries of Environment and of Agriculture. This class describes the creation of two Executive Orders that authorized the commercialization of the 2003/2004 and 2004/2005 crops.

Table 2. *Number of articles on transgenics published by section and by year.*

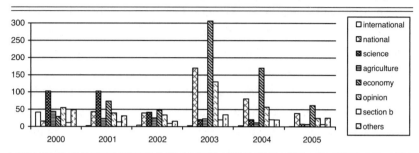

The latter was released after a one-year delay, caused by the negotiation process necessary for the approval of the Bio-Safety Law, which finally took place in March 2005. This class also describes the negotiations toward the new rules; it shows the divisions inside the government, presidential pressure on the National Congress, and public dissatisfaction about the "liberation" of GM crops.

The class "Landless Workers Movement – MST" describes MST's protests and planned actions against transgenics, which involves the burning of seeds, the destruction of plantations and even the distribution of informative brochures in supermarkets to convince the middle class of the threat posed by GM products. This class also presents MST's arguments against transgenics, such as: the decrease in varieties of crops to a few cultures, the supremacy of multinationals companies, and the decline of production by small producers. Most protests took place in 2001, during the World Social Forum in Porto Alegre, and revealed the group's integration with international movements such as Via Campesina.

Another interesting analysis is to consider the evolution of how this theme was treated during the considered period of six years. Table 2 shows the distribution of articles published each year within the different newspapers.

As Table 2 shows, in the year 2000 most of the articles were published in the science section. In 2001, science was still important, but an increase of articles published in the economy section is noticed. From

2003 onward, economy was the dominant section for the publication of the articles. These results point to the fact that classes "research" and "science, technology, and society" discussed transgenics by presenting their history, processes, and possible social and environmental risks and impacts upon society. Classes "Bio-Safety Law 1" and "Landless Workers Movement – MST" show the beginning of a civil movement against this new technology. All these four classes are typical of the years 2000, 2001, and 2002. It seems that from 2003 on – with the inception of the Lula administration, which coincided with the political shift from a preventive to a promotional policy, as discussed in Part II – that this kind of critical discussion lost space in the media to the debate about the economic gains this technology might bring. It is also important to remember that in 2003 the Brazilian media gave much more space to this topic.

IV. Conclusion

The complexity of the environmental crisis requires a complex communication solution that should originate from the different languages of Ecology, Economics, Science, and Politics.[39]

A "system," such as Economics, Politics, or Science is emergent, in that it comes into existence as soon as a border can be drawn between a set of communications and the system's environment. A system is always less complex than its environment – if a system does not reduce the complexity in its environment, then it cannot perform any function. A system effectively defines itself by creating a binary language to maintain a border between itself and the environment. For instance, Economics is related to "having" or "not having" money, Politics to "being in power" or "not being in power," Science to a theory "being" or "not being" true.

---

[39] LUHMANN, Niklas. *Ecological communication*. Translation of John Bednarz Jr. (Chicago: University of Chicago, 1989), 51–105.

The binary code (having/not having or being/not being) "is the condition of the system's being set in motion and keeping it going."[40]

The circumstances of the Brazilian economy, including its agricultural activities with a large production of soya, corn, and cotton, which could potentially benefit from biotechnology, showed the importance of Economics. The reduced costs that would contribute to improve Brazil's international competitiveness emphasized this system. Thus, there were difficulties in making the other systems relevant to allow communication between them and Economics.

The complexity of the GM crops debate and its solution require a policy that deals with the different languages of the connected systems (Ecology, Economics, Science, and Politics). The infrastructure linked to GM crops demands, as Science shows, different long-term experiments to measure the long-term effects of pesticide exposure on non-target organisms. Economics tries to solve immediate allocation problems and doesn't understand long-term effects (externalities). Ecology, on the other hand, demands knowledge of long-term effects to guarantee biodiversity conservation, in the present and in the future. Unfortunately, Brazilian policy makers deal only with Economics (the regular market approach) thinking exclusively of maximizing profit in the allocation of GM crops that are ready to be traded.

Therefore, Brazilian politics was not able to pursue such an elaborate policy. There was a lack of public opinion and pressure in favor of safe standards.[41] In the beginning of the public debate about GM crops, the main issue was Science; by 2003, Economy. Simultaneously, there was a discussion shift from preventive to promotional policies regarding GM crops in the Brazilian media. By focusing on the economic gains rather than on the risk aspects, and by not promoting a "social amplification of

---

[40] LUHMANN, Niklas. *Ecological communication*. Translation of John Bednarz Jr. (Chicago: University of Chicago, 1989), 51.

[41] "Political resonance arises because 'public opinion,' as the true sovereign, suggests the chance of re-election." (Luhmann, Niklas. *Ecological communication*. Trans. John Bednarz Jr. (Chicago: University of Chicago, 1989), 89).

risks" among the population, as in other countries, the Brazilian media may have contributed to maintain the "attitude of resignation or indifference towards risks" among the Brazilian population.

The case of Brazil is a good example of how international economic pressure undermines the autonomy of developing countries when they develop policy for a new technology, and how the prospect of benefits from international trade overpowers other societal interests and the safety concerns of their citizens. In particular, this pressure and its economic promise has even more advantage when there is a lack of public discourse and mobilization for addressing safety and other concerns raised by GM agriculture.

REFERENCES

Bauer, M. (1994). A popularização da ciência como imunização cultural: a função de resistência das representações sociais. In: P. A., Guareschi & S. Jovchelovitch (Orgs.), *Textos em representações sociais* (pp. 229–257). Petrópolis: Vozes.

Beck, Ulrich. (1999). *World Risk Society*. Cambridge: Polity Press.

Einsiedel, E. & Kamara, W. (2006). The Coming of Age of Public Participation. In: G. Gaskel & M. Bauer (Eds.), *Genomics and Society: Legal, Ethical, and Social Dimensions*. (pp. 95–112). Londres: Earthscan.

Frewer, L., Miles, S., & Marsh, R. (2002). The media and genetically modified foods: evidence in support of social amplification of risk. *Risk Analysis*. 22(4): 701–711.

Gaskell, G., Allum, N., & Stares, S. (2002). Europeans and biotechnology in 2002. Eurobarometer 58.0. Report to the EC Directorate General for Research from the project 'Life Sciences in European Society' QLG7-CT-1999–00286. London School of Economics: Londres.

Guivant, J. (2001). A teoria da sociedade de risco de Ulrich Beck: entre o diagnóstico e a profecia. *Estudos Sociedade e Agricultura*. n. 16. pp. 95–112.

Guivant, J. (2006). Transgênicos e percepção publica da ciência no Brasil. Ambiente & Sociedade – Vol. IX, n°. 1 Jan./Jun. 2006.

Gutteling, J. et al. (2002). Media coverage 1973–1996: trends and dynamics. In: M. Bauer & G. Gaskel (Eds.), *Biotechnology: The Making of a Global Controversy*. Cambridge: University Press.

International Centre for Trade and Sustainable Development. (2006). ISAAA Report: Developing Country Biotech Plantings Continue to Expand, Trade BioRes Main Page, vol. 6, n.1 (Jan. 2006), at http://www. ictsd.org/biores/06–01–20/story3.htm.

Jodelet, D. (1986). La representación social: fenómenos, concepto e teoría. In: S. Moscovici (Org.), *Psicología social II*. Barcelona: Ediciones Paidós.

Lopes, Ignez Vidigal et al. (2006). *Factors Affecting Brazilian Growth or Are There Limits to Future Growth of Agriculture in Brazil?* Rio de Janeiro: Getulio Vargas Foundation.

Luhmann, N. (1984). *Social Systems, trans.* J. Bednarz, Jr. with D. Baecker. Stanford: Stanford University Press.

Luhmann, N. (1993). *Risk: A Sociological Theory, trans.* Rhodes Barrett. New York: Aldine De Gruyter.

Luhmann, N. (1989). *Ecological communication, trans.* John Bednarz Jr. Chicago: University of Chicago.

Moscovici, S. (2000). The phenomenon of social representations. In: S. Moscovici & G. Duveen (Orgs.), *Social representations: Explorations in social psychology* (pp. 18–77). Cambridge: Polity.

Nascimento-Schulze, C. M. & Camargo, B. V. (2000). Psicologia social, representações sociais e métodos. *Temas em Psicologia da SBP*, 08 (03), pp. 287–299.

Reinert, M. (2000). *Alceste: Analyse de données textuelles*. Manuel d'utilisateur. Toulouse: IMAGE, 1998.

Soskin, A. B. (1988). *Non-Traditional Agriculture and Economic Development: The Brazilian Soybean Expansion, 1964–1982*. New York: Praeger.

Wathern, P., ed. (1992). Environmental Impact Assessment: Theory and Practice. London: Routledge.

Wu, F. & Butz, W. P. (2004). *The Future of Genetically Modified Crops: Lessons from the Green Revolution*. Santa Monica, CA: Rand.

Part II FUTURE CHALLENGES

6 Coexistence and Traceability of GMOs in the Agro-Food Sector

Klaus Menrad, Tobias Hirzinger,
and Daniela Reitmeier

1. Introduction and Regulatory Framework

The worldwide acreage of genetically modified (GM) plants is growing year by year and amounted to more than 114 million hectares in 2007 (ISAAA, 2008; James, 2005, 2006). In contrast to the globally growing use of GM plants in agriculture, the acceptance of GM food is still low in the European Union (EU) (Gaskell et al., 2006) as well as in Germany (Frank, 2004). In the opinion of most EU consumers there is nothing to gain by applying GMO ingredients but serious disadvantages may occur. Some of the often-mentioned concerns of EU consumers are negative long-term health and/or environmental impacts, the extreme difficulties of reversing GMO technology as soon as it becomes widespread, and a rising monopolization of huge seed and food processing companies resulting in a larger dependency of farmers as well as ethical concerns. Furthermore, the share of people thinking that it is useful to apply biotechnology to food production decreased in the recent years (Gaskell et al., 2006). It is interesting that there are significantly more consumers concerned about GM food than about medical applications of biotechnology (Frank, 2004; European Commission, 2002; Gaskell et al., 2006). In the case of GM food the high opposition of European consumers "is accompanied by perceptions of relatively high risk" (Gaskell et al., 2006) which is unacceptable for many EU consumers.

Therefore, the EU adopted a series of regulations related to GMOs (see Chapter 3) of which the regulations (EC) No 1829/2003 and 1830/2003 dealing with the admission, labeling, and traceability of GMOs have special impact on the food and feed industry (Jany and Schuh, 2005). Important targets of these regulations are to ensure freedom of choice for consumers and users of GM and non-GM products as well as to avoid environmental and health risks associated with the commercial use of GM products. However, it is important to consider that the afore-mentioned regulations deal with GM food and feed products that have been approved in the EU either for commercial use, import, or export. GM food and feed should only be authorized for placing on the EU market after a scientific evaluation of any risks that they present for human and animal health and for the environment (i.e., GM food and feed that are approved for commercial use in the EU are regarded by the regulatory authorities to be safe for consumers and do not cause any adverse effects to the environment or ecosystems) has been done at least at the current stage of knowledge (European Parliament and the Council of the European Union, 2003a, b).

According to regulations (EC) No 1829/2003 and 1830/2003, food and feed products have to be labeled to contain GMOs or GM material when a tolerance threshold of 0.9 percent is exceeded for EU authorized GMOs, and 0.5 percent for unauthorized GMOs if they have already received a favorable EU risk assessment. Products containing traces of GMOs below the appropriate regulatory thresholds are exempt from labeling, provided that compliant traceability systems are in place and traces of GMOs are adventitious and technically unavoidable. Also animal products that were produced with GM feed compounds do not have to be labeled. Products containing GMOs above the thresholds must be labeled as such, even if the GM material is undetectable by analytical tests. In these cases, product traceability has to be mandated through documentation systems and implementation of these systems for the entire supply chain (Fagan, 2004; European Parliament and the Council of the European Union, 2003a, b).

Furthermore, there is an intensive discussion in the EU about how to ensure freedom of choice between farmers in agricultural production. In July 2003, the European Commission (DG Agriculture) released Commission Recommendation 2003/556/EC on general coexistence guidelines and asked member-states to set up national strategies and best practices to ensure the coexistence of GM crops with conventional and organic farming. The national member-states of the EU are responsible for setting rules for coexistence that are in line with Commission Recommendation 2003/556/EC.

In recent years EU member-states have developed a variety of coexistence rules and regulations that may influence the adoption of GM crops in the different regions. Thus the institutional environment for planting GM crops in Europe is heterogeneous (Beckmann et al., 2006). Poland discusses a ban of planting GM crops while Bt maize is cultivated in Spain since the mid-1990s (James, 2005). One hundred and twenty communities in Belgium have declared themselves to be GMO-free, whereas a regional grain trader and feed producer has announced to pay the same price for Bt maize and conventional varieties (Beckmann et al., 2006). Farmers in Upper Austria have to apply authorization for each field intended to be planted with GM crops and farmers in Denmark have to pay a levy of 100 DK for each hectare of GM crops. Taking all together this indicates that so far there is no clear regulatory framework in the EU concerning the concrete implementation and handling of coexistence measures in the different EU member-states. The situation is further complicated by the fact that general and GMO-specific liability rules (if existing) differ significantly between member-states.

Several studies analyzed the possibilities of coexistence schemes and its economic effects in Europe (e.g., Bock et al., 2002; Tolstrup et al., 2003; Messéan et al., 2006) showing a wide set of measures to minimize pollen flow to neighboring fields (Table 1). The recent studies also show that potential costs of coexistence schemes occur on different levels (e.g., on a single farm, a region, the agricultural sector, or the agro-food chain of a specific country or internationally) and that different types of costs have to be distinguished when assessing the economic impacts of coexistence measures in agricultural production (Menrad, 2003). However, a lot of questions could not be clarified in these studies, in particular with respect to production of certified seeds. Therefore, thresholds for the adventitious presence of GM seeds in conventional seeds are still under discussion in the EU.

2. Economic Effects of Coexistence Measures in Maize Crop and Seed Production in France

France is the leading maize producer in Europe (EU 15). The Poitou-Charentes region has been chosen for a case study for maize crop production because it represents the third largest grain maize producing region and accounts for about 11 percent of the area under maize in France. Furthermore, GM maize varieties are an alternative for farmers with problems of controlling weeds and European or Mediterranean corn borer infestations.

Both in the case of maize crop and maize seed production, the coexistence MAPOD® gene flow model (Angevin et al., 2001) was used to estimate adventitious presence of GM maize varieties due to cross-pollination. This model was developed during a study that aimed to assess the economic relevance and technical feasibility of non-GM supply chains in France (Le Bail & Meynard, 2001). Input data of the model refer to field structure (e.g., form and size of fields, location of specific plant varieties), climate (e.g., temperature, rain, speed, and direction of the wind), cropping systems (like e.g., sowing dates, drought stress before and during flowering), and the variety (e.g., quantity of pollen per plant, pollen sensitivity to temperature, genotype of GMO, tassel height of the variety). The model estimates the rate of variant impurities due to cross-pollination in maize as well as changes in these rates due to changes in cropping techniques (Angevin et al., 2001).

Table 1. *Measures to Prevent Pollen Flow to Neighboring Fields*

Measures to prevent pollen flow to neighboring fields		
On farm measures	Preperation for sowing, planting, and soil cultivation	Isolation distance
		Buffer zones
		Pollen traps or barriers, e.g., hedgerows
		Suitable crop rotation systems
		Planning crop production
		Reducing size of the seed bank through adequate soil tillage
		Managing populations in field borders through appropriate cultivation methods, use of selective herbicides
		Choosing optimal sowing dates
		Careful handling of seeds to avoid admixture
		Using varieties with reduced pollen production or male sterile varieties
		Cleaning of seed drills
		Sharing seed drills only with farmers using the same production type
		Preventing seed spillage when traveling to and from the field
		Control/destruction of volunteers
	Harvest and postharvest field treatment	Saving seeds only from suitable fields and field areas
		Minimizing seed loss during the harvest
		Cleaning of harvesting machinery
		Sharing harvesting machinery only with farmers using the same production type
		Separately harvesting of field margins
	Transport and storage	Ensuring the physical segregation
		Adequate seed storage arrangements and practices
		Avoiding spillage during transport
	Field monitoring	Monitoring of seed spillage sites, fields, and field margins for volunteer development

Source: Reitmeier et al., 2006.

Simulations were carried out on landscapes representing two French regions: the *département*[1] of "Pyrénées-Atlantiques" in southwest France for seed production and the "Poitou-Charentes" region in western France for crop production. Two scenarios were built for the presence of GMOs in the landscape (10 percent and 50 percent share of GMOs in the relevant crop), three agricultural production systems (GMO-based, conventional, and organic) as well as different thresholds for adventitious GM presence: 0.1 percent and 0.9 percent for crop production and 0.1 percent, 0.3 percent, and 0.5 percent for seed production. In a first step the economic performance of the different crops is investigated by reviewing literature, collecting publicly available statistical information, and searching databases as well as contacting and interviewing experts. The costs of coexistence measures for the different crops, farm types, and regions as suggested as outcome agronomic analysis were calculated in a second step using publicly available data sources of costs of agronomic practices.

2.1 Economic Effects in Maize Crop Production

Variable production costs of 687 €/ha and an income of 950 €/ha form the baseline for the calculation of costs of coexistence measures in maize crop production in France resulting in a gross margin of 743 €/ha if compensation payments were taken into consideration (Theyssier, 2004). Because the costs of several coexistence measures differ depending on the potential economic performance of the cultivated GM maize (for which no empirically sound data are available for France so far) it is assumed in a first case that GM maize has the same gross margin as non-GM maize, while an economic advantage of 43 €/ha of GM maize compared to non-GM varieties is considered in a second case (Menrad and Reitmeier, 2006).

---

[1] French administrative district.

There are moderate opportunity costs of increasing isolation distances in maize crop production due to the small differences in the gross margins of alternative crops whereas the changing of flowering times causes substantial income losses for farmers active in maize crop production. The opportunity costs of discard widths on the non-GM field (which is separately harvested) differ significantly depending on the width of the discard width as well as the size of the non-GM field (Table 2). High differences in the per-hectare costs can also be observed for non-GM buffer zones around GM fields mainly depending on the GM adoption rate in a region and the estimated economic performance of GM maize.

The comparison of our results with the results of other studies dealing with coexistence issues is complicated by the fact that other regions with other cropping systems are analyzed as well as due to differing methodological approaches. Tolstrup and colleagues (2003) assumed that for silage/feed maize production in Denmark it might be sufficient to fulfill the required threshold of 0.9 percent by cleaning machinery what results in significantly lower per-hectare coexistence costs compared to the suggested measures for the French region of Poitou-Charantes. Bock and colleagues (2002) analyzed coexistence costs in maize crop production for feed purposes in France and Italy. For a farm producing in an intensive maize cultivating region that is comparable to the analyzed region of Poitou-Charantes, costs of changing agricultural practices were estimated to 45.4 €/ha due to changing flowering time of the cultivated varieties (Bock et al., 2002). This result is in line with the time isolation costs of changing from late to mid-early varieties (Table 2).

To identify the effects of different coexistence measures in a landscape, several scenarios of GM adoption were simulated with the MAPOD® model in the region of Poitou-Charantes (France). The costs of an existing farm in this region were calculated for this purpose assuming that non-GM buffer zones are used as coexistence measure because they seem to be a cost-effective measure to reach the defined threshold of 0.9 percent GM adventitious presence in maize crop production.

Table 2. *Economic Effects of Coexistence Measures in Maize Crop Production*

Additional Measure	(Opportunity) Costs of Singular Measures
Clean the machines a) single seed driller b) harvest – combine c) transport – trailer or truck	Costs of shared machinery: 38.38 56.84 1.48
Isolation distance	GMA[1] of GM maize = GMA[1] of non-GM maize: 0 €/ha GMA[1] of GM maize > GMA[1] of non-GM maize: 2.19 €/ha
Time isolation	Change from very late to late (30°days): 201 €/ha Change from late to mid-early (60°days): 46 €/ha
Discard width on the non-GM-field – extra harvest	6 m wide discard width: 1.27–2.85 €/ha[2] 12 m wide discard width: 2.55–5.70 €/ha[2] 24 m wide discard width: 5.10–11.40 €/ha[2]
Non-GM buffer zones around the GM field – extra sowing	GMA[1] of GM maize = GMA[1] of non-GM maize: 17.54–35.07 €/ha[3] GMA[1] of GM maize > GMA[1] of non-GM maize: 60.54–78.07 €/ha[3]

[1] GMA = Gross margin
[2] The first figure refers to a neighboring non-GM field of 5 ha, and the second to a non-GM field of 1 ha.
[3] The first figure refers to a 50 percent GM adoption rate in the region with clustered fields, whereas the second figure refers to a 10 percent GM adoption rate with dispersed fields.
Source: Menrad and Reitmeier, 2006.

In this context the effects of non-GM buffer zones on the level of GM adventitious presence in neighboring fields have been simulated for two differing locations of GM fields:

- GM fields are scattered among the non-GM fields ("dispersed fields")
- GM fields are concentrated on one part of the farm ("clustered fields")

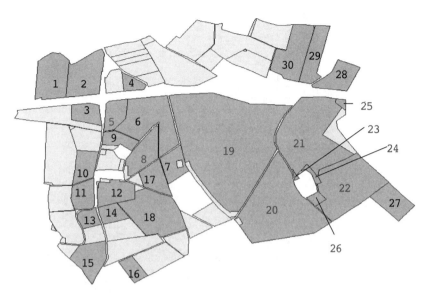

Figure 1. Example of field pattern used for the landscape scale study: 10 percent GM maize adoption.

The economic effects of non-GM buffer zones were analyzed in a landscape with GM maize production (Figure 1). Based on the simulations of the level of adventitious presence of GM pollen in different fields, big variations can be observed in the additional costs of non-GM buffer zones, depending on the sizes of the GM fields, the width of the buffer zones as well as the underlying assumptions concerning the economic performance of GM maize in France: in the case of a 10 percent GM adoption rate in the region, the per-hectare costs of non-GM buffer zones range between around 4 €/ha and 17 €/ha for a 9-m wide buffer zone and between around 7 €/ha and 30 €/ha in the case of an 18-m wide buffer zone (Table 3). Significant cost savings (of up to 29 percent) can be achieved if the fields producing GM crops are clustered in the region under investigation, in particular if small GM fields are concerned.

Table 3. *Costs of Buffer Zones in Maize Crop Production in France (10 percent GM maize in region)*

| GM Fields | | Neighboring Non-GM Fields | | No Difference in Gross Margins of GM and Non-GM Maize | | | | Gross Margin of GM Maize Higher than Non-GM Maize | | | |
| | | | | Costs per Field (€/GM Field) | | Costs per ha (€/ha) | | Costs per Field (€/GM Field) | | Costs per ha (€/ha) | |
Number	ha	Number	ha	9 m	18 m	9 m	18 m	9 m	18 m	9 m	18 m
5	3.6	6	12.8	28.06	49.10	7.79	13.64	62.16	108.78	17.27	30.22
8	5.5	No fields with thresholds > 0.9		42.08	70.14	7.65	12.75	93.24	155.4	16.95	28.25
22	17	24	0.6	73.65	126.25	4.26	7.30	163.17	279.72	9.43	16.17
26	1										
27	5.2										
8	5.5			42.08	70.14	7.65	12.75	93.24	155.4	16.95	28.25

Source: Menrad and Reitmeier, 2006.

2.2 Economic Effects in Maize Seed Production

Maize seed production in Europe covered 126,311 ha in 2003, with France being the leading seed producer in Europe (49,822 ha). In France 50 percent of seed production is concentrated in the southwest region and two "*départements*" (Landes and Pyrénées-Atlantiques) account for 25 percent of the national production. To estimate the economic effects of the suggested coexistence measures, it was assumed that a yield of 3.5 t of maize seed per hectare generates a total income of 3,365 €/ha of maize seed production in France (Hugger, 2004). Taking into account variable production costs of 2,177 €/ha and additional compensation payments, a gross margin of 1,488 €/ha was taken as the baseline for the cost calculations of maize seed production (Hugger, 2004). The economic effects of increasing isolation distances were calculated for a kind of worst-case scenario in which the farmer producing GM maize seed has to reduce his seed producing area and plant the most economic crop (i.e., wheat) as an alternative. This results in gross margin losses of almost 22 percent in the case of an additional 100-m isolation distance and almost one-third of the gross margin if an extra 150-m isolation distance is added (Table 4). Substantial opportunity costs of around 16 percent of the gross margin have to be added, particularly if 18 additional male rows have to be cultivated. Changing the flowering time of the cultivated seed maize varieties also has negative effects on yield, which are quite substantial in the case of switching from very late to late varieties (30° days). Farmers' loss of income due to this measure would total to around 30 percent of the gross margin of maize seed production. The income losses are significantly lower if the flowering time is switched from late to mid-early varieties (Table 4).

In a subsequent step of our study the economic effects are calculated for combinations of different measures in case that GM and non-GM seeds are produced in a region. The lowest per-hectare costs of such combinations of measures necessary to meet a defined threshold differ considerably, depending on the sizes of neighboring non-GM seed

Table 4. *Economic Effects of Coexistence Measures in Maize Seed Production*

Additional Coexistence Measure	Costs/income Losses in €/ha	Percent of Variable Production Costs	Percent of Gross Margin
Increasing isolation distance by:			
100 m (wheat as alternative crop)	322	14.8	21.6
150 m (wheat as alternative crop)	483	22.2	32.5
Planting additional male rows on non-GM seed maize field			
6 additional male rows	80.85	3.7	5.4
18 additional male rows	242.5	11.1	16.3
Changing flowering time of cultivated maize varieties from...			
Very late to late (30° days)	446.8	20.5	30.0
Late to mid-early (60° days)	114.0	5.2	7.6

Source: Menrad and Reitmeier, 2006.

production plots. To meet a threshold of 0.5 percent in maize seed production, costs of around 410 €/ha have to be assumed (almost 28 percent of the gross margin) in the case of non-GM seed plots of 0.5 ha, whereas this threshold can be met without any additional costs in the case of 5 ha non-GM seed plots (Figure 2). The same picture emerges if a 0.3 percent threshold has to be met: in the case of 0.5 ha non-GM seed plots, additional costs of around 650 €/ha (around 44 percent of the gross margin) have to be expected, which fall to 114 €/ha in the case of non-GM seed plot sizes of 5 ha. The costs of additional measures to meet a 0.1 percent threshold add up to more than 650 €/ha even in the "best case" 5 ha non-GM seed plots (Figure 2).

Taken all together, it can be summarized that in maize grain production, levels of adventitious presence below 0.9 percent can be achieved without any cooperation between farmers in neighboring clusters. When fields are located in the same cluster, additional measures have to be taken with very differing cost effects depending on the specific characteristics of the measure. Additional measures should also be taken (either by the seed company or by the commercial GM grower) for ensuring

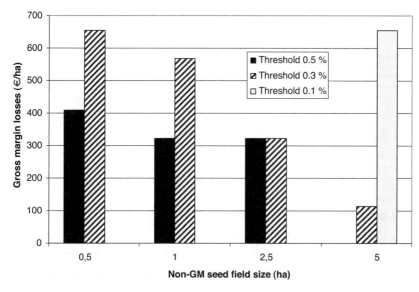

Figure 2. Gross margin losses due to the most effective coexistence measures for different thresholds and field sizes of non-GM neighboring fields in maize seed production. *Source:* Menrad and Reitmeier, 2006.

coexistence between commercial GM fields and non-GM seed production clusters, whereas current practices would be sufficient for ensuring coexistence between GM and non-GM maize seed production plots for a threshold of 0.5 percent adventitious presence.

3. Regional Costs of IP Systems for Bt Maize in Bavaria (Germany)

Coexistence costs do not only occur on single farms but have a regional dimension as well. To quantify the effects of specific measures (in particular buffer zones) necessary to keep adventitious presence of GM material under the defined thresholds, the costs of such measures for Bt maize are quantified in the federal state of Bavaria (Germany), which is characterized by small-scale farms and landscape patterns. Data sources of this analysis are digitized maps and official data from the federal Ministry of Agriculture that include information about field size, crop cultivation on field, and user of field. The analysis has been done in two model regions

Table 5. *Characteristics of the Analyzed Model Regions in Bavaria*

Model Region	Agricultural Area in Use	Agricultural Crop Land	Maize share[1]	Permanent Crops and Pasture Land	Average Field Size
	ha	ha	percent	percent	ha
I	30,812	20,900	44	32	2.17
II	47,572	31,511	19	34	1.89

Source: Reitmeier and Menrad, 2006.

that have agricultural areas in use (AAU) of between 30,800 ha in model region I and nearly 50,000 ha in model region II (Table 5). Agricultural crop land (ACL) is between 20,000 and 30,000 ha with high shares of maize in model region I (44 percent of ACL) and low maize cultivation in model region II (19 percent of ACL) (Table 5).

So far, there are no definite rules concerning the width of the isolation distances between Bt maize and conventional maize fields to comply with the legal threshold of 0.9 percent in Germany. Therefore, a variety of buffer zones around Bt maize fields are considered in the analysis ranging from 20 m to 100 m. A buffer zone of 20 m is in line with the results of the German field trial experiments (so-called "Erprobungsanbau") where out-crossing rates of Bt maize were analyzed under German conditions in 2005. According to this experience, an isolation distance of 20 m for maize is sufficient to comply with the threshold of 0.9 percent GM adventitious presence (Weber et al., 2005a, b). Furthermore, the effects of adoption rates of 10 percent, 30 percent, and 50 percent Bt maize were analyzed in both model regions.

In an initial scenario with 10 percent Bt maize adoption in the region I, it can be observed that between 1 percent and 7 percent of the conventional maize area is affected by neighboring Bt maize fields depending on the isolation distance required. With increasing adoption rates of Bt maize the proportion of the affected conventional maize area increases up to 31 percent (Table 6). With respect to potential conflicts among

Table 6. *Impact of Growing Bt Maize in Model Region I (with high proportion of maize in crop rotation)*

Adoption Rate	Isolation Distance	Initial Situation			Bt Maize is Growing of			Bt Maize Affects		
Percent	m	Total Maize Area (ha)	Number of Fields	Number of Farms	Bt maize Area (ha)	Number of Fields	Number of Farms	Affected Conventional Maize Area (percent)	Percentage of Fields (percent)	Percentage of Farms (percent)
10	20	9101	4224	869	851	394	87	1	10	19
	50							3	16	22
	100							7	24	25
30	20				2420	1211	261	3	31	47
	50							8	46	51
	100							20	71	57
50	20				3921	1755	435	4	46	64
	50							13	67	70
	100							31	100	100

Source: Reitmeier and Menrad, 2006.

153

farmers growing Bt maize or conventional varieties in the same region, not only the area grown with specific varieties is a point of interest but also the percentages of farmers that are influenced by neighboring Bt maize fields. The simulations in model region I indicate that already with a low adoption rate of 10 percent for Bt maize farmers, a substantial part of the farmers growing non-GM varieties (around 19 percent to 25 percent) might be influenced by cross-pollination of neighboring Bt maize fields. If adoption of Bt maize increases to 30 percent, this figure rises to around half of the "conventional" farmers and to more than three quarters in case of a 50 percent adoption rate of Bt maize (Table 6).

Comparing the results of model region II (with lower relevance of maize in crop rotation) with those of model region I, it can be observed that regions with low maize cultivation show lower affection rates with respect to conventional maize areas, fields, and farms. In model region II, affection rates for isolation distances of 20-m range from 1 percent to 3 percent over all Bt maize adoption levels regarding the affected conventional maize area. In analogy to the results observed in model region I, the percentage of influenced farms is substantially higher than those of affected areas ranging from 13 percent (in case of 10 percent Bt adoption and 20-m isolation distance) to 66 percent (if we have a 50 percent Bt maize adoption rate and 100-m isolation distance) (Table 7).

3.1 Economic Impact of Buffer Zones

According to the Recommendations on coexistence measures of the European Commission of July 2003 the GM farmers are responsible for applying and bearing the costs of coexistence measures (Commission of the European Communities, 2003). Spatial isolation of GM and non-GM crops is regarded as being an effective measure of decreasing adventitious presence by cross-pollination: Farmers have to maintain an isolation distance (or "buffer zone") between GM and non-GM crops. This could result in a reorganization of fields used for production of a specific crop and may lead to a reduction of the total area used for production

Table 7. *Impact of Growing Bt Maize in Model Region II (with low proportion of maize in crop rotation)*

Adoption rate	Isolation Distance	Initial Situation			Bt Maize is Growing of Bt Maize Affects			Affected Conventional Maize Area	Percentage of Fields	Percentage of farms
Percent	m	Total Maize Area (ha)	Number of Fields	Number of Farms	Bt Maize Area (ha)	Number of Fields	Number of Farms	(percent)	(percent)	(percent)
10	20	6105	3083	936	530	279	94	1	6	13
	50							2	8	15
	100							5	12	19
30	20				1557	781	281	1	15	29
	50							4	20	34
	100							11	30	40
50	20				2427	1161	468	3	24	51
	50							8	33	56
	100							19	49	66

Source: Reitmeier and Menrad, 2006.

of this specific crop in a region depending on the size of the isolation distance. Because most agricultural production is not organized according to a centralized plan (e.g., the case in seed production) this requires additional time and activities as well as rising bureaucracy costs among farmers within a region, the willingness and ability of farmers to cooperate with each other, new rules and contractual forms to organize this type of cooperation as well as modes for conflict solving. Furthermore, the freedom of the single farmer to organize his farming business might be reduced through this type of activity. This relates in particular to regions with small-scaled farms and fields in which multiple farmers might have to coordinate their activities.

Among other methodological approaches we have the possibility of calculating the costs of buffer zones by assuming that the GM farmer cultivates conventional maize or another crop with lower gross margins on the isolated buffer zone area (Menrad and Reitmeier, 2006). In the case of growing conventional maize varieties, additional costs of coexistence measures are differences in the gross margins of Bt maize and conventional maize varieties, in particular differences in seed prices, insecticide treatment, yields and prices of the crop, extra machinery costs, and efforts concerning cleaning machineries. To quantify the costs of the suggested coexistence measure, it is necessary to make assumptions concerning the economics of Bt maize because no empirical evidence exists with respect to the economic performance of Bt maize in Germany due to lack of commercial planting of this crop. According to the reported experiences, it can be assumed that the yields of Bt maize might increase in particular in regions with a high infestation level of the European Corn Borer. Due to the resistance of Bt maize against this insect, insecticide use is often reported to decrease when cultivating Bt maize. In contrast, the seed costs of Bt maize will increase due to the technology fee that farmers have to pay to the seed breeding companies. However, there is no final conclusion possible concerning positive or negative changes in gross margins of Bt maize in comparison to non-GM varieties (Menrad and Reitmeier, 2006).

To estimate potential coexistence costs, we took data from Degenhardt et al., who analyzed the impact of existing pest management systems against the European Corn Borer and compared the efficiency of the differing systems. Compared to biological and chemical pest management methods, Bt maize had the highest impact on larvae of the European Corn Borer with efficiency rates of nearly 100 percent. Cost calculations of Degenhardt and colleagues (2003) result in economic benefits of around 84 to 93 €/ha for cultivating Bt maize by considering higher yields in the range of up to 15 percent and seed costs of plus 35 €/ha compared to conventional seeds. Users of synthetic insecticides gain between 18 and 55 €/ha when applying common insecticide management methods. Non-insecticide users do not benefit from their ecological insecticide treatment (trichogramma application) in case of high infestation levels. In such a situation their losses amount to 52 to 57 €/ha (Degenhardt et al., 2003).

To quantify the costs of the buffer zone, we assumed a profit of 38 €/ha to 66 €/ha, which equals to 3.4 percent and 6.2 percent of variable costs of conventional maize. This profit implies higher yields[2] between 3 percent and 4 percent for Bt maize, higher seed costs of 35 €/ha and insecticide savings of 40 €/ha (Degenhardt et al., 2003).

The additional costs of buffer zones around Bt maize fields are increasing with higher adoption rates as indicated in Table 7. In case of a 20-m buffer zone the aggregated costs in the region range from 19,289 € (10 percent scenario) to 76,134 € (50 percent scenario) in model region I. These result in additional costs of 222 € per farm in the 10 percent scenario and 175 € per farm in the 50 percent scenario. In model region II where only half of the maize is grown compared to region I additional costs per farm range from 48 €/farm to 33 €/farm (Table 8).

The additional costs increase consequently when higher isolation distances of 50 m and 100 m, respectively, have to be applied to meet the 0.9 percent threshold of adventitious presence of GM maize (Table 8). In

[2] Price for conventional maize in five-year average is 117.7 €/tonne (tax included).

Table 8. Additional Costs of Buffer Zones Around Bt Maize Fields in Two Model Regions in Bavaria

	Model Region I – Intensive Maize Production				Model Region II – Extensive Maize Production			
Adoption Rate	Buffer Zone	Bt-maize Farms in Region	Accumulated Additional Costs[1]		Buffer Zone	Bt-maize Farms in Region	Accumulated Additional Costs	
percent	Area (ha)	n	€/region	€/farm	Area (ha)	n	€/region	€/farm
			Isolation distance of 20 m					
10	292	87	19289	222	118	94	4499	48
30	722	261	47680	183	256	281	9741	35
50	1154	435	76134	175	411	468	15625	33
			Isolation distance of 50 m					
10	494	87	32576	375	233	94	8869	95
30	1122	261	74085	284	523	281	19888	71
50	1658	435	109409	252	866	468	32898	70
			Isolation distance of 100 m					
10	634	87	41868	482	320	94	12178	130
30	1575	261	103930	399	755	281	28695	102
50	2364	435	156053	359	1219	468	46306	99

1) Region I: Gross margin of Bt maize is 66 €/ha higher than those of conventional varieties.
2) Region II: Gross margin of Bt maize is 38 €/ha higher than those of conventional varieties.
Source: Reitmeier and Menrad, 2006.

case of a 100-m buffer zone costs of 482 € per farm are observed in case of a 10 percent Bt adoption and 359 € per farm in case of a 50 percent adoption rate in model region I (Table 8). In model region II (with lower relevance of maize production) the respective figures amount to 130 € per farm in case of the 10 percent adoption scenario and to 99 € per farm in case of the 50 percent adoption (Table 8).

4. Effect of EU Regulations on the German Food and Feed Industry

In addition to the effects of coexistence measures in agriculture, there are impacts of the EU regulations in place for the food and feed industry as well, although only small surfaces of GM plants are cultivated in the EU (mainly around 60,000 hectares of Bt maize in 2005 in Spain). To analyze these effects, a comprehensive written survey was carried out in Germany with a total of 1,700 questionnaires mailed to food and feed processing companies to investigate and analyze the effects of regulations (EC) No 1829/2003 and 1830/2003 on the German food and feed industry in May 2005. The response rate to this survey was around 20 percent resulting in 333 filled-in questionnaires (Hirzinger and Menrad, 2006). For this chapter the answers of those branches of the food and feed industry were separately analyzed that were defined as key branches to be affected by the application of GMOs. Thus the empirical basis of this analysis are filled-in questionnaires of thirty-two bakery companies, four oil mills, twenty-nine dairy companies, twenty-seven confectioneries, and forty feed producers located in Germany.

According to the survey, the German food and feed industry is already affected by the worldwide increasing use of GMOs and the European GMO legislation. In Figure 3 the main strategies of the German food and feed industry are illustrated to fulfill legal requirements of Regulations (EC) No 1829/2003 and 1830/2003.

If the food and feed industry is willing to avoid GMO labeling, they face higher production costs to keep adventitious GM presence under

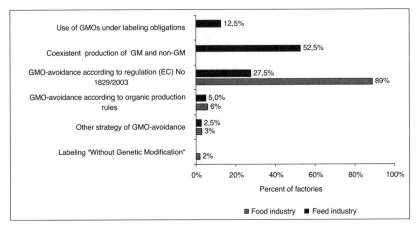

Figure 3. Strategies of German food and feed producers to fulfill legal require-ments of Regulation (EC) No 1829/2003 and 1830/2003. *Source:* Hirzinger and Menrad, 2005.

the 0.9 percent threshold. Main cost drivers of GMO-free production are additional personnel costs, higher costs of raw materials, and costs for GMO analytics. In feed industry additional costs of GMO-free raw materials can reach 1.4 percent of the turnover, additional personnel costs can amount to 0.3 percent of the turnover, and additional costs of GMO analytics can rise up to 0.6 percent of the turnover (Hirzinger and Menrad, 2006). In the food industry a factory of margarine and special fats obtained the highest additional costs of GMO-free raw materials with about 0.4 percent of the turnover. A factory of confectionary prod-ucts obtained the highest additional personnel costs of around 0.2 per-cent of the turnover and a factory of soy products indicated they had the highest costs as a result of GMO analytics of around 0.1 percent of its turnover (Hirzinger and Menrad, 2006). In this context it is impor-tant to mention that raw materials and food ingredients derived from soybean (e.g., soy oil, flour, and lecithin), corn (e.g., flour, starch, starch-derived sugars, and isoglucose) and rapeseed (e.g., oil and flour) are main sources of unintended GMO admixture because around 60 percent of the worldwide soy, 14 percent of the worldwide corn, and 18 percent of the worldwide rapeseed production were GM in 2005 (Transgen, 2005).

An overview of the costs of GMO testing regimes in different branches of the German food and feed industry is given in Table 9. Although there are only rather small differences in the average costs of single tests (both for qualitative and quantitative GMO testing), the number of tests carried out differs significantly by the different branches. Although the total costs of GMO testing differ strongly between the branches (with around 1,200 €/year in the bakery industry and 14,600 €/year in the feed industry), these differences are widely smoothened when setting these costs in relation to the turnover of the companies, being the highest with 0.02 percent in the milling industry (Table 9). This indicates that the direct costs of GMO testing are rather limited so far in the German food and feed industry – not least due to the limited number of approved GM varieties in the EU. However, it should be considered that higher costs of raw materials, additional personnel costs, or costs for changing the organization or the processing regime in a factory are not included in the costs shown in Table 9.

5. Conclusions

In recent years there have been several studies targeting to analyze the cost effects and wider economic impacts of coexistence of GM crops with conventional and organic crops in Europe and overseas (e.g., Bock et al., 2002; Tolstrup et al., 2003; Messéan et al., 2006). In addition, there are two EU-financed integrated projects in place (SIGMEA and Co-Extra) that intend to analyze organization and costs of coexistence measures between GM and non-GM crops in agriculture and the food industry. These studies show that potential costs of coexistence schemes occur on different levels (e.g., on a single farm, a region, the agricultural sector, or the agro-food chain of a specific country or internationally) and that different types of costs have to be distinguished when assessing the

Table 9. Costs of GMO Testing Regimes in Different Branches of the German *Food and Feed Industry*

	Bakery	Dairy	Milling	Confectionary	Feed
Number of quantitative GMO tests per year and company	6	28	61	44	17
Average costs of one quantitative GMO test	207 €	169 €	179 €	155 €	176 €
Number of qualitative GMO tests per year and company		26		13	80
Average costs of one qualitative GMO test		157 €		163 €	145 €
Total costs of GMO testing per year and company	1,224 €	8,814 €	10,919 €	8,939 €	14,592
Costs in percent of company turnover	0.01	0.002	0.02	0.01	0.011
	percent	percent	percent	percent	percent

Source: Survey of FHW, 2005.

economic impacts of coexistence measures in agricultural production (Menrad, 2003):

- Short-term financial losses in case of contamination with GM material (e.g., via cross-pollination, volunteers, mixture of GM and non-GM crops).
- Insurance and liability costs.
- In case a contamination with GM material has happened, mid-term costs for reducing or removal of the GM contamination.
- Costs of establishing and handling monitoring, segregation, and labeling systems.
- Wider impacts of coexistence of GM crops on agricultural and food markets, production, and processing structures as well as trade flows.

The estimation of cost effects or economic impacts of coexistence schemes or measures is further complicated by the fact that agricultural production systems and structures differ significantly between EU member countries and regions. This is one important reason why so far no generally accepted coexistence schemes and measures have been suggested by agronomists due to differing biologic characteristics of farm crops and regional production systems (Menrad, 2003). Furthermore, the necessary coexistence measures highly depend on the adoption rate of GM crops in a specific region as well as the threshold levels of adventitious admixture that are tolerated by existing regulations. Case studies on the regional effects of differing coexistence measures indicate that there might be a substantial proportion of fields that are cultivated with non-GM varieties likely to be influenced by cross-pollination of a GM crop (e.g., herbicide-tolerant rapeseed, Bt maize). In particular, this refers to regions with small-scale fields and high relevance of the potential GM crop in crop rotation. Generally, the affection rates of conventional crop areas are substantially lower compared to the rate of affected farms, indicating the high potential of conflicts among farmers particularly in regions with intensive growing of arable crops and dispersed landscape pattern. To quantify the exact costs of coexistence measures in different regions of the EU, the lack of empirical data concerning the economic performance, yields, and costs of growing GM crops in Europe needs to be filled, such as by using (privately or state-organized) field trials experiments in several EU member-states to collect such information.

For seed production, the threshold of GM adventitious presence is still under discussion in the EU so that it is difficult to assess the potential cost impact (Messéan et al., 2006). However, the results of model simulation and cost calculations in maize certified seed production in France show the substantial effects on costs that might be caused by defining very low thresholds on GM adventitious presence in seeds (Menrad and Reitmeier, 2006). On the other hand, such thresholds facilitate the work of farmers in a sense that it is easier for them to meet the thresholds of GM adventitious presence defined in crop production.

Concerning potential insurance or liability costs of GM contamination, there is only limited empirical evidence available in the published studies for the EU (Menrad, 2003). Generally spoken, studies are lacking so far, that intend to assess the overall impacts of coexistence measures on agricultural production and the food processing chain (e.g., of a specific country). In addition, the costs of specific stewardship or training programs for farmers to introduce and implement the suggested coexistence measures in agricultural practice are mostly not included in available studies (Menrad, 2003).

The differences in the developed coexistence rules at EU member-state level as well as the relevant liability rules for market introduction and cultivation of GMOs in the single member-states highly influence the potential adoption of GM crops in the twenty-seven member-states of the EU. These factors will also have a significant influence on the costs that seed breeding companies, farmers, food processors, retailers, and finally consumers will have to face for coexistence and traceability measures in case GM crops are widely planted and used in the EU agro-food sector. In this sense an important target of the EU to organize EU-wide harmonized markets will not be realized in this field unless additional measures are taken to harmonize the rules between member-states.

Furthermore, the impacts of introducing and implementing the new EU regulations after 2000 on consumer attitudes and acceptance of agro-food biotechnology and GM foods have not been analyzed in detail. However, the still low and gradually decreasing consumer acceptance in several EU member-states seems to indicate that there was no strong positive impact in this respect. Altogether Gaskell and colleagues (2006) come to the conclusion that recent communication activities and "the introduction of new regulations on the commercialization of GM crops and the labeling of GM food (EC regulation 2001/18) appears to have done little to allay public anxieties about agri-food biotechnology in Europe." This view is substantiated by the fact that nearly all food processing companies, at least in Germany, currently try to avoid the use of GM products and materials that need to be labeled in food production and food processing.

REFERENCES

Angevin, F., Klein, E. K., Choimet, C., Meynard, C. M., de Rouw, A., & Sohbi, Y. (2001). Modélisation des effets des systèmes de culture et du climat sur les pollinisations croisées chez le maïs. In: INRA-FNSEA (Ed.), *Pertinence économique et faisabilité d'une filière sans utilisation d'OGM.* pp. 21–36.

Beckmann, V., Soregaroli, K., & Wesseler, J. (2006). Coexistence rules and regulations in the European Union. *American Journal of Agricultural Economics* 88, No. 5, pp. 1193–1199.

Bock, A.-K., Lheureux, K., Libeau-Dulos, M. et al. (2002). Scenarios for coexistence of genetically modified, conventional, and organic crops in European agriculture. Report EUR 20394EN, Seville.

Commission of the European Communities. (2003). Commission Recommendation of 23 July 2003 on guidelines for the development of national strategies and best practices to ensure the coexistence of genetically modified crops with conventional and organic farming, Amtsblatt der Europäischen Union K, p. 2624.

James, C. (2005). *Global review of commercialized transgenic plants 2005.* ISAAA: Ithaca, NY.

James, C. (2006). *Global review of commercialized transgenic plants 2006*. ISAAA: Ithaca, NY.

Degenhardt, H., Horstmann, F., & Mülleder, N. (2003). Bt-Mais in Deutschland – Erfahrungen mit dem Praxisanbau von 1998 bis 2002. *Mais* 31, No. 2, pp. 75–77.

Directorate-General for Agriculture European Commission. (2002). Economic Impacts of Genetically Modified Crops on the Agri-Food Sector – A Synthesis. http://www.ec.europe.eu/comm/agriculture/publi/gmo/gmo.pdf. Call date 25/05/06.

European Parliament and the Council of the European Union (2003a). Regulation (EC) No 1829/2003. *Official Journal of the European Union*.

European Parliament and the Council of the European Union (2003b). Regulation (EC) No 1830/2003. *Official Journal of the European Union*.

Fagan, J. (2004). Without a trace? New GMO labelling rules. In: *The European Food & Drink Review*, Special Feature. http://www.efdreview.com. Call date 27/05/06.

Frank, R. (2004). European Consumer Study 2004. In: Themenbereich: Ernährung und Gesundheit. Nürnberg. Gesellschaft für Konsum-, Markt- und Absatzforschung e.V.

Gaskell, G. et al. (2006). Eurobarometer 64.3 – Europeans and Biotechnology in 2005: Patterns and Trends. Report to DG Research of the European Commission.

Hirzinger, T., Menrad, K. (2005). Effects of the regulation (EC) No 1829/2003 and 1830/2003 on the German food industry. In: Messéan, A. (Ed.) (2005). *Proceedings, Second International Conference on Co-Existence between GM and non-GM-based agricultural supply chains*, pp. 125–130.

Hirzinger, T., & Menrad, K. (2006). Implementation of EU legislation concerning GMOs in the German food and feed industry. Paper presented at the 10th ICABR-Conference "Agricultural Biotechnology: Facts, Analysis and Policies" from June 29–July 2, 2006, in Ravello (Italy).

Hugger, H. (2004). Personal communication on economics of maize seed production in southwest Germany. Regional Commission/Council of Fribourg, August 2004.

ISAAA. (2008). Global status of commercialized biotech/GM crops: 2007. ISAAA Brief 37–2007: Executive Summary.

Jany, K.-D., & Schuh, S. (2005). Die neuen EU-Verordnungen Nr. 1829/2003 und Nr. 1830/2003 zu genetisch veränderten Lebens- und Futtermitteln: die Kennzeichnung. *Journal für Ernährungsmedizin*, *2*, 6–12.

Le Bail, M., & Meynard, J. M. (2001). Isolement des collectes et maitrise des dissémination au champ. Rapport du groupe 3 du programme de recherche ≪ Pertinence économique et faisabilité d'une filière sans utilisation d'OGM ≫. INRA – FNSEA, 56 p.

Menrad, K. (2003). Strategies and economic assessments. In: Boelt, B. (Ed.) (2003). Proceedings of the 1st European Conference on the coexistence of genetically modified crops with conventional and organic crops (GMCC 03) dated 13.-14.11.2003, Slagelse (Dänemark), pp. 137–139.

Menrad, K., & Reitmeier, D. (2006). New case studies on the coexistence of GM and non-GM crops in European agriculture. Economic assessment of coexistence schemes and measures. Final report to IPTS, Seville, Science Centre Straubing.

Menrad, K., & Reitmeier, D. (2006). New case studies on the coexistence of GM and non-GM crops in European agriculture. Economic assessment of coexistence schemes and measures. Science Centre Straubing.

Messéan, A., & Angevin, F., Gomez-Barbero, M., Menrad, K., Rodriguez-Cerezo, E. (2006). New case studies on the coexistence of GM and non-GM crops in European agriculture. Final report to the European Commission. Seville.

Reitmeier, D., & Menrad, K. (2006). Coexistence costs under German regulation – Case Study of Bt maize. Paper presented at the 10th ICABR-Conference "Agricultural Biotechnology: Facts, Analysis, and Policies" from June 29th to July 2nd, 2006 in Ravello (Italy).

Reitmeier, D., Menrad, K., Demont, M., Deams, W., & Turley, D. (2006). *Guidelines of work package 5 concerning task 5.2 and 5.3 within Project SIGMEA*. Science Centre Straubing.

Teyssier, D. (2004). Index des prix et des normes agricoles 2004–2005, 20e édition, Paris, 2004.

Tolstrup, K., Andersen, S. B., Boelt, B., et al. (2003). Report from the Danish working group on the coexistence of genetically modified crops with conventional and organic crops. DIAS report Plant production No. 94. Tjele, Denmark.

Transgen (2005 B). Weltweiter Anbau von transgene Pflanzen 2005. In: http://www.transgen.de/gentechnik/pflanzenanbau/531.doku.html.

Weber, W. E., T. Bringezu, et al. (2005a). Koexistenz von gentechnisch verändertem und konventionellem Mais – Ergebnisse des Erprobungsanbaus zu Silomais 2004. Mais 1(32), pp. 1–5.

Weber, W. E., T. Bringezu, et al. (2005b). Koexistenz von gentechnisch verändertem und konventionellem Mais – Ergebnisse des Erprobungsanbaus Körnermais 2004. Mais 2(32), pp. 1–3.

7 The "Pharming" Challenge

Armin Spök

Introduction

Since the mid-1990s, an increasing number of research papers have described the production of substances of industrial interest from genetically modified (GM) plants, also referred to as "molecular farming."[1] As a fundamental difference to present-day industrial crops, most of these substances are not naturally occurring in these plants. The majority of R&D activities have so far focused on high-value proteins and especially on biopharmaceuticals (plant-made pharmaceuticals or PMPs) such as vaccines, monoclonal antibodies, therapeutic enzymes, hormones, and interferon.[2] Furthermore, plants are used for the production of enzymes and other substances such as fatty acids, bioplastics, spider silk, and gelatine (plant-made industrials or PMIs) that can be used in various industrial sectors.[3]

---

[1] Some authors are using the terms pharming or biopharming. Pharming also refers to the production of pharmaceuticals in animals. The term "molecular farming" is used in this chapter to specifically refer to crops and to include nonpharmaceutical products.

[2] J. K. Ma et al., Plant Derived Pharmaceuticals – the Road Forward, 10 *Trends in Plant Science* 580–585 (2005).

[3] F. Arcand & P. G. Arnison, Development of Novel Protein-Production Systems and Economic Opportunities & Regulatory Challenges for Canada (2004) available at http://archives.cpmp2005.org/pdf/NPPS_040412.pdf.; E. E. Hood et al., Criteria for High-level Expression of a Fungal Laccase Gene in Transgenic Maize. 1 *Plant Biotechnology Journal* 129–140 (2003); K. Neumann et al., Production of Cyanophycin, A Suitable Source for the Biodegradable Polymer Polyaspartate, in Transgenic Plants. 3 *Plant Biotechnology Journal* 249–258 (2005); J. Scheller & U. Conrad, Plant-based

For producing these substances, a broad range of such GM crops have been successfully grown in the open field including maize, tobacco, rice, safflower, potato, rape, soybean, and barley.[4]

The main drivers of molecular farming seem to be economic and technical in nature: scaling-up of production of substances by simply enlarging the cultivated area for such crops is considered an asset over presently used bioreactors that require expensive high-tech buildings, machinery, and equipment and a time-consuming process for optimizing production. This enables producers to quickly adjust to changing market requirements.[5] Plant molecular farming would also provide sufficient capacity to manufacture biopharmaceuticals well beyond 10,000 kg/year – which constitutes the highest annual tonnage presently derived from microbes or mammalian cell lines. This is considered by the pharmaceutical industry as especially important for producing novel high-dose antibodies[6] in annual tonnages of 10,000 to 50,000 kg. For such antibodies, a shortage of conventional production capacities is anticipated if relying on production in bioreactors only.[7] Beyond these high-volume biopharmaceuticals, most presently used therapeutic proteins are sold at tonnages of much less than 1,000 kg/year. Even in these cases, it seems tempting to produce this amount by planting a total area of 2 to 40 hectares.

Plants are also an interesting alternative for making proteins that are difficult or impossible to be produced in microbial systems. The protein resulting from the same gene might be slightly different in structure and

Material, Protein, and Biodegradable Plastic. 8 *Current Opinion in Plant Biology* 188–196 (2005).

[4] A. Sauter & B. Hüsing, Grüne Gentechnik – Transgene Pflanzen der 2. und 3. Generation (2006), available at www.tab.fzk.de/de/projekt/zusammenfassung/ab104.pdf.

[5] I. Raskin et al., Plants and Human Health in the Twenty-first Century. 20 *Trends in Biotechnology* 522–531 (2002).

[6] Monoclonal antibodies are widely used as diagnostic and research reagents. Their introduction into human therapy has been much slower. Still, more than 150 antibodies are presently in preclinical and clinical development, many of them aiming at the treatment of cancer.

[7] K. Ko & H. Koprowski, Plant Biopharming of Monoclonal Antibodies, 111 *Virus Research* 93–100 (2005).

function depending whether it is expressed in microbes, mammals, or plants. Bacteria for instance, do not add certain sugar residues (glycosylation) and might not be able to correctly process some human glycolproteins.[8]

Product safety is another reason frequently reiterated by industry, as PMPs are claimed to be free of contaminating human or animal viruses, which is a concern in case of production from mammalian cell lines.[9] Although a presence of such viruses in mammalian cell lines might pose risks to human health, plant viruses are not known to infect humans.

Potential savings in production costs have been strongly emphasized,[10] although industry has more become less optimistic in recent years. In fact the agricultural production of plant biomass that includes the target protein is likely to be much cheaper compared to conventional production with microbes and mammalian cells in high-tech facilities. According to earlier and very optimistic estimates, recombinant proteins could be produced in plants at 2 to 10 percent of the cost of microbial fermentation systems and at 0.1 percent of the cost of mammalian cell cultures, although this depends on the product yield.[11] Cut down in costs would, however, only affect the production of the crude protein, whereas the purification of the protein and formulation of the biopharmaceutical in subsequent downstream processing amounts to 50 to 80 percent of the total production costs.

The preclinical and clinical trials of new biopharmaceuticals are already long-term, very expensive procedures required by pharmaceutical legislation. Higher compliance costs have to be anticipated for approval of PMPs compared to conventional biopharmaceuticals under

[8] R. Twyman et al., Molecular Farming in Plants: Host Systems and Expression Technology, 21 *Trends in Biotechnology* 570–578 (2003).

[9] U. Commandeur et al., The Biosafety of Molecular Farming in Plants. 5 *AgBiotechNet* 1–9 (2003).

[10] J. H. Seon & M. M. Moloney, A Unique Strategy for Recovering Recombinant Proteins from Molecular Farming: Affinity Capture on Engineered Oil Bodies, 4 *Journal of Plant Biotechnology* 95–101 (2002).

[11] G. Giddings, Transgenic Plants as Protein Factories. 12 *Current Opinions in Biotechnology* 450–454 (2001).

GMO legislation and medicinal product legislation. Furthermore, PMP companies are still facing uncertainties with regard to how drug regulators, who are used to dealing with contained production facilities and strictly controlled and validated production processes, will deal with open-field agricultural production environments that will be influenced by weather, climate, soil, and pests. Finally, potential humanitarian benefits to developing countries are frequently mentioned by manufacturers and scientists, that is to say the availability and applicability of drugs might be improved (e.g., for oral vaccines, storage conditions of PMP's in kernels).[12]

Until a few years ago, most activities have centered in the United States and Canada, with far fewer activities in the EU. As this chapter shows, the picture in the EU is changing and challenges for regulators are looming.

In the first section of this chapter, the driving forces of the technology are discussed. Then, in the second section, the present status of commercialization and the most important aspects of the North American public debate are reviewed. Third, evidence is presented that molecular farming is about to gain a foothold in Europe. In the fourth section, it is argued that specific hazards and risk dimensions are associated with molecular farming. The subsequent sections identify policy challenges for the EU and explore possible repercussions from very stringent rules for open field cultivation to the innovation process. In the concluding section, it is argued that policy development for molecular farming will have to be pursued in a complex environment where unresolved problems with the first generation of such GM crops[13] are still prevalent. The overall focus of the article is on PMPs but frequent reference is given to PMIs.

---

[12] J. K. Ma et al., Plant Derived Pharmaceuticals – the Road Forward, 10 *Trends in Plant Science* 580–585 (2005).

[13] First-generation GM crops comprise so-called output traits that are not aimed to directly benefit the final consumer. This group comprises various types of tolerance traits, mainly herbicide and insect tolerance.

United States and Canada: Early Starters

Most commercial activity has so far been centered in North America. More than four hundred experimental field trials in the United States and Canada with GM crops producing PMPs or PMIs[14] have been conducted, which indicates commercial interests. Another indicator is clinical trials: sixteen PMPs were recently reported to be in various stages of clinical trials[15] with about ten products – including veterinary drugs – moving closer to market stage (see Table 1).[16] Horn[17] anticipates market approval for twelve products from plants, including vaccines, antibodies, and enzymes by 2009. The process of market commercialization, however, turned out to be much slower. In 2006, a poultry vaccine from plant cell culture was the first PMP that achieved regulatory approval.[18] Another promising PMPs, a safflower-derived human insulin advanced to phase 3 clinical trials[19] and a carrot-cell culture-derived human glucocerebrosidase for treating Gaucher's disease, successfully completed phase 3 clinical trials in 2009. Some enzymes and other substances are already produced on a small scale through molecular farming for commercial use as fine chemicals.[20]

Consequently, the North American PMP developers are now eager to obtain a green light for commercial production, which would include open field production in food crops. Therefore, they hope to

[14] See www.isb.vt.edu/cfdocs/fieldtests1.cfm; www.inspection.gc.ca/english/plaveg/bio/mf/sumpnte.shtml.

[15] PHARMA-PLANTA, Molecular Farming for New Drugs and Vaccines. 6 *EMBO Reports*, 593–599 (2005).

[16] This also includes two products from EU-based companies, Meristem Therapeutics and Cobento, the former of which is conducting field trials in the USA, Chile, and Europe.

[17] M. E. Horn et al., Plant Molecular Farming: Systems and Products. 22 *Plant Cell Reports* 711–720 (2004).

[18] See www.dowagro.com/newsroom/corporatenews/2006/20060131b.htm.

[19] A. Spök et al., Evolution of a regulatory framework for pharmaceuticals derived from genetically modified plants. 26(9) *Trends in Biotechnology* 506–517 (2008).

[20] A. Spök & M. Klade, Molecular Farming. Novel Challenges for Risk Management and Legislation (Office of Technology Assessment at the German Parliament 2005).

Table 1. *Plant-made Pharmaceuticals Approaching Market Stage*[a]

Product	Application	Plant Host(s)	Status[b]	Company
Biopharmaceuticals and nutraceuticals for humans				
AB	AB cancer vaccine	Tobacco	Phase 2 clinical trials	Large Scale Biology Corp., USA[d]
CaroRx™	AB carries prophylaxis	Tobacco	Phase 2 clinical trials[e]	Planet Biotechnology, USA
Gastric lipase	Cystic fibrosis	Maize	Phase 2 clinical trials	Meristem Therapeutics, France[f]
Hepatitis antigen	Oral vaccine against Hepatitis B	Potato	Phase 2 clinical trials	Arizona State University, USA
Human glucocere-brosidase	Gaucher's disease	Carrot cells	Phase 3 clinical trials completed in 2009 (US Food and Drug Administration)	Protalix Biotherapeutics, Israel
Human intrinsic factor	Food supplement; Vitamin B_{12} deficiency	Arabidopsis thaliana	Approval from Danish national authorities for commercial production in greenhouse; approval as food supplement under the EU Regulation for GM food and feed pending	Cobento Biotech AS, Denmark

Insulin	Diabetes	Safflower	Phase 3 clinical trials	SemBioSys, Canada
Human lactoferrin	Anti-infection, anti-inflammatory and iron-binding properties	Rice	Advanced[c]	Ventria, USA
Human lysozyme	Anti-infection, anti-inflammatory and iron-binding properties	Rice	Advanced[c]	Ventria, USA
Biopharmaceuticals for animals				
HN protein of Newcastle Disease Virus	Poultry vaccine	Plant cell culture	Approved by USDA	Dow Agro Sciences, USA
Antigen	Vaccine against feline parvovirus	Tobacco	Advanced	Large Scale Biology Corp., USA[d]
Immunosphere™	Carp somatotropin to be used as feed additive for shrimps	Safflower	Major shrimp exporting regions are outside the USA, Canada, and the EU; only import permits for food products required	SemBioSys, Canada

[a] This table only includes PMPs that are in the advanced stages; [b] For human biopharmaceuticals: phase of clinical trials; [c] Already commercially available as fine chemicals; [d] Large Scale Biology filed bankruptcy in 2006; [e] Approved as medical device in the EU in 2003; [f] According to most recent information Meristem Therapeutics has ceased its operational activities for financial reasons and it remains unclear whether at all and how development of their flagship product, the dog lipase from maize, will continue.
Source: company websites, Spök (2007), Spök et al. (2008; modified).

175

establish a regulatory framework that would allow for commercialization. The United States Department of Agriculture (USDA) and the Canadian Food Inspection Agency (CFIA) have become active quite early in the process. Support for this technology has come from certain growers' organizations, such as National Corn Growers Association (2001) and medical patients' alliances, such as IAPO (2005).[21] Confronted with strong pressure from the food industry, environmentalists and consumer organizations, regulators are however proceeding slowly and with care.[22]

Given the preference of some PMP developers for maize and other food crops as production platforms in the United States, the key policy issue obviously is the risk of contamination, that is, that pharm crops would end up in the food or feed chain.[23] Environmentalists and consumer organizations are highlighting health and environmental risks and the food industry is – on top of that – also concerned about the impacts of perception – recalling the consequences and costs of recent cases of accidental contamination (see further below). These concerns had been amplified by initiatives to grow pharm maize in the corn-belt region.

[21] See www.ncga.com/news/CC/volume10/ccVol10n03.html.

[22] B. Cassidy & D. Powell, Pharmaceuticals from Plants: The ProdiGene Affair (2002), www.extension.iastate.edu/grain/pages/grain/news/newsarchive/02biotechnews/021202 bionews.html; N. C. Ellstrand, Going to "Great Lengths" to Prevent the Escape of Genes that Produce Specialty Chemicals. 132 *Plant Physiology* 1770–1774; H. Miller, Will We Reap What Biopharming Sows? 21 *Nature Biotechnology* 480–481 (2003); H. Kamenetsky, GM Crop Controls. New USDA Pharming-test Rules Leave Biotechs Unfazed, Food-Protection Groups Unsatisfied, *The Scientist*, March 10, 2003, available at www.biomedcentral.com/news/20030310/05.

[23] California Council on Science and Technology, A Food Foresight Analysis of Agricultural Biotechnology: A Report to the Legislature for the Food Biotechnology Task Force (2003), available at www.cdfa.ca.gov/exec/pdfs/ag_biotech_report_03.pdf; A. S. Felsot, "Pharm Farming." It's Not Your Father's Agriculture. 195 *Agrichemical and Environmental News* 1–23 (2002); Pew Research Center, Pharming the Field: A Look at the Benefits and Risks of Bioengineering Plants to Produce Pharmaceuticals, available at http://pewagbiotech.org/events/0717/ConferenceReport.pdf.

Canadian authorities are taking a more precautionary approach. Unlike the United States, they explicitly recommended the use of nonfood crops for PMPs and are limiting the size of experimental field trials per applicant to 1 hectare per province and year.[24]

The sensitivity of certain actors results from contamination incidents, especially the StarLink[25] and the ProdiGene incidents,[26] which are also discussed in Chapter 2.

StarLink is a GM maize variant harboring the bacterial protein Cry9C. This protein is specifically toxic to a variety of pests and thereby renders the maize insect resistant. In 1998, the U.S. Environmental Protection Agency (EPA) did not exclude the possibility of an allergic potential in humans, and therefore granted a tolerance exemption for feed and industrial use only (i.e., not for human food). The EPA required a buffer zone of 200 meters between the GM and any conventional maize to avoid pollen contamination. StarLink maize and maize derived from the buffer zone were to be processed separately from food maize. Despite such safety measures Cry9C was detected in taco chips, a human food product, in September 2000 and subsequently also in maize

[24] Canadian Food Inspection Agency: Interim Amendment to Dir 2000–07 for Confined Research Field Trials of PNTs for Plant Molecular Farming (2003), available at www.inspection.gc.ca/english/plaveg/bio/dir/dir0007ie.shtml.

[25] See Ellstrand, supra. See also B. Freese, Manufacturing Drugs and Chemicals in Crops: Biopharming Poses New Threats to Consumers, Farmers, Food Companies and the Environment (2002) www.foe.org/camps/comm/safefood/biopharm/BIOPHARM_REPORT.pdf; A. Spök et al., Toxicity and allergenicity of GMO products – Part 2B: Regulation of risk assessment for genetically modified food in the EU and the USA (2003); EPA, EPA Preliminary Evaluation of Information Contained in the October 25, 2000, Submission from Aventis CropScience (2000) available at www.epa.gov/scipoly/sap/2000/november/ prelim_eval_sub102500.pdf.

[26] B. Cassidy & D. Powell, Pharmaceuticals from Plants: The ProdiGene Affair (2002), www.extension.iastate.edu/grain/pages/grain/news/newsarchive/02biotechnews/021202 bionews.html; C. Q. Choi, Black Eye for Ag-biotech: Texas Company Under Fire for Possibly Contaminating Food Crops, *The Scientist*, November 20, 2002, available at http://www.biomedcentral.com/news/20021120/03; C. Q. Choi, BIO Backpedals. Politics Push Biotech Organization to Withdraw Heartland Policy on GM Crops, *The Scientist*, December 11, 2002, available at www.biomedcentral.com/news/20021211/04.

flour. USDA eventually detected Cry9C in 9 to 22 percent of all maize samples. Given the huge variety of processed maize products, millions of people are assumed to have consumed contaminated maize products before those products were recalled and removed from supermarket shelves. Despite a considerable number of consumer reports about allegedly allergic symptoms, in no case were actual allergic symptoms proven to be caused by the GM maize. Nevertheless, recalls and compensations were reported to amount to US$1 billion.

It was later revealed that the contaminations occurred from commingling after harvest. Commingling might happen for instance, if storage facilities, equipment, and machinery are used for both GM and conventional maize varieties without properly cleaning them between these uses. Moreover, farmers or wholesalers handling such material might not have been aware of the need to keep these types of maize separate. In fact, it was determined that some of the farmers and farm workers had not received appropriate information and training on both sowing and trading restrictions. In addition, there were indications of pollen flow to conventional maize varieties.

Although the StarLink case was about a GM feed maize grown on large acreages, the ProdiGene incident was about a GM pharm maize grown in small areas. In 2002, USDA's Animal and Plant Inspection Service (APHIS) staff recorded two cases of violations of conditions for deliberate release of GM pharm crops. In both cases, GM maize resulting from field trials of the U.S. molecular farming company ProdiGene were detected in conventional soybean fields.

In the Iowa case, GM maize "volunteers"[27] were detected in a late stage of development. Given the possibility of pollen flow to surrounding maize fields, more than 60 hectares of maize had to be incinerated.

---

[27] A crop that sprouts unexpectedly in a surprise location. Birds and animals often plant them in their droppings, or the seeds are carried by wind or humans to new locations. In the case of maize, kernel might remain in the soil, survive the winter, and sprout in the next growing season. If the field is being used for some other cultivars, the maize might be a weed.

In Nebraska, ProdiGene did not remove the volunteers despite the order to do so issued by inspectors of the USDA-APHIS. Thus, the volunteer pharm maize was harvested together with the soybean plants. About 14,000 tons of soybeans were subsequently put in quarantine by APHIS and ProdiGene reportedly purchased the entire batch of soybeans. The U.S. Food and Drug Administration (FDA) stated that the incident caused only minimal risks, if any. Nevertheless, economic damages in this case were considerable: fines and financial damage were reported to have amounted to some US$3 million and eventually led to the bankruptcy of ProdiGene. In this case total economic damage was small compared to StarLink but, according to several commentators, the incident nevertheless caused a severe setback for the molecular farming industry – in particular for those developing food crops as production platforms for nonfood substances.

European Union: Catching Up

In the EU, commercial R&D activities in molecular farming have been increasing over recent years: some twenty-four companies are active in this field, most of them specialized in this technology.[28] Recently, Bayer and BASF, two large EU-based multinational companies, moved into the arena. Two SMU-type companies, Cobento and Meristem Therapeutics, seem to be closer to market commercialization (see Table 1). Cobento recently filed an application under EU Regulation 1829/2003 on GM food and feed for producing human intrinsic factor protein from *Arabidopsis thaliana* cultivated in greenhouses. The protein is intended to be used as a nutraceutical food supplement against vitamin B12 deficiency. Meristem is producing its gastric lipase in open field production using maize (presently on 20 hectares in France) and anticipates

---

[28] A. Spök, Molecular Farming on the Rise–GMO Regulators Still Walking a Tightrope, 25 *Trends in Biotechnology* 74–82 (2007).

full-scale production on 1,000 hectares.[29] The gene for the enzyme lipase was derived from dogs and the product is intended to be used for treating Cystic Fibrosis.

Pharma-Planta, a research consortium under the European Commission's 6th Framework Programme, is pioneering academic research activities in partnership with a small number of firms.[30] The European Technology Platform "Plants for the Future," which is advising the European Commission on research topics for the upcoming 7th Framework Programme,[31] set a particular focus on industrial crops, including molecular farming.[32] These activities have very recently brought molecular farming into the radar of EU regulators and risk assessors.

Why Risks Might Differ from First-Generation GM Crops

In principle, most of the potential risks discussed for first-generation GM crops[33] apply to molecular farming as well. Nevertheless, three reasons are suggested here as to why risks associated with molecular farming could have different characteristics:

---

[29] D. Burtin, Presentation in the course of the IPTS Workshop 'Molecular farming in plants – opportunities and challenges': Recombinant Gastric Lipase, Antibodies, and Allergen Production in Transgenic Plants., June 19, 2006; according to most recent information Meristem Therapeutics has ceased its operational activities for financial reasons and it remains unclear whether at all and how development of their flagship product, the dog lipase from maize, will continue.

[30] See www.pharma-planta.org.

[31] EU Technology Platforms are led by industry and serve as frameworks for stakeholders, to define research and development priorities, timeframes, and action plans on a number of strategically important issues where achieving Europe's future growth, competitiveness, and sustainability objectives is dependent upon major research and technological advances in the medium to long term. The European Technology Platform "Plants for the Future" is coordinated by European Plant Science Organisations and EuropaBio and is advising the European Commission on biotechnology and plant genomics.

[32] Plants for the Future: Input to the European Commission online consultation to FP7 by the Technology Platform (October 2004), www.epsoweb.org/Catalog/TP/TP_FP7_1.pdf.

[33] Mostly herbicide-tolerant and insect-resistant crops.

First, unlike first-generation GM crops, PMPs are designed to have a physiological effect on man and/or higher animals, hence the hazard characteristics of the introduced protein might be of greater concern.

Secondly, an entirely different breeding rationale applies. Plants will be designed, for example, for maximum yield, special morphology, and growth habit suited to a specific harvesting method that can be used with the PMP application, absence of metabolites that may compromise product integrity or quality during bioprocessing.[34] Pharm crops are considered production facilities that have to be optimized for maximum yield of the target substance. Human and environmental exposure could therefore be increased compared to first-generation GM crops. Depending on the expression system maximum yields of up to 25 and 31 percent of total soluble protein (TSP)[35] and 80 percent TSP[36] have been achieved (the latter of which in greenhouse experiments). This would constitute a 700- to 5,000-fold increase in yield of transgene products compared to first-generation GM crops.[37]

Thirdly, the likelihood of unintended secondary effects might be higher, and the hazard characteristics of GM plants might thus be of

[34] H. M. Davies, Plant-made Pharmaceuticals: An Overview and Update. in Agricultural Biotechnology: Beyond Food and Energy to Health and the Environment, 59–70 (National Agricultural Biotechnology Council 2005).

[35] H. Daniell et al., Breakthrough in Chloroplast Genetic Engineering of Agronomically Important Crops, 23 *Trends in Biotechnology* 238–245 (2005); R. Fischer et al., Plant-based Production of Biopharmaceuticals. 7 *Current Opinion in Plant Biology* 152–158 (2004); R. Fischer et al., Plant-based Production of Biopharmaceuticals. 7 *Current Opinion in Plant Biology* 152–158 (2004).

[36] D. Gleba, Use of Plant Roots for Phytoremediation and Molecular Farming. 96 *Proceedings of the National Academy of Sciences* 5973–5977 (1999); S. Marillonnet et al., In Plant Engineering of Viral RNA Replicons: Efficient Assembly by Recombination of DNA Modules Delivered by Agrobacterium. 101 *PNAS* 6852–6857 (2004).

[37] The yield of 80 percent of TSP was achieved using a production system that is not intended for open field cultivation. It nevertheless shows what is technically feasible at present. For open field cultivation, yields of 10 to 35 percent might be more realistic – but might also be optimized as technology improves. See A. Spök, Presentation in the course of the IPTS Workshop 'Molecular farming in plants – opportunities and challenges': Molecular Farming, Environmental Health Aspects and Coexistence with Conventional Crop Plants (June 19, 2006).

concern. Unintended secondary effects are already a big issue with single gene insertions of first-generation GM crops, but the number and significance of genomic changes in the forthcoming generation of crops increase the likelihood of unintended effects and the associated uncertainties, all of which will need to be addressed by regulation. This is because these plants are likely to include several genetic modifications at the same time – some of which might interfere to a larger extent with plant metabolism. Resistance genes might be introduced to avoid problems with pests, pathogens, and weeds that would otherwise require applying pesticides and herbicides. These substances might cause concerns as drug contaminants. Moreover, genetic modification for easy and unambiguous visual identification of seeds and plants are suggested that would enable a simple differentiation of plants, seeds, or fruits not intended for consumption.[38] In addition, molecular confinement technologies are being introduced involving several complex changes in the plant genome. Molecular confinement aims at avoiding gene dispersal via pollen or rendering plants infertile.[39]

Whether this would translate into higher health and environmental risks would, however, depend on the particular case and also on the category. With many PMIs – in contrast to PMPs – there might be no intention of a biological effect in humans or animals. Nevertheless, hazardous properties could also be associated with this category. Avidin, for instance, which is presently produced as a fine chemical, is toxic to many insects and might cause Vitamin H deficiency in higher animals and humans. Aprotinin, to take another plant-derived fine chemical, is considered a reproductive hazard. In contrast, enzymes like lipases or trypsin might pose less health risks in case of food contamination, because

---

[38] U. Commandeur et al., The Biosafety of Molecular Farming in Plants. 5 *AgBiotechNet* 1–9 (2003). N. C. Ellstrand, Going to "Great Lengths" to Prevent the Escape of Genes that Produce Specialty Chemicals. 132 *Plant Physiology* 1770–1774.

[39] H. Daniell, Molecular Strategies for Gene Containment in Transgenic Corps, 20 *Nature Biotechnology* 581–586 (2002).

both types of enzymes are ubiquitous in nature.[40] Moreover, trypsin is considered safe and used in food production in the United States and elsewhere. Health risks might not necessarily be restricted to toxic or allergenic effects, though. A human hormone could have detrimental effects if it contaminates the food chain, and a vaccine, such as a virus protein, might lead to desensitization in that those affected would perhaps not develop a desired immune response when vaccinated.[41] Thus, the hazards depend on the particular PMI involved.

Exposure, another key issue in risk assessment, will not only depend on the amount of protein produced but also on the area of land used for cultivation. Commercial production of PMPs could take place on 10 to 1,000 hectares, which is in the range of larger U.S. field trials with first-generation GM crops. Beyond possible contamination in the open environment, accidental exposure may also occur in processing or handling the crops. Environmental exposure will also be different due to the higher concentration of proteins/unit area. Environmental exposure and spread could, however, be diminished by molecular, physical, and organizational confinement measures, while worker exposure could be reduced by other protective measures. Unintended secondary effects (see below) might be of less concern in the case of small cultivation areas, especially if confinement measures are effective.

Key Problem: Managing Confinement

Regulatory and industry experts are thus focusing on confinement. In the United States and Canada, regulators have been working with industry on a variety of physical and organizational confinement measures

---

[40] B. Freese, Manufacturing Drugs and Chemicals in Crops: Biopharming Poses New Threats to Consumers, Farmers, Food Companies, and the Environment (2002) www.foe.org/camps/comm/safefood/biopharm/BIOPHARM_REPORT.pdf.

[41] D. D. Kirk & K. McIntosh, Social Acceptance of Plant Made Vaccines: Indications from a Public Survey. 8 *AgbioForum* 228–234 (2005).

that can be applied to avoid outcrossing, spillage of seeds or biomass, and commingling with food or feed crops (see Table 2), and researchers are working on molecular confinement mechanisms that aim at avoiding gene dispersal.[42] Most of the molecular confinement mechanisms being proposed,[43] however, are "leaky," that is, not working 100 percent, and still far from being used for commercial production.[44] Standard Operating Procedures and other organizational or physical measures can fail due to human error or mismanagement. Even more frequent and thorough inspections of production sites, as promised by the USDA, may fail.[45] It has therefore been proposed that a combination of several different confinement measures have to be applied at the same time to establish a redundant system that could provide an acceptable level of safety.

What is considered by the biotech industry and regulatory experts as sufficient risk mitigation measures might, however, not be sufficient for the food industry or consumer and environmental groups, and perhaps also for the general public. Beyond and independent of any health or environmental harm, considerable economic damage might occur in case of contamination of the food and feed chain. Given the lessons of the StarLink and ProdiGene incidents, serious economic consequences might result from accidental commingling even if no relevant health or environmental risks are anticipated. Anxieties of civil society and the food and feed sector might also be sparked by discussions to use

---

[42] H. Daniell, Molecular Strategies for Gene Containment in Transgenic Corps, 20 *Nature Biotechnology* 581–586 (2002); a more comprehensive review is provided in J. M. Dunwell & C. S. Ford, Technologies for Biological Containment of GM and Non-GM Crops. DEFRA Contract CPEC 47. Final Report. Reading (2005).

[43] Union of Concerned Scientists, Pharm and Industrial Crops: The Next Wave of Agricultural Biotechnology (2003).

[44] N. C. Ellstrand, Going to "Great Lengths" to Prevent the Escape of Genes that Produce Specialty Chemicals. 132 *Plant Physiology* 1770–1774.

[45] Union of Concerned Scientists, Pharmaceutical and Industrial Crops. UCS uncovers lax USDA oversight of pharma crops (2006), available at http://www.ucsusa.org/food_and_environment/genetic_engineering/usda-ventria-oversight.html.

Table 2. *Physical and Procedural Confinement Measures Proposed[a]*

- Distinct visual markers
- Time shift in planting compared to food/feed crops nearby
- Cultivation in remote areas
- Fencing, restrictions to enter
- Extended isolation distances (e.g., 1600/800 m for normal pollinating maize), fallow zones, temporal shifts in planting (e.g., 21 days for maize), other plants as pollen barriers, detasseling (maize), covering of inflorescence
- Dedicated equipment, machinery, and processing facilities
- Preliminary on-farm processing
- Postrelease monitoring
- SOPs[b] for
  - seeding, transplanting, side-maintenance, harvesting, seed cleaning
  - storage, drying, and processing of biomass
  - disposal of biomass, e.g., autoclaving, incineration, etc.
  - handling and cleaning of machinery, equipment, and containers
  - monitoring during growing seasons and postharvest land use
  - dealing with noncompliance with terms and conditions for confinement
- SOPs[b] for records and reporting of all activities dealing with the cultivation and transport to processing facility, documentation, and logs for seeds and biomass
- SOPs[b] for training of staff and workers to adequately handle the plant material
- Emergency response/contingency plans
- Strict control of compliance to measures imposed – either by regulators or by other independent institutions (third-party audits)
- Test for GMO detection in raw agricultural commodity

[a] *Source:* BIO (2005), Burtin (2006), CFIA (2003, 2004a, 2004b, 2004c, 2005), Spök et al. (2004).
[b] SOP: Indicates that Standard Operating Procedures are developed/required.

the remainders of biomass after the pharmaceutical component has been separated for feed purposes instead of expensive incineration, also referred to as "dual-use."[46]

---

[46] B. Freese, Manufacturing Drugs and Chemicals in Crops: Biopharming Poses New Threats to Consumers, Farmers, Food Companies and the Environment (2002) www. foe.org/camps/comm/safefood/biopharm/BIOPHARM_REPORT.pdf.

Policy Challenges Posed to the EU

Pharm crop operations will be similar to production facilities and will primarily be designed for maximum yield of intact proteins. Risk characteristics are likely to differ from first-generation GM crops, and risk mitigation requirements will become a focal issue. These specifics are likely to pose a number of challenges to policy makers and regulators in the EU.[47]

First, there is the need to thoroughly review and update current risk assessment approaches and guidelines established for first-generation GM crops. Possible challenges for risk assessment approaches include the applicability of the concepts of substantial equivalence and familiarity, discussed in Chapters 3 and 4, which play important roles for structuring risk assessment of current GM crops. Familiarity, for instance, also refers to environmental and agricultural experiences gathered with the host crop in conventional agriculture.[48] Familiarity might however be less important if the crops have been subjected to multiple and perhaps more substantial changes of genotype (see above) or if non-food/nonfeed plants with which there is less experience are used, such as safflower in Canada. Likewise, "substantial equivalence" understood as referring to the degree of compositional, morphological, and agronomic differences between the GM crop and its conventional counterpart might no longer be considered appropriate to guide risk assessment. Furthermore, with PMPs another step might be added to risk assessment: to thoroughly assess and to advise on the appropriate level of

---

[47] A. Sauter & B. Hüsing, Grüne Gentechnik – Transgene Pflanzen der 2. und 3. Generation (2006), available at www.tab.fzk.de/de/projekt/zusammenfassung/ab104.pdf; A. Spök & M. Klade, Molecular Farming. Novel Challenges for Risk Management and Legislation (Office of Technology Assessment at the German Parliament 2005).

[48] K. Barret & E. Abergel, Genetically engineered crops. Breeding familiarity: environmental risk assessment for genetically engineered crops in Canada. 27 (1) *Science and Public Policy* 2–12 (2000).

confinement and containment measures. In response to this challenge the European Food Safety Authority (EFSA) has recently published an Opinion.[49]

Second, and perhaps the most important goal of EU regulation, might be to address the issue of "coexistence" between industrial crops and food and feed crops, and the avoidance of any cross-contamination (confinement). In the case of open field production of food crops with PMPs and perhaps with PMIs, there is a clear need for mandatory and harmonized rules at the EU level. These rules need to include threshold limits in case of accidental contamination that will have liability implications. The present threshold limits of 0.9 percent for GM crops in non-GM agricultural food products will clearly not be generally applicable to pharm crops and only be envisaged for PMIs that do not have hazardous properties and have been authorized as GM food/feed under EU Regulation 1829/2003 (on GM food and feed). Conversely, it is difficult to envisage a zero tolerance policy, which is being pursued by the USDA.[50] Even thorough on-site risk mitigation measures and safety distances (e.g., 1 mile for maize-producing PMPs)[51] are not considered to be 100 percent effective by many commentators and by Canadian regulators.[52] Given the huge differences that can be assumed for the hazardous properties

---

[49] EFSA, Scientific Opinion on Guidance for the risk assessment of genetically modified plants used for nonfood or nonfeed purposes (22 April 2009), available at http://www.efsa.europa.eu/en/scdocs/doc/1164.pdf.

[50] United States Department of Agriculture, BRS Factsheet (2006), available at www.aphis.usda.gov/publications/biotechnology/content/printable_version/BRS_FS_ pharmaceutical_02–06.pdf; Howard, J. A., and Donnelly, K. C., 2004. A quantitative safety assessment model for transgenic protein products produced in agricultural crops. *Journal of Agricultural and Environmental Ethics*, 17, 545–558.

[51] United States Department of Agriculture, BRS Factsheet (2006), available at www.aphis.usda.gov/publications/biotechnology/content/printable_version/BRS_FS_ pharmaceutical_02–06.pdf.

[52] Canadian Food Inspection Agency's Plant Biosafety Office, Developing a Regulatory Framework for the Environmental Release of Plants with Novel Traits Intended for Commercial Plant Molecular Farming in Canada (2005), available at www.inspection.gc.ca/english/plaveg/bio/mf/fracad/commere.pdf.

of PMPs, substance-specific threshold limits would be more likely. In analogy to the limit values for pesticide residues (EU Regulation 396/2005), limit values will need to be harmonized across the EU, either for specific substances or for particular categories of PMPs, as differences in limits between EU member-states would hamper food and feed trade. Limit values would not only be an issue regarding contamination of conventional or organic crops, it would also pertain to GM food/feed crops. Such a scenario would render food control a more complex matter.

A related issue would be the question of liability that is of paramount interest to the food and feed industry, as well as to farmers.[53] Who would be liable in case of accidental commingling of pharm crops with food or feed crops? Who would be responsible for the economic damages from low levels of pharm crops found in food crops when producers fully comply with the rules? In such cases, compensation might cover a broad range of direct and indirect costs including[54]

- lost export earnings
- retrieval of contaminated grain
- reduced value of nonpharma grain or oilseeds
- recall of products from grocery shelves
- cleaning of grain elevators and processing plants
- testing expenses
- added transportation and handling costs
- lost storage and merchandising income
- long-term market loss resulting from increased foreign competition
- rejected supplies of meat, dairy products, and eggs
- animal or human illnesses

[53] S. Smyth et al., Liabilities and Economics of Transgenic Crops. 20 *Nature Biotechnology* 537–541. (2002).
[54] R. Wisner, The Economics of Pharmacutical Crops. Potential Benefits and Risks for Farmers and Rural Communities, (Union of Concerned Scientists, 2005).

An even more unfavorable scenario could emerge from possible contaminations of food or feed crop seed supplies. The recent contaminations of conventional U.S. rice varieties by GM rice lines[55] and the controversial cultivation of a GM rice producing a PMP nearby a research station where rice varieties are tested before introduction into the U.S. rice breeding programs[56] show that this is not an entirely hypothetical scenario. Clarification would also be needed whether and to what extent liability risks might be shifted to the contract farmer growing the pharm crops.

Conversely, companies making and using PMPs can be expected to strive to avoid contamination of their drugs or other products by food and feed crops, pests, and pesticides, to maintain the purity and safety standards of validated production processes. In certain areas concerns might, however, differ between food and drug producers. For instance, outcrossing via pollen transfer might be a particular concern for seed producers of pharm crops but less so for the commercial production stage – especially if the PMP will be purified from the green plant material. In case of PMIs, there might, however, be less incentive for confinement. This type of product might be considered in many cases as lower risk, but will also be of lower value compared to PMPs and occupy (much) larger acreages. Thus, strict confinement measures may neither be economically justified nor required.

With its already existing framework on coexistence for GM and non-GM agriculture, the EU appears to be in a better starting position to deal with such issues than the United States. However, it has to be questioned

---

[55] Pew Research Center, Pharming the Field: A Look at the Benefits and Risks of Bioengineering Plants to Produce Pharmaceuticals, available at http://pewagbiotech.org/events/0717/ConferenceReport.pdf.

[56] Union of Concerned Scientists, Pharmaceutical and Industrial Crops. UCS uncovers lax USDA oversight of pharma crops (2006), available at http://www.ucsusa.org/food_and_environment/genetic_engineering/usda-ventria-oversight.html.

whether the different coexistence and liability regimes in the EU member-state, which are of continuing importance because of nonmandatory EU recommendations, would be a sensible basis for molecular farming. Furthermore, different from first-generation GM farming contamination by PMPs and PMIs would be an issue for all food and feed farmers of organic, conventional, and GM crops.

Even before the first PMP or PMI will be commercially cultivated in the EU, if this technology advances further in the United States, Canada, or any other agricultural or food export country, EU regulators may have to deal with questions of threshold limits earlier than expected. The recent contamination incidents from noncommercial field trials on limited acreages of GM crops show that even in such cases, commingling with conventional food crops can occur.[57]

Third, there is no equivalent procedure in the EU to what is envisaged for commercial molecular farming in the United States. EU Directive 2001/18/EC foresees two different authorization tracks: time- and area-limited field trials (Part B) and placing on the market of GM crops including import, transport, processing, handling, storage, and cultivation (Part C). Part B authorization can be granted by the respective member-state only, though derived products must not be used for commercial purposes. Conversely, Part C authorizations would allow for commercialization, but have to be granted at the EU level by a process involving all member-states in both risk assessment and decision making. Both procedures are not appropriate for PMPs. At least these procedures would need to be applied differently compared to first-generation GM food and feed crops.

Perhaps most PMPs could be produced on limited acreages, such as 100 to 10,000 hectares that compare to large-scale field trials and do

---

[57] E.g., The GMO Contamination Register, US GM rice trials contaminate world rice supplies, available at http://www.gmcontaminationregister.org/index.php?content= nw_detail2.

not necessarily needed to be grown, transported, and processed in more than one member-state. In all likelihood, such seeds and plants will also not be traded on the market. Cultivation or processing of such plants might even be conducted in-house or by contractors under supervision of the manufacturer. Given the U.S. experience, companies may want to stay under strict regulatory oversight during the commercial production stage, which is not foreseen in the present EU regulatory regime (see e.g., www.bio.org/healthcare/pmp/factsheet4.asp).

Part C authorization procedures would be more proportionate for the increased rigor of their risk assessment and their demand for mandatory monitoring, but in the complex EU environment there may be continued unpredictability regarding eventual authorization decisions. National-level Part B procedures would be more straightforward but would not be considered sufficient in terms of risk assessment and monitoring, and perhaps not as acceptable if there is a chance that possible contamination might affect commercialization of food and feed products for other EU member-states.

One could therefore argue that the characteristics of PMPs require a separate authorization track in the EU. However, given the sensitivity of the issue, it is difficult to envisage such a procedure becoming established at any national level without the involvement of the EU or national authorities. EU regulators might also reconsider the Part B track in case of field trials of pharm crops. In contrast to GM crops for food and feed use, pharm crops are to be cultivated for long periods of up to fourteen years and are likely to be grown in larger areas to collect data and produce sufficient amounts of substances necessary for testing in the course of their authorization as biopharmaceuticals.

Fourth, a related issue could emerge from the fact that EU-based companies tend to conduct their field trials in part outside of the EU, such as in Chile, the United States, and elsewhere – supposedly because of the more difficult regulatory environment and the less favorable public perception in the EU, but also because this makes it possible to get more than one harvest per year. Such a practice could include both the export of seeds that are produced in the EU and the import of processed or unprocessed biomass. EU economists might still be happy with this practice if production and marketing of the drugs (and thus the vast majority of value added) can still be kept within the EU. In the case of maize or in other cases of PMP production in seeds, it would, however, be tempting to store and ship the PMP-enriched kernels because of protein stability and the ease of handling. Companies wishing to take advantage of this may need to clarify whether it would constitute the import of a GMO into the EU requiring market authorization under Part C of EU Directive 2001/18/EC. If so, they may be forced to relocate processing activities as well.

Fifth, most of what is said here pertains to open field cultivation using food/feed crops. Producing PMPs or PMIs in tobacco leaves might be of less concern, although many of the challenges mentioned previously would, in principle, apply. There are, moreover, alternative production approaches in contained facilities, using, for example, plant cell culture, duckweed, moss, algae, or root exudation (see Box 1). Contained production would drastically reduce the physical and economic risks of food and feed contamination but lack some of the advantages of open field production (cost savings, flexibility for scaling up, possibility to produce large tonnages, etc.). Furthermore, whereas confinement measures for open field production of PMPs are likely to be discussed and agreed at the EU level, commercial production under contained conditions is still under regulatory oversight of the particular member-state according to EU Directive 2009/41/EC. Greenhouse production would also be an alternative option, because greenhouses are normally considered as contained facilities. Greenhouse space for contract cultivation is presently available up to some 30 hectares,[58] which would be sufficient for producing significant quantities of several high-value proteins.

---

[58] See e.g., http://www.bevoagro.com/index.html.

Box 1: Contained Production Approaches in Plant Molecular Farming

Plant Cell Culture

Plant cell lines, mainly from tobacco cultivars, are grown in a way very similar to mammalian cell lines. In the last fifteen years, production of more than twenty different recombinant proteins have been demonstrated including antibodies, hormones, growth factors, and cytokines. Purification of the target protein might be simpler compared to agricultural-scale production.[59] The first commercially approved PMP, a poultry vaccine, is being produced from plant cell culture (see fn. 18).

Root Exudation

The formation of hairy roots can be induced by genetic modification and enable root tissue to be cultured in liquid medium. A variety of plant metabolites have been produced from hairy roots and excreted into the liquid medium that makes purification easier. Proteins produced so far include antibodies, phosphatase, and ricin B fusion protein.[60]

Moss

A particular moss variety that is very susceptible to transformation with recombinant DNA is cultured in bioreactors. Proteins cannot only be secreted into the medium but also – via additional genetic

---

[59] P. M. Doran, Foreign Protein Production in Plant Tissue Cultures, 11 Current Opinion in Biotechnology 199–204 (2000); S. Hellwig, Cell Cultures for the Production of Recombinant Proteins, 22 *Nature Biotechnology* 1415–1422 (2004).

[60] D. A. Fitzgerald, Reviving Up the Green Express: Companies Explore the Use of Transgenic Plants for Economical, Large-scale Protein Expression, *The Scientist*, July 14, 2003, available at www.the-scientist.com/yr2003/jul/lcprofile1_030714.html; D. Gleba, Use of Plant Roots for Phytoremediation and Molecular Farming. 96 *Proceedings of the National Academy of Sciences* 5973–5977 (1999); S. Guillon et al., Harnessing the Potential of Hairy Roots: Dawn of a New Era. 24 *Trends in Biotechnology* 403–409.

Box 1 (continued)

modification – can be modified to change from plant to human glyco-sylation pattern.[61]

Lemna

Lemna or duckweed are small plants growing on the surface of ponds, lakes, and rivers. The plant has been genetically modified to produce twelve monoclonal antibodies including small peptides and large mul-timeric enzymes.[62]

Algae

Algae have been tested to express a broad range of biopharmaceu-tical proteins including antibodies, interleukins, neurotrophic factors, and cholera toxin B unit.[63] Single-cell algae can be grown under high density and large volumes. Downstream processing might be easier and therefore less costly compared to higher plants because algae are much simpler organisms.[64]

---

[61] E. Decker, Moss – An Innovative Tool for Protein Production, 02/2003 BIOfo-rum Europe 96–97 (2003). A. Schaaf et al., Use of Endogenous Signal Sequences for Transient Production and Efficient Secretin by Moss (Physcomitrella patens) Cells, 5:30 *BMC Biotechnology* doi: 10.1186/1472–6750–5–30 (2005) available at http://www.biomedcentral.com/content/pdf/1472–6750–5–30.pdf.

[62] D. A. Fitzgerald, Reviving Up the Green Express: Companies Explore the Use of Transgenic Plants for Economical, Large-scale Protein Expression, *The Scientist*, July 14, 2003, available at www.the-scientist.com/yr2003/jul/lcprofile1_030714.html; J. R. Gasdaska et al., Advantages of Therapeutic Protein Production in the Aquatic Plant, *BioProcessing Journal*, Mar/Apr 2003 at 49–56.

[63] Mera Pharmaceuticals, c.f. Dunwell & Ford 2005, supra; M. Sun et al., Foot-and-mouth disease virus VP1 protein fused with cholera toxin B subunit expressed in Chlamy-domonas reinhardtii chloroplast. 25 *Biotechnol Lett* 1087–1092 (2003); The applica-tion of algae for PM farming has been reviewed by M. M. El-Sheekh, Genetic engi-neering of eukaryotic algae with special reference to Chlamydomonas. 29 *Turk J Biol* 65–82 (2005); S. E. Franklin & S. P. Mayfield, Prospects for molecular farming in the green alga Chlamydomonas reinhardtii. 7 *Curr Opin Plant Biol* 159–165 (2004), S. E. Franklin & S. P. Mayfield, Recent developments in the production of human thera-peutic proteins in eukaryotic algae. 5 *Expert Opin Biol Ther* 1225–1235 (2005); T. L. Walker et al., Microalgae as bioreactors. 24 *Plant Cell Rep* 629–641 (2005).

[64] T. L. Walker et al., Microalgae as bioreactors. 24 *Plant Cell Rep* 629–641 (2005).

That said, some PMPs (e.g., allergens for diagnostics or medical therapy, vaccines, or hormones) might call for higher levels of containment than others. EU member-states might also have different opinions about what would constitute an appropriate level of containment for a particular substance. There might even be different ideas about the borderline between contained production and deliberate release. For instance, a commercial production using nethouses (saranhouse), as is envisaged with potatoes in Denmark[65] might be considered by some EU member-states as a rather unproblematic authorization under the contained use EU Directive 2009/41/EC, whereas other member-states might classify the same practice as deliberate release that would require an application under Directive 2001/18/EC and a much more cumbersome EU procedure. Such differences will need to be reviewed and perhaps harmonized by EU regulators.

Possible Repercussions on Innovation

The United States and Canada are each developing a separate regulatory track for molecular farming with requirements for risk assessment, risk mitigation, and monitoring that will be much more rigorous than such requirements for first-generation GM crops. Under pressure by the powerful food industry, the USDA is promising a highly precautionary approach, a zero-tolerance policy, for both PMPs and PMIs with regard to accidental contaminations, to prevent detectable traces of pharm or industrial GM crops in human food and animal feed.

Europe can reasonably be expected to follow this approach. Hence, much higher compliance costs can be expected for open field production of PMPs compared to first-generation GM crops. Together with the prospect of huge liabilities following contamination incidents, this may drive innovation into nonfood crops or strictly confined or contained

[65] United States Department of Agriculture, BRS Factsheet (2006), available at www.aphis.usda.gov/publications/biotechnology/content/printable_version/BRS_FS_pharmaceutical_02–06.pdf.

production. Perhaps even more significant, regulatory uncertainty that translates into extended timeframes and higher regulatory costs can be expected for authorizing pharmaceutical products from GM crops.[66] Technology platforms that are similar to presently used contained production systems – highly controlled and sterile environments for development of cell lines and microbes – may therefore be facing lower regulatory hurdles – at least for the first wave of PMPs. This approach may also be more attractive for the pharmaceutical industry, which seems to be reluctant to adopt PMPs from open fields.[67] Such production platforms could work well for high value products that would not be needed in very large amounts.

For PMPs such as insulin, certain antibodies, and vaccines that need to be produced at larger scales, open field production in food crops may still be considered as the only feasible approach. This may hold true for those PMIs that require larger volumes at much lower overall costs, such as those to be used for food supplements or feed additives that confer health benefits (nutraceuticals), or for making bioplastics.

Another Scenario for a Public Debate

Previous discussion has illustrated the characteristics of molecular farming and its associated health, environmental, and economic risks, as compared to first-generation GM crops. Increased activities in European R&D and the proximity to the market stage of the first products of plant molecular farming are now confronting EU regulators. Several challenges are posed to regulators to allow for commercialization of molecular farming in the EU, including contamination of the food and

---

[66] A. Spök & M. Klade, Molecular Farming. Novel Challenges for Risk Management and Legislation (Office of Technology Assessment at the German Parliament 2005).

[67] A. Spök & S. Karner, Plant molecular farming. Opportunities and challenges. Technical Report Series, Joint Research Centre Institute for Prospective Technological Studies, EUR 23383 EN, DOI 10.2791/30861, European Communities 2008; available at

feed chain and threshold limits, associated questions with respect to liability, and establishment of an authorization track that is appropriate for commercial open field production. Risk assessors are expected to reconsider their assessment concepts and approaches and include confinement measures as a particular focus of their risk assessment tasks (see Chapter 6 for analysis of some confinement considerations).

At the time the research process on which this chapter is based was being conducted, EU institutions and some stakeholders have become active including EFSA,[49] the European biotech industry association EuropaBio (Barber, personal communication), the European Plant Science Organisation,[68] and the Institute for Prospective Technology Studies of the EU Joint Research Centres. So far, most of these activities are designed as expert, technical initiatives. Neither environmental/consumer NGOs nor food industry representatives have participated in these activities. Some of the issues associated with molecular farming definitely will, however, require public debate that encompasses a broad range of stakeholders. In that sense, the hearing at the German Parliament in 2006[69] where different stakeholder groups and members of parliament could respond to and discuss the findings of a technology assessment project on molecular farming[70] was a first move toward broadening the policy debate. In June 2008, EFSA conducted a public consultation on its draft opinion on how to adapt its risk assessment guidance on GM plants to address GM crops that produce PMPs and PMIs.[71] Given the experience of the United States and Canada, a broad debate can be expected to take up some key questions of acceptable risks that

[68] www.epsoweb.org/Catalog/epsopercent20workshops/EPSOpercent20handoutpercent 20300106.pdf.
[69] Deutscher Bundestag, "Zukunftspotenziale der Grünen Gentechnik" – öffentliches Fachgespräch des Ausschusses für Bildung, Forschung und Technikfolgenabschätzung, Press Release available at www.bundestag.de/aktuell/presse/2006/pz_0606191 .html.
[70] A. Sauter & B. Hüsing, Grüne Gentechnik – Transgene Pflanzen der 2. und 3. Generation (2006), available at www.tab.fzk.de/de/projekt/zusammenfassung/ab104.pdf.
[71] EFSA 2008, supra.

cannot be resolved on a purely technical level: under what circumstances, if any, will it be acceptable to use food to make PMPs and PMIs? Under what circumstances will it be possible to move into open field production?

These questions and issues about risks, benefits, and regulatory authority and decision making are to be dealt with in a complex EU setting of conflicting strategic agendas. Molecular farming is likely to be linked to other contentious policy arenas of renewables, greening of industry, and even more broadly, of sustainable development and globalization of commerce.

The sustainability issue often involves consideration of substituting traditional (e.g., chemical) production processes by processes that are more environmentally sound. Consequently, this is more relevant to non-proteinous PMIs, produced on a larger scale as plant metabolites that might be produced more efficiently. In this case, the potential environmental advantages might conflict with the specific environmental and health risks associated with open field production of industrial GM crops. In that sense molecular farming would find itself located at the crossroads of two debates: the risk debate on agricultural biotechnology and the sustainability debate on renewables and greening of industry.

The issue of agricultural problems and reform is not only of a hypothetical nature: in the United States, some rural states, where cropland is abundant and jobs are scarce, anticipate that pharm crops will generate economic benefits. In the EU, which is struggling with heavily subsidized agricultural production, industrial crops are considered an interesting option to diversify European agriculture. In that context pharm crops have been explicitly welcomed by some commentators.[72] Individual farmers who – in some EU member-states – are receiving compensation for not cultivating parts of their land are nevertheless coming under pressure and might be tempted to explore other agricultural products,

---

[72] APA, Agrartechnologie: Pharma-Landwirtschaft wäre Weg aus der Krise (2005), available at http://www.bmgf.gv.at/cms/site/news_einzel.htm?channel=CH0262&doc=CMS1112689973243.

especially if these products would promise a higher added value. As this analysis suggests, a higher added value by cultivating pharm crops might, however, be restricted to a few contract farmers and relatively small areas. GM crops for PMIs that would be grown on a larger scale might in fact provide an interesting alternative, if the problem of coexistence can be solved.

Beyond these complexities there is another issue that deserves particular attention. Molecular farming sits at the crossroad between "green" (agricultural) biotechnology and "red" biotechnology (use of genetic engineering for medical and pharmaceutical purposes). From this setting, an interesting situation emerges because the public has generally been more supportive of red biotechnology than green biotechnology.[73] Thus new lines of reasoning and new value conflicts are expected. There is preliminary evidence from public perception studies that consumers would be more supportive of PMP or PMI production than of first-generation GM crops.[74] This crossroad situation is also reflected by a more complex pattern of policy actors. The molecular farming industry may receive support from certain growers' and patients' associations, whereas environmental and consumer organizations may be supported by the food and feed industry.

The EU food industry, in particular, will be put on alert. The food industry and its big retailers in many EU member-states are presently still struggling to keep first-generation GM crops out of the food supply and avoid exceeding the labeling threshold to satisfy their GM

---

[73] G. Gaskell, In the Public Eye: Representations of Biotechnology in Europe. in Biotechnology 1996–2000: The Years of Controversy 53–79 (G. Gaskell & M. Bauer (Eds.); T. V. Nielsen et al., Traditional Blue and Modern Green Resistance, in Biotechnology: The Making of a Global Controversy (M. Bauer & G. Gaskell eds., Cambridge University Press 2002).

[74] A. Elbehri, Biopharming and the Food System: Examining the Potential Benefits and Risks. 8 AgbioForum 18–25 (2005); E. F. Einsiedel & J. Medlock, A Public Consultation on Plant Molecular Farming, 8 *AgbioForum* 26–32 (2005); D. D. Kirk & K. McIntosh, Social Acceptance of Plant Made Vaccines: Indications from a Public Survey. 8 *AgbioForum* 228–234 (2005).

crop-adverse customers. It appears that the anticipated demand in the EU for non-GM food stabilizes conventional crop supplies and that the food industry and food retailers are thus far able to handle this. With molecular farming in the open field and especially in use of food crops, the EU food industry may consider themselves in an entirely different situation that would be much more difficult to control and where they have nothing to gain but much to lose in case of accidental contamination of the food chain.

Given the characteristics of molecular farming, its inherent business rationale, and its differences from first-generation GM crops, policy development on molecular farming in the EU is likely to require a broad public debate.

8 GMO as a Sustainability Issue

The Role of the Global Reporting Initiative

Philip J. Vergragt[1] and Halina Szejnwald Brown[2]

Introduction

Genetically Modified Organisms (GMOs) have been introduced in the agricultural system and on the market of consumer goods in the last ten to twenty years, initially in the United States but, increasingly, in developing countries as well. Since the discovery of genetic engineering with its potential to modify DNA of living organisms, discussion and controversy have been abundant.[3] Europe has witnessed a particularly strong resistance to the introduction of GMOs in agriculture and for consumer food products, both from consumers, national governments, and from the EU. The public objections had numerous causes, including concerns about food safety, risk assessment, ethics and equity issues, power relations, and mistrust of technocrats and public authorities. The resistance in Asia, Latin America, and North America has been weaker than in Europe, although some authors have voiced scathing criticism of the U.S.

[1] Professor Emeritus of Technology Assessment, TU Delft, Netherlands; Research Professor, Marsh Institute, Clark University, Worcester, MA, USA; and Senior Associate, Tellus Institute, Boston, MA, USA, pvergragt@tellus.org

[2] Professor of Environmental Science and Policy, Clark University, Worcester, MA, USA, hbrown@clarku.edu

[3] See M. F. Singer & D. Soll, DNA Hybrid Molecules, 181 *Science* 1114 (1973); See also P. Berg et al., Potential Biohazards of Recombinant DNA Molecules, 185 *Science* 303 (1974).

governments and the industrial lobby for allegedly using famine in Africa to foster the spread of GM food to developing countries.[4]

In response to the criticism, European governments have attempted to improve risk assessment methods and their scientific basis and to tailor public policies to the growing demand for transparency, accountability, and public participation. The form such public participation might take, how it would contribute to greater transparency and accountability, and how it would shape more effective and legitimate public policies have yet to be fully resolved.

This chapter attempts to clarify these poorly articulated concepts, starting with the assumption that discourse and public engagement are indeed positive and necessary for solving the GMO controversy. We believe that the growing practice of voluntary sustainability reporting by companies can serve to enhance a discourse, including the widest possible range of participants, some of whom have been until now kept outside the debate. A multi-stakeholder discourse so created enhances societal participation in the strategic corporate decisions regarding the research and development trajectories for agricultural GMOs – constructive technology assessment – and elevates the idea of social accountability and social responsibility of producers of GMOs. We suggest that bounded sociotechnical experiments (BSTEs), small-scale experiments for introducing new GMOs technology designed for the purpose of enhancing social learning, are a suitable instrument for enhancing and enriching the societal discourse and for improving technology assessment.

GMOs in Agriculture and Food: Risks, Public Perceptions, and Regulation

In food biotechnology, genetic modification techniques have been extensively applied to enhance enzymes production by microorganisms used

---

[4] N. Zerbe, Feeding the Famine? American Food Aid and the GMO Debate in Southern Africa, 29 *Food Policy* 2593–2608 (2004).

in food manufacture.[5] In agriculture the focus has been on producing genetically modified crops that are resistant to insects, viral pathogens, and commonly used herbicides, such as Monsanto's Roundup.[6] Experiments are also under way to produce crops with enhanced nutritional and health benefits ("functional foods" and "nutriceuticals") and with the capacity to produce pharmaceuticals ("pharming"). The metaphor of "crops becoming factories, producing vaccines, plastics, industrial starches, and feed supplements and enzymes" captures the trajectory of this type of research.

Major Issues

The concerns about the introduction of GMOs in crops and in food concentrates on four mutually overlapping areas: environmental concerns; public health concerns; ethical concerns about "tampering with nature" and individual choice; and a combination of ethical and socioeconomic concerns related to the issue of patenting.

The environmental risks include the possibility of a transfer of the introduced genes to wild plants and nontarget insects and the subsequent emergence of resistant or highly invasive insects and weeds. There is also the possibility of harmful changes in the nutritional status of foods and decline of the biodiversity of wildlife as a result of changes in the availability of food.[7] Among the health concerns, allergenicity and antibiotic resistance are most often mentioned.[8] Some scientists also discuss the

[5] D. Barling et. al., The Social Aspects of Food Biotechnology: A European View, 7 *Environmental Toxicology and Pharmacology* 85–93 (1999).

[6] See R. S. Hails, Genetically Modified Plants – The Debate Continues, 15 *Tree* 14–18 (2000); See also Barling, supra., and A. K. Deisingh & N. Badrie, Detection Approaches for Genetically Modified Organisms in Food, 38 *Food Research International* 639–649 (2005).

[7] See A. K. Deisingh, supra.; D. Barling et al., The Social Aspects of Food Biotechnology: A European View, 7 *Environmental Toxicology and Pharmacology* 85–93 (1999); H. Gaugitsch, Experience with Environmental Issues in GM Crop Production and the Likely Future Scenarios, 127 *Toxicology Letters* 351–357 (2002).

[8] See D. Barling et al., The Social Aspects of Food Biotechnology: A European View, 7 *Environmental Toxicology and Pharmacology* 85–93 (1999); See also Y. Endo &

possibility of horizontal gene transfer (HGT) of recombinant DNA from
GM crop-derived foods to human gut microflora or the human or animal genome, as gene transfer between different organisms is quite common in nature and a driving force in evolution.[9] However, transfer from
food upon ingestion is a rare event and only consequential if the trait is
expressed and confers selective advantage.

In relation to the ethical concerns about "tampering with nature,"[10]
three major ethical paradigms exist: consequentialism (acceptable outcomes for most people), ethics of autonomy/consent (everybody should
have a choice), and ethics of virtue/tradition (based on traditions of the
community).[11] In the consequentionalist ethics, the first generation of
GM technology is acceptable because it generally focuses on improving efficiency, if applied with enough foresight about possible adverse
consequences. It is unclear if the same holds for second-generation
GMO products, because they add new properties and thus goes beyond
efficiency.

In the ethics of autonomy/consent, each person should have the right
to avoid GMO products. The policy implication is the need to separate
GMO from non-GMO food and to label them accordingly and to create
rules for optimal traceability.

The ethics of virtue/tradition can take different forms, depending on
the tradition. In the "agrarian" tradition, agriculture is a "way of life"
and its adherents oppose GMOs as part of the broader resistance to
modern biotechnology-based agriculture. In the "nature-ism" tradition,
transspecies of genetic material can upset the operations of ecosystems,
with unknown consequences, and thus are ethically unacceptable. Consequentionalist ethics dominated the early years of the GMO debate,

E. Boutrif, Plant Biotechnology and its International Regulation–FAO's Initiative, 74
Livestock Production Science 217–222 (2002).

[9] H. A. Kuiper et al., Concluding Remarks, 42 *Food and Chemical Toxicology* 1195–1202
(2004).

[10] L. Frewer et al., Societal Aspects of Genetically Modified Foods, 42 *Food and Chemical Toxicology* 1181–1193 (2004).

[11] Burkhardt, J., 2001, The GMO debate: taking ethics seriously, http://www.
farmfoundation.org/news/articlefiles/120-burkhardt.pdf (accessed Aug 5, 2008).

focusing on risks, costs, and benefits, while the other perspectives have been marginalized. During the 1990s, consumer activists and environmental groups injected the other ethical perspectives into the debate.

The issue of patenting living organisms has been hotly debated since the 1980s. The controversial U.S. Supreme Court ruling,[12] which upheld the companies' claim to patent life forms, supplied additional visibility. The arguments against patenting life forms have been summarized by Krimsky as follows:[13] It does not ".... promote the progress of science and useful arts,"[14] and often even interferes with the development of new technologies[15]; the knowledge of crop and food production, which underlies the development of GMOs, has accumulated over thousands of years of human development and is taken for free to enrich the GMO manufacturers, and thus it is '.... little more than blatant piracy from cultures whose history has long demonstrated the "utility" of such plants."[16] The clash of values between those who consider life as another form of property ("genes are basically chemicals") and those who consider the knowledge about the functioning of a genome as something that fundamentally should be shared by everyone[17] is unresolved; plants and genes represent cultural artifacts that cannot be claimed as inventions or discoveries;[18] life forms are simply part of nature, and no ownership can be claimed over them.[19] The impacts of patenting on the livelihood of small farmers, who lose their free access to an essential public good, crop seed, also enters the debate. Monsanto has taken farmers to court many times for planting seeds obtained from genetically engineered plants.[20]

---

[12] Diamond vs. Chakrabarty, 447 U.S. 303 (1980).

[13] S. Krimsky & P. Shorett, *Rights and Liberties in the Biotech Age: Why We Need a Genetic Bill of Rights* (Rowman and Littlefield Publishers 2005).

[14] US Constitution, article 1, section 8, as cited by Albright, M., *Life Patents and Democratic Values*, in Krimsky et al., supra. At 30.

[15] J. King & D. Stabinsky, *Life Patents Undermine the Exchange of Technology and Scientific Ideas*, in Krimsky et al., supra, at 53.

[16] Albright, supra, at 33–34.

[17] Id. at 35.

[18] Id.

[19] Id. at 36.

[20] King et. al., supra, 53.

These concerns regarding GMOs in food production and agriculture are further magnified by the uncertainty associated with the high speed and large scale of adoption of GMOs around the world[21] such as the hazards of potential GMO monocultures, as well as with the rapid developments in the science and technology of GMOs.

Public Resistance to GMOs

Whereas the introduction of GMOs in food and agriculture engendered debate around the world, the European public has been the most resistant to the new technology. The difference between the United States and Europe is especially striking because it is the reverse of the acceptance of cigarette smoking on the two sides of the Atlantic. Some attribute the greater U.S. acceptance to the fact that "Americans perceive farming as yet another industry. . . . on par with cars or steel, and do not harbor the same sentimental ties and ethical concerns for the preservation of rural life" as Europeans do.[22] Others explain the difference by pointing to American trust in the government agencies with oversight of the GMOs: EPA, FDA, and USDA. The Europeans, according to this view, doubt the competence of regulatory agencies, especially after the recent mad cow disease episode.[23] The differences may

---

[21] Harvey Brooks, *The Typology of Surprises in Technology, Institutions, and Development, in International Institute for Applied Systems Analysis, Development of the Biosphere* 325–348, (William C. Clark & R. E. Munn eds., Cambridge University Press 1986).

[22] P. Kurzer, Who Steers the Field of Consumer Protection and Environmental Regulations? An American-European Comparison, European Response to Globalization: Resistance, Adaptation, and Alternatives, 88 *Contemporary Studies in Economic and Financial Analysis* 41–63 (2006); See also M. A. Echols, Food safety regulations in the European Union and the United States: Different Cultures, Different Laws, 4 *Columbia Journal of European Law* 525–544 (1998).

[23] See Bray, F., 2003, *GM Foods: Shared Risks and Global Action, in Risk, Culture, and Health Inequality* (B. H. Harthhorn & L. Oaks eds., Praeger 2003); See also G. P. Gaskell et. al., *Worlds apart? Public Opinion in Europe and the USA, in Biotechnology-the making of a global controversy,* (M. W. Bauer and G. Gaskell eds., Science Museum

also be attributed to the opposing dominant principles of "substantial equivalence" (USA) and "precaution" (EU); or, even more succinctly, as "innocent until proven guilty" in the United States versus "guilty until proven innocent" in the EU.[24]

The European public's reaction to GMOs has been characterized by mistrust of both regulatory institutions and the technocratic approach to risk assessment and management. Whereas the Eurobarometer surveys conducted between 1991 and 2002, and other sources[25] register the familiar concerns about "tampering with nature" and environmental and health consequences (allergens, outcrossing, super-weeds), the public appears to recognize and accept the scientific uncertainty with which regulatory agencies must deal.[26] Rather, the public questions the ability of scientists to serve the public good, as well as the ability of government agencies to produce wise policies. A European researcher recently[27] used focus groups to decipher public opinions about risks, experts, and regulations in five European countries. The study concluded that there is little knowledge of regulatory institutions and a lot of skepticism about them, especially since the mad cow disease incident. The study also documented widespread feelings that the bureaucracies favor formal procedures over actual safety and big corporations over small firms. The extreme specialization of scientific research also came under fire, in addition to the strong connections between science and industry. The study indicated the public's overarching mistrust of ambition-driven

2002); L. Pellizoni, Democracy and the Governance of Uncertainty. The Case of Agricultural Gene Technologies, 82 *Journal of Hazardous Materials* 205–222 (2001).

[24] S. Lieberman & T. Gray, The So-called 'Moratorium' on the Licensing of New Genetically Modified (GM) Products by the European Union 1998–2004: A Study in Ambiguity, 15 *Environmental Politics* 592–609 (2006).

[25] Frewer et al., Societal Aspects of Genetically Modified Foods, 42 *Food and Chemical Toxicology* 1181–1193 (2004).

[26] L. Pellizoni, Democracy and the Governance of Uncertainty. The Case of Agricultural Gene Technologies, 86 *Journal of Hazardous Materials* 205–222 (2001).

[27] Id.

scientists, experts, regulators, and policy management of risk and uncertainty. Unfortunately, the study lacked data on the positions of focus groups on specific aspects of risk and uncertainty in the GMO debate.

Those results are consistent with the results of other focus groups, which uncovered public resentment of decision-making procedures and unease about the prevalent direction of the agro-food system. Researchers also mention the perception of an institutional failure to address public concerns, mistrust in these institutions, and specific concerns about the balance of power between producers and consumers, and between the industrialized and developing worlds.[28] Notably, the public appears to favor the idea of "societal usefulness" as the criterion for judging the acceptability of GMO technologies over the economic efficiency criterion. The increased demands for public participation and the rise of the "consumer citizen" movement in Europe since the mid-1990s (through purchasing decisions and consumer boycotts), and the attendant need for labeling foodstuffs and traceability of food components feed into the GMO debate.

Public Policies

Regulation of GMOs in agriculture and food in Europe has been difficult, owing to the legislative and regulatory complexity of the EU, the technical complexity of the issue, its economic and industrial importance, and the inherent uncertainties.[29] The initial wave of regulation during the 1980s engendered so much criticism from the member-states and various stakeholder groups that it resulted in a 1998 a *de facto* moratorium on all GMOs, first adopted by France and Greece, then Italy, Denmark,

---

[28] See L. Levidov & C. Morris, Science and Governance in Europe: lessons from the case of agricultural biotechnology, *Science and Public Policy* 345–360 (2001). See also Frewer et al., supra, and D. Barling et al., The Social Aspects of Food Biotechnology: A European View, 7 *Environmental Toxicology and Pharmacology* 85–93 (1999).

[29] S. Borras, Legitimate Governance of Risk at the EU level? The Case of Genetically Modified Organisms, 73 *Technological Forecasting and Social Change* 61–75 (2006).

and Luxembourg, and finally by the EU Commission.[30] The proximate trigger for the moratorium was the highly publicized shipment of GMO maize by Monsanto to a European harbor.

Since 1998, the EU has been tackling the issue along three lines: developing specific GMO regulations; reinterpreting the precautionary principle; and improving transparency and public trust through institutional changes. In 2003, it adopted more stringent regulations concerning authorization procedures, and the labeling and traceability of food components. The precautionary principle was extended from environmental protection to consumer and health protection. The most important innovations in the 2003 regulations include: explicitly incorporating "consumer choice," by making the labeling and traceability requirements mandatory; formalizing the distinction among risk assessment, risk management, and risk communication; and recognizing that risk communication means a two-way dialogue with a goal of making the general public an active participant in both the technical and policy discourse.[31] These reforms were enacted after extensive informal consultations with numerous stakeholder groups.

Some have also sought to create an effective barrier between GM and non-GM crops by creating GMO-free zones. For example, one proposal would create a GMO-free zone in the Alps region of Upper Austria, Biosphere Reserve, for the following reasons:

- The active promotion of alternative technologies, as opposed to following a single direction of technological innovation (like the case of nuclear energy)

---

[30] R. Von Schomberg, 1998, An appraisal of the working in practice of directive 90/220/EEC on the deliberate release of genetically modified organisms: final study, European Parliament, DG research, Directorate B: the STOA programme, Luxembourg; S. Lieberman & T. Gray, The So-called 'Moratorium' on the Licensing of New Genetically Modified (GM) Products by the European Union 1998–2004: A Study in Ambiguity, 15 *Environmental Politics* 592–609 (2006).

[31] See Borras, supra.

- The creation of a protected space (a 'niche') for experimentation and learning about alternatives
- "Endogenous response" to globalization by "less favored regions," meaning the mobilization of local knowledge and solutions to ensure sustainable development

In 2003 the EU Commission rejected this request, and the decision is being contested in the courts.[32]

Greenpeace has generally supported the 2003 EU regulations and voiced opposition to the United States' attempt to challenge the EU regulations through the World Trade Organization (WTO).[33] The United States, Canada, and Argentina initiated proceedings against the EU over its *de facto* moratorium on GMOs at the WTO.[34] The WTO ruled in 2006 that it is illegal for individual countries to ban specific GMOs, although strict laws are still possible.[35]

One of the key features of the European policy with regard to GMOs – the labeling and traceability requirements – has proven to be difficult to implement. For one thing, there is no consensus about the definition of no-GMO-containing foodstuffs. Greenpeace has been campaigning against companies that lobbied the EU to allow increasing amounts of "contamination" by GM food. Second, incidents of mixing during storage, transport, and processing are bound to occur, as exemplified by the widely publicized case of Starlink corn in the United States, where GMO corn, strictly limited to use for animal feed, found its way into supermarket cereals and other grain products. In 2005, there was the highly publicized case of GMO-producing company Syngenta misleading the public and regulators by withholding information about GM maize contamination. Recently, Greenpeace created a Contamination

---

[32] PlanetArk Factbox, www.planetark.org/dailynewsstory.cfm/newsid/34942/story.htm Feb 8 (last visited June 25, 2008).

[33] Greenpeace, www.greenpeace.org (last visited June 25, 2008).

[34] PlanetArk Factbox, www.planetark.org/dailynewsstory.cfm/newsid/34942/story.htm Feb 8 (last visited June 25, 2008).

[35] Bite Back, http://www.bite-back.org (last visited June 25, 2008).

Index describing 113 incidents and has consistently argued that "coexistence" of fields with GM and non-GM crops is impossible without contamination.

The third problem is that once cross-contamination is detected, tracing the source of GMOs is difficult, which calls into question the capacity to enforce labeling policies. Finally, not all foods are covered, for instance there are no procedures to label meat and dairy.

One way the technical and policy communities responded to the public concerns about GMOs and institutional ability to control the attendant risks has been to develop increasingly sophisticated methods for testing, monitoring, early problem detection, and risk assessment.[36] They also concentrated on modifying and refining existing expert-based assessments. One expert-based assessment technique, proposed by the Food and Agriculture Organization and World Health Organization, is the concept of "substantial equivalence."[37] Substantial equivalence embodies the concept that " ...if a new food or food component is found to be substantially equivalent to an existing food or food component, it can be treated in the same manner with respect to safety."[38] This concept has been criticized on the grounds that "....the degree of difference between a natural food and its GM alternative before its 'substance' ceases to be 'equivalent' is not defined anywhere, nor has an exact definition been agreed [upon] by legislators." Moreover, it is ironic that the same actors who endorse the concept of "substantial equivalence" also endorse the present right to patent new GMO life forms.

An EU-funded project proposes a more elaborate method for the safety assessment of foods derived from GM crops: ENTRANSFOOD.

---

[36] A. K. Deisingh & N. Badrie, Detection approaches for genetically modified organisms in food, 38 *Food Research International* 639–649 (2005).

[37] Y. Endo, & E. Boutrif, Plant Biotechnology and its International Regulation – FAO's Initiative, 74 *Livestock Production Science* 217–222 (2002); S. Lieberman & T. Gray, The So-called 'Moratorium' on the Licensing of New Genetically Modified (GM) Products by the European Union 1998–2004: A Study in Ambiguity, 15 *Environmental Politics* 592–609 (2006).

[38] See Endo, supra.

Using the substantial equivalence approach, this procedure also includes a thorough description of all aspects of the products and the process and a study of unintended side effects. According to the authors, this method is applicable to both the first- and second-generation GMO crops, the latter including nutritionally enhanced crops, those with improved performance under environmental stress conditions (salt tolerance, heat resistance), and others.

Whereas these proposals may be steps in the right direction, they are still, in essence, expert-based, technocratic approaches, limited by scientific uncertainties and technocratic judgment. As such, they do not go far enough in addressing many public concerns. Perhaps for that reason, the project[39] also called for "research on new ways of public participation in the risk analysis process for foods and new food producing technologies" as well as the establishment of a Permanent Evaluation and Discussion Platform for the scientific and societal assessment of the development and introduction of future foods in Europe. The call did not clarify how such participation would contribute to either the risk assessment or risk management of GMOs.

The establishment of the European Food Safety Agency (EFSA) has been a promising step in the direction of greater transparency, accountability, public participation, and restoring trust in public institutions.[40] Nonetheless, many consider it inadequate. According to some critics[41] the informal process of consultation and contestation creates problems of unequal access and influence, largely related to the inequality or the stakeholders' resources. Also, the EU parliament and the national parliaments have no involvement in the authorization process. Thus it is unclear if the new GMO rules will gain social acceptance. Now that the

[39] H. A. Kuiper et al., Concluding Remarks, 42 *Food and Chemical Toxicology* 1195–1202 (2004).

[40] L. Levidov & C. Morris, *Science and Governance in Europe: Lessons from the Case of Agricultural Biotechnology, Science and Public Policy* 345–360 (2001).

[41] S. Borras, Legitimate Governance of Risk at the EU level? The Case of Genetically Modified Organisms, 73 *Technological Forecasting and Social Change* 61–75 (2006).

moratorium on GM foods is effectively lifted in most countries of the EU, it remains to be seen how consumers will respond to the appearance of GM products on the supermarket shelves.

The Unresolved Question of Public Participation

Whereas most participants in the debate agree about the central role of broadly based, inclusive societal discourse on policy making and risk assessment and management, there is much less clarity in the literature on how to create an effective discourse and participation, or what exactly its objectives would be.[42] With regard to the objectives of public participation, the open questions include: would it seek to reduce the public mistrust of the public institutions, and thus empower these institutions to act in the public interest? Would it seek to educate the public about the benefits and risks of GMOs, and thus help them make individual choices as consumers? Would it help the regulatory agencies to understand public concerns, and thus make more informed and possibly more effective public policies? Or perhaps other objectives should be chosen?

Several studies have in fact shown that better education and outreach to the general public does not necessarily reduce controversy or increase public trust in regulatory agencies. For example, one study[43] showed that more information polarizes the existing attitudes rather than opening peoples' minds to other views; consumers with initially negative values become even more negative, while consumers with initially positive values become even more positive. In another study[44] it appeared that more

---

[42] See Kuiper et. al, supra. 2004; See also Frewer et al., Societal Aspects of Genetically Modified Foods, 42 *Food and Chemical Toxicology* 1181–1193 (2004) and Borras, supra.

[43] Frewer et al., supra.

[44] J. Scholderer, & L. J. Frewer, The Biotechnology Communication Paradox: Experimental Evidence and the Need for a New Strategy, 26 *Journal of Consumer Policy* 125–127 (2003).

information had no effect on the attitude toward GMOs, either positive or negative, but led both the proponents and opponents to recommend reducing the use of GMOs. Additional research[45] showed that the perception of high risk was greater among the individuals with greater "objective" knowledge of the GMO technology and those who recently discussed biotechnology.

This chapter aims to contribute to clarifying the poorly elaborated concepts of inclusive societal discourse and public participation. Assuming that discourse and public engagement are indeed good things and necessary for solving the GMO controversy, the following four propositions are put forth:

- The concept of sustainability offers a helpful framing of the debate about the multiple controversial aspects of GMOs in food and agriculture.
- The rapidly growing practice of voluntary sustainability reporting by companies provides a powerful instrument for serving the goal of creating a discourse that includes the widest possible range of participants, some of whom have been, until now, kept outside the debate.
- A multi-stakeholder discourse so created opens an opportunity for increasing societal participation in strategic corporate decisions regarding the research and development (R&D) trajectories for agricultural GMOs,[46] and elevates the idea of social accountability and social responsibility of GMO producers.
- Small-scale experiments with introducing GMO technologies, designed for the purpose of enhancing social learning, or Bounded Socio-Technical Experiments (BSTEs), are suitable instruments for enhancing and enriching the societal discourse and for improving technology assessment.

---

[45] D. Barling et al., The Social Aspects of Food Biotechnology: A European View, 7 *Environmental Toxicology and Pharmacology* 85–93 (1999).

[46] Constructive Technology Assessment, Managing Technology in Society: The Approach of Constructive Technology Assessment, (A. Rip et al., eds., Pinter 1995).

Taken together, these approaches – sustainability, reporting, and BSTEs – advance social learning about the agricultural GMO technology.

The Role for Sustainability Reporting

During the past decade, the ideas of transparency and accountability in environmental and sustainability performance have taken root in the discourse on corporate social responsibility.[47] Voluntary sustainability reporting has emerged as part of this trend and has rapidly diffused among large global corporations.[48] By 2002, the Global Reporting Initiative (GRI) has rapidly become the leader among voluntary worldwide performance reporting programs on corporate responsibility and a gold standard by which sustainability reporting is judged.

GRI introduced three key institutional innovations: (1) creating the guidelines through collaborative efforts of a wide range of actors, who had not previously thought of themselves as members of the same political or policy networks, in a maximally transparent Internet-based manner; (2) putting in place a self-replicating, inclusive, multi-stakeholder international network of organizations and individuals for producing successive generations of the guidelines, which assures their adaptability and long-term survival; (3) creating an organization that serves as the steward of the guidelines and the process by which they will evolve. GRI's meteoric rise on the global scene – in scope, visibility, name recognition, and prestige – speaks to the broad acceptance of these ideas. For that reason, and because of some of GRI's unique features, we use GRI as

---

[47] See Wolfgang H. Reinicke & Francis Deng, *Critical Choices: The United Nations, Networks, and the Future of Global Governance*, (International Development Center 2000); See also *World Bank, Greening Industry: New Roles for Communities, Markets, and Government* (Oxford University Press 2000).

[48] See A. L. White, Sustainability and the Accountable Corporation. 41 *Environment* 3–43 (1999). See also Corporate Storytelling: Non-financial Accounting is Now Too Serious to be Left to Amateurs, *The Economist* Nov. 6–12, 2004, 13–14.

a case in point for discussing the role that sustainability reporting might play in the debate over agricultural GMOs.

At its most explicit, the social argument in favor of reporting is that it empowers all stakeholders to hold companies accountable for their actions and to exert pressures for changing behaviors, either through political action, market mechanisms, or through more collaborative mechanisms.[49] A less often discussed, but crucial, argument for reporting is that it forces the reporting companies to gather and critically examine data about themselves, and, in the cases of serious commitment to producing a high-level report, to engage with their most important stakeholders: those who experience, and have an interest in, the impacts of the company's activities. This, in turn, may lead to considerable organizational learning and may create dialogue between the company and the rest of society.

A third key benefit of reporting is that the collective process of reaching a consensus on what and how to report creates a platform for a discourse among many different types of societal actors while providing a common language for conducting it. It is these two aspects of reporting – its potential to create a platform for a multi-stakeholder engagement and a broader societal discourse on many dimensions of agricultural GMOs – that we address in this section.[50]

---

[49] N. Gunningham et al., Social License and Environmental Protection: Why Businesses Go Beyond Compliance. *Law and Social Inquiry* 29(2): 307–341 (2004).

[50] For a more extensive discussion of the historical foundations, development, and institutionalization of GRI, see: Brown, H., De Jong, M., and Levy, D. 2009. "Building Institutions Based on Information Disclosure: Lessons from GRI's Sustainability Reporting." *Journal of Cleaner Production* 17(4): 571–580; Levy, D., Brown, H. S., and de Jong, M. 2010. "NGO Strategies and the Politics of Corporate Governance: the Case of Global Reporting Initiative." *Business and Society* 49: 88–115; Halina Brown et al., The Rise of Global Reporting Initiative (GRI) as a Case of Institutional Entrepreneurship, Working Paper #36. Cambridge, MA: John F. Kennedy School of Government, Harvard University; http://www.hks.harvard.edu/m-rcbg/CSRI/publications/workingpaper_36_brown.pdf; (last accessed Aug 8, 2008).

Three features of GRI are of particular interest for the GMO case: its inclusiveness and interactive character, its focus on social impacts, and its global scope. The inclusiveness and participatory character are structurally built into the GRI system in the following manner: the framework for reporting (Reporting Guidelines) is developed through a collaborative effort of the widest possible range of international actors, including the manufacturing and service sectors, institutional investors, financial rating sector, banks and insurance industry, accountancy organizations, religious organizations, social activists, environmental and labor organizations, governments, communities, and others. Since the birth of the idea of GRI within the Boston-based CERES organization in 1997, more than three thousand individuals and organizations worked together through various working groups on figuring out what to report, how to report, and how to account for the individual sectoral and regional activities, needs, and interests. This collaboration has produced three generations of generally applicable Reporting Guidelines (known as G1, G2, and G3), and half a dozen of supplemental guidelines tailored to specific sectors (Sectoral Supplements for automotive, telecommunications, financial services, tour operators, mining and metals, and public agencies) as well as countless discussion papers and discussion forums.

Furthermore, because the GRI Guidelines are a perpetual work in progress – the work on a subsequent version of the guidelines commences as soon as one is officially released – causing a self-replicating process of social discourse over the issues that are of interest to a widely ranging constituency. This process can be applied to the emerging GMO industry.

The process by which GRI Guidelines have evolved – intense interaction, wide range of views and ideas, and a shared goal – has been conducive for social learning (see section 4 for a theoretical discussion on learning). Our own research has uncovered several dimensions of that learning:

- GRI has contributed to the operationalization of the abstract concept of social impacts (within the sustainability framework), demonstrated that communicating social performance in a systematic and comparable way is in fact possible, and showed that broadly based consensus can be reached on how to do it;
- GRI illustrates how a very broad multi-stakeholder process can serve to build consensus on a difficult and possibly divisive issue such as sustainability indicators;
- GRI has legitimated the idea of sustainability reporting and created an expectation that such a report will be comprehensive, responsive to its stakeholders, verifiable, and based on mutual engagement with the key stakeholders;
- The concept of a multi-stakeholder process has been adopted by other visible global institutions. For example, the International Standards Organization is using this process to develop its new sustainability reporting standard, ISO 26,000.

Although the GRI Guidelines do not seek to establish norms of behavior, the process they set in motion is likely to contribute over time to a societal consensus on what constitutes the proper use of a technology and fair treatment of interested parties. Most importantly, the relatively unthreatening process of developing reporting guidelines brings together societal actors, who would not otherwise engage with one another if the topic focused on actual performance or other divisive topics. The experience of creating the GRI Supplement for the Mining and Metal Processing Sector, briefly described in the Appendix, illustrates this signature GRI phenomenon of discourse creation and consensus making.

For application of this process to the GMO problem, the GRI organization would embark on producing a "Sector Supplement" for the agricultural GMO industry. This would automatically create a platform, the language and framing for a discourse, and a widely ranging constituency.

The participants would go beyond the "usual suspects," namely regulatory agencies, industry, technical experts, environmentalists, and public health, consumer and civil society advocates. They would also include the insurance industry and various members of the financial sector who have not so far been part of the debate but who have great stakes in its outcome.

This inclusive multi-stakeholder process would certainly lead to new ideas and new perspectives on the issue of agricultural GMOs. As illustrated by the story of the Mining Supplement in the Appendix, it would have a good chance of accomplishing an important goal, mobilizing the key stakeholders to discuss, in a nonadversarial environment, their concerns. Because the process bypasses any discussion on what constitutes socially acceptable performance, it could produce an agreement on the agenda for a social discourse about the impact of the GMO industry. In time, it might contribute to a societal consensus about what constitutes acceptable norms of behavior with regard to the development of specific types of agricultural GMOs and the mode of their application into commerce. It might also contribute to the development of formal policies.

This type of participation and democratic deliberation over the trajectory of technological development is not a new idea. In the 1980s, it received considerable attention under the umbrella of "Constructive Technology Assessment" (CTA).[51] CTA aimed to mitigate unforeseen and socially undesirable effects of new technologies by increased stakeholder participation in the process of technology development. What is new here is the proposal to employ the process for encouraging corporate accountability – namely, sustainability reporting as defined by the GRI – to create an instrument for implementing such technology assessments.

---

[51] *Managing Technology in Society: The Approach of Constructive Technology Assessment*, (A. Rip et al. eds., Pinter 1995).

To consider the types of questions that might be scrutinized in the process, and by whom, we take a closer look at the GRI guidelines. The system uses three categories of sustainability indicators:

1. *Social performance indicators* center on how an organization contributes to the well-being of its employees, customers, other stakeholders, and the society through its labor, human rights, governance, and product responsibility practices. It includes such topics as labor and human rights, diversity and use of fair hiring practices, board members and suppliers, workplace safety, transparency, ethics, corporate governance, social impacts on host communities, product safety, and others.

2. *Economic performance indicators* address the organization's and its host community's economic prosperity, by focusing on its economic impacts on customers, suppliers, employees, providers of capital, and the public sector. Some topics include sales, profits, capital expenditures, debt and interest, wages, community donations, taxes, local purchasing, and brand strength.

3. *Environmental indicators* concern environmental performance and impacts, both now and for future generations. They cover such topics as: resource conservation, waste prevention and management, environmental risk control and restoration, supply chain impacts, waste disposal, recycling, energy conservation, greenhouse gases, biodiversity, water and materials use; renewable energy; and wildlife conservation.

Clearly, the three categories create an opportunity to ask companies to engage in some of the most vexing questions about this technology, not only after it is developed and/or introduced into the market but especially earlier in its development at the R&D stage. Questions such as, what types of social goods are expected to emerge from a particular new trait in agricultural GMOs? How will the GMOs impact the socioeconomic well-being of indigenous communities? What are the compensatory mechanisms for free access to the indigenous knowledge? and others, can be addressed at this stage.

Some of the current GRI indicators are well designed for these questions; others could serve only as rough proxies. A GMO-specific Sector Supplement would be necessary to refine the system to serve the purpose of technology assessment.

Whereas the process of developing Agricultural GMO Sector Supplements of GRI Guidelines could be the engine for creating an interactive multi-stakeholder discourse, application of the Guidelines to prepare a sustainability report by GMO manufacturers might be another avenue to prompt that discourse. The recent experience of Nike, which, in 2005, produced a highly regarded GRI Report, illustrates this alternate path. To report on the impacts of its products on labor conditions and human rights, the company engaged with all its global vendors and sought their input. It is simply impossible to report human rights, community development, labor relations, and other issues without involving the affected constituencies.

In short, taking advantage of the growing popularity of voluntary sustainability reporting like the GRI framework would enrich and increase the effectiveness of the current discourse about agricultural GMOs. GRI need not be the specific mechanism. Rather, the GRI system serves to illustrate how a reporting system that emphasizes both the product and the process, the inclusive multi-stakeholder engagement and the ever-evolving Guidelines, can serve that purpose.

Is there a sufficient will to create sustainability reporting guidelines for the agricultural GMOs sector, and then use them? The answer is not easy. A recent review[52] cites research reports showing that, in a knowledge-based economy, the returns on investments into technology developments are becoming increasingly important, which creates powerful incentives for protecting intellectual property and for

---

[52] A. L. White, Sustainability and the Accountable Corporation. 41 *Environment* 3–43 (1999).

avoiding transparency. On the other hand, the same review also shows that the current system of financial reporting, which does not account for knowledge-based assets, adversely affects the functioning of markets by creating abnormal gains to informed investors at the expense of everybody else, which erodes investor confidence, leads to high share-price volatility, and increases the cost of capital. These findings make an economic and political case for greater transparency with regard to technological developments within companies like GMO producers. The difficulty with resolving these competing objectives is the idea that the financial sector and other hitherto neglected stakeholders must participate in the social discourse about the science, policy, and economics of agricultural GMOs.

It is possible that these pressures will result in actions by GMO companies to engage in the process of establishing a sector supplement for agricultural and food GMO companies. The initiative could be taken by the companies themselves, by a collaboration of companies and NGOs, or, indirectly, through pressure from governments or financial institutions, similar to the case of the mining industry. Government agencies that regulate food safety and security could play a catalytic role by bringing together companies with the GRI secretariat and its networks and procedures.

There are also signs of mounting social expectations for companies to engage with the society through meaningful and verifiable sustainability reporting. Over the past decade, this practice has taken on the characteristics of an institution, in other words, it is beginning to resemble a self-sustaining and highly resilient system of shared values, norms, and taken for granted behavioral patterns and assumptions that actors hold about "how the game is played."[53] A good institution inculcates responsibilities, provide societal actors with validated standards

---

[53] Paul DiMaggio & Walter Powell, Introduction, in *The New Institutionalism in Organizational Analysis* 1–40 (Paul DiMaggio & Walter Powell eds., University of Chicago Press 1991); See also W. R. Scott, *Unpacking Institutional Arguments in The New Institutionalism in Organizational Analysis* 164–182 (Paul DiMaggio & Walter Powell

for desirable and expected behaviors, and produce outcomes that are beneficial to society.[54] Research on GRI and similar reporting frameworks indicates that they possess numerous characteristics of a global institution.[55] Some illustrations of this phenomenon include the increasing consensus about what constitutes a high quality sustainability report and what process should underlie its preparation, the incorporation of the concept of reporting into the discussions of corporate accountability and social responsibility, the emergence of new professions (such as social investment financial analyst) and new enterprises (consultancies and think tanks) that depend on sustainability reporting and that specialize in their preparation and verification, and stabilization of a wide network of diverse stakeholders, ranging from market analysts to shareholder activists to labor, civil rights, and environmental organizations, who have developed a sense of shared enterprise with regard to the expectation of sustainability reports by companies.

In short, GRI's most salient promise is that it can help create transparency in an early phase of the R&D process, where new GMO products and GMO-based production processes are still under development, and also create powerful incentives for compliance with emerging codes of conduct.

The Role for Bounded Sociotechnical Experiments

For controversial technologies with potential adverse consequences for society, it is wise to conduct small-scale experiments before scaling up for commercial introduction. The literature on GMOs shows wide support for pre-market experimentation, both among its proponents and

eds., University of Chicago Press 1991) and W. R. Scott Institutions and Organizations (Sage 1995).

[54] Claus Offe, Designing Institutions in East European Transitions, in *The Theory of Institutional Design* 199–224 (Robert E. Goodin ed., Cambridge University Press 1996). G. Paquet, Governance Through Social Learning (University of Ottawa Press 1999).

[55] See Brown et al., note 50; Levy et al., note 50.

opponents. One of the key rationales for experimentation is that it allows the scientists, technologists, policy makers, and other concerned parties to learn about the technology and its unanticipated impacts and to find ways to respond to them. This section expands on the concept of learning through experimentation beyond the characteristics of the technology. Specifically, it addresses the problem framing and policy-oriented discourse needed for higher-order learning.

Higher-order learning is a change in approaches to interpreting observations and framing problems and situations. It entails changes in the assumptions, norms, and interpretive frames that govern the actions of individuals, communities, and organizations, or that underlie a policy discourse. The term "higher order" denotes what in organizational sciences has been dubbed "double loop"[56] or "generative" learning,[57] and in policy sciences as "conceptual" learning.[58] It contrasts with lower order/single loop/adaptive/technical learning in which problems are corrected or policies altered without changes in problem framing, assumptions, or norms.

Learning occurs through a feedback-stimulus mechanism when the well-accepted, time-tested, and trusted assumptions and competences receive feedback on their problem-solving performance. If the feedback reveals poor problem-solving performance, the original assumptions are reevaluated and replaced. This broad concept of feedback stimulus is consistent across a wide range of disciplinary writings about learning from the cognitive, organizational, and policy sciences. Working within the context of cognitive science on how individual professionals learn through problem solving, a seminal study showed that learning among

[56] See C. Argyris, Double-loop learning in organizations, 55 *Harvard Business Review* 115–125 (1977); See also C. Argyris & M. Schön, *Organizational Learning: A Theory of Action Perspective.* (Addison-Wesley 1978).

[57] P. M. Senge, Building learning organizations, 32 *Sloan Management Review* 7–23 (1990).

[58] Pieter Glasbergen, *Learning to Manage the Environment, in Democracy and the Environment: Problems and Prospects* 175–212 (William M. Lafferty & James Meadowcroft eds., Edward Elgar Publishing 1996).

professionals occurs by way of a "conversation" between an individual and the problem, through trial and error, which in turn leads to increasingly higher-order reassessments.[59] First, the tools are questioned (lower order learning), then, the problem is defined, and, finally, the systems and overarching theories are analyzed (higher order). In the context of organizations, the stimuli necessary for higher-order learning come from threats to organizational survival and success, failures, disasters, and other surprises.[60]

A 1998 study[61] examined the mechanisms by which external stimuli induce learning in social organizations, both formal and informal (communities of practice). The feedback process that is central to learning takes place, according to the authors, by means of interaction between the deep competency possessed by a community of practice and the experience it acquires by interacting with the outside world. These "boundary processes" produce learning. Several factors can enhance learning at the boundaries, for example, having something to interact about, such as a specific project or a problem to solve; the ability to communicate in a common language; and the presence of individuals who serve as brokers of new ideas among different communities of practice.

In policy sciences, higher-order learning is broadly understood as a collective change in prevalent views, norms, problem definitions, relationships among groups, and the collective approaches to common problems. Like organizational and cognitive sciences, this school of thought attributes learning to the presence of feedback loops between the existing interpretive frames and problem definitions, and new experiences.

---

[59] D. A. Schön, *The Reflective Practitioner, How Professionals Think in Action* (Basic Books 1983).

[60] See Argyris, supra. See also Argyris & Schön, supra, and S. B. Sitkin Learning Through Failure: The Strategy of Small Losses, 14 *Research in Organizational Behavior* 231–266 (1992). P. M. Senge, Building learning organizations, 32 *Sloan Management Review* 7–23 (1990), describes group techniques that generate feedback on the accepted assumptions and behaviors, as the means to stimulate higher-order learning in organizations.

[61] Etienne Wenger, *Communities of Practice: Learning, Meaning, and Identity* (Cambridge University Press 1998).

Some authors emphasize the role of new knowledge in providing the feedback, while others[62] emphasize interactions among groups with different belief systems and interpretive frames as the means for learning. There is widespread agreement that crises, a sense of urgency, the availability of platforms for interaction, accumulation of new knowledge, and experimentation are important facilitators of social learning.[63]

Higher-order learning may be employed to solve intractable policy controversies. Such controversies usually arise as a result of an irreconcilable clash between the adversaries on the levels of problem definitions, norms, values, and belief systems. Learning manifests itself in a collective re-framing of the problem so as to accommodate the fundamentally irreconcilable differences on the other levels, which in turn leads to conflict resolution.[64]

Our study[65] used a four-level conceptual scheme to examine higher-order learning in interactive project teams working on technological innovations, building on previous researchers' works.[66] It presupposes that the participants bring to the interactive process a range of competencies and belief systems, which in turn affect the meaning they attach to the project at hand and the ways in which they seek to contribute to it.

---

[62] *Theories of the Policy Process* (P. Sabatier ed., Westview Press 1999); A. Wildawski, Choosing Preferences by Constructing Institutions: A Cultural Theory of Preference Formation, 81 *American Political Science Review* 3–21 (1990); Pieter Glasbergen, *Learning to Manage the Environment, in Democracy and the Environment: Problems and Prospects* 175–212 (William M. Lafferty and James Meadowcroft, eds., Edward Elgar Publishing 1996); Schön, supra.

[63] T. Birkland, *After Disaster: Agenda Setting, Public Policy, and Focusing Events.* (Georgetown University Press 1997); G. Paquet, *Governance Through Social Learning,* (University of Ottawa Press 1999).

[64] D. A. Schön & M. Rein, *Frame Reflection: Towards the Resolution of Intractable Policy Controversies* (Basic Books 1994).

[65] See H. S. Brown et al., Learning for Sustainability Transition through Bounded Socio-technical Experiments in Personal Mobility. *Technology Analysis and Strategic Management* 15, 291–315 (2003). See also Halina Brown and Philip Vergragt 2008. Bounded Socio-Technical Experiments as Agents of Systemic Change: The Case of a Zero-Energy Residential Building. *Technological Forecasting and Social Change* 75: 107–130.

[66] J. Grin & H. Van de Graaf, Technology Assessment as Learning, 20 *Science, Technology, and Human Values* 72–99 (1996).

Factors such as institutional membership, professional training, self-interest, socialization through membership in political and professional groups as well as deeply held values and beliefs contribute to the variability. These differences can be grouped into four categories: (1) Problem solving according to predetermined objectives; (2) Problem definition; (3) Dominant interpretive frames; (4) Worldview.

Worldview denotes deeply held values with regard to the preferred social order, including such issues as justice, fairness, equality, freedom, and private versus public good. Discourse at this level rarely occurs, is unlikely to produce changes, and is most dangerous for a collaborative project. This is because the views of this order are very stable within each participant group. Rather than closing gaps in deeply held beliefs, an open discourse in this domain may lead to a deadlock. Of course, differing worldviews do play a role in the overall process. They do so indirectly, by impacting the way individual participants interpret the meaning of the project *vis-à-vis* the private and public interests, or how they define a problem.

By interpretive frame we mean the approaches to making sense of observations and to identifying the most salient characteristics of a particular situation. It is strongly linked to institutional and professional affiliations of its holder, his/her self-interest, as well as the worldview. Well-established professional assumptions and norms of behavior can strongly influence one's interpretive frame. Interpretive frames resists change but can support change, especially in crisis situations.

Problem definition denotes specifying the task at hand or problem to be solved. Participants do so by examining the features of a particular situation through the lens of their respective interpretive frames and worldviews. Discourse on this level is a struggle or negotiation about how to pair a problem definition with a problem solution. For instance, professionals with a technical background are inclined to define the problem as technical whereas social scientists or public agency employees would develop a more social problem definition. Learning on this level is adjusting problem definitions to reach consensus or at least congruence. This is first-order learning.

When interactions among participants take place on levels 2, 3, and 4, differences in problem definitions, motivations for engaging in the project, individual interests and organizational missions, and ideologies are exposed. The nature and the extent of the resulting higher order learning depend on how the participants confront their differences and the ways they are mediated. Interactions at the level of problem definition are the most common, and this is the type of learning that most often occurs. Our 2008 study[67] showed that a turnover in the team membership took place until all the participants reached congruency in their worldviews. Learning occurred mostly in problem definition and partially in interpretive frame.

In summary, the disparate bodies of scholarship on learning can be distilled down to this: learning takes place when key actors representing a range of interpretive frames, problem definitions, and core competences engage in intense interactions around an issue, a problem, or an idea. The question here is how to create an environment or a setting in which this form of higher-order learning could occur. Clearly, the type of interaction represented by acrimonious press reports, blockades, and secretive shipping practices is not the right setting. The process of creating a GMO sector supplement, which involves representation and action by all stakeholders, ranging from GMO companies to activist NGOs, could be an approach and a process in which higher order learning could take place. In conceptual terms, the process could be described as an experiment or, more specifically, a "Bounded Socio-Technical Experiment" (BSTE), bounded by scope and time, but with a wide range of inputs for inducing higher-order learning among the participants.[68]

---

[67] Halina Brown and Philip Vergragt 2008. Bounded Socio-Technical Experiments as Agents of Systemic Change: The Case of a Zero-Energy Residential Building. *Technological Forecasting and Social Change* 75: 107–130.

[68] See H. S. Brown et al., Learning for Sustainability Transition through Bounded Sociotechnical Experiments in Personal Mobility. *Technology Analysis and Strategic Management* 15: 291–315 (2003).

Apart from creating an opportunity for testing and critically evaluating a new technology before its readiness to face the market, a BSTE allows for development of new social arrangements among actors, and to consider them as templates for other societal contexts. It is also a way to draw into the sustainability agenda actors who would otherwise not see a place for themselves in the types of projects in technological and system innovation that are often sponsored by powerful corporate, governmental, or NGO entities. A successful BSTE creates a socially embedded new configuration of technology or service that can serve as a starting point for further innovation and that, at a minimum, informs the policy-making process.

The GMO case presents an opportunity to apply such sociotechnical experimentation to increase learning, reduce controversies, and advance the policy process. The GMO controversy includes many technical and risk assessment problems to investigate, thus providing an anchor (the 'boundary') for the experiment, and a wide range of views and interpretive frames. Many of the parties to the controversy, notwithstanding their public positions, recognize both the inevitability of GMO technology and its considerable potential to produce social good as well as harm. Developing wise public policy on the GMO subject necessitates a broad-based discourse and mutual learning.

In our view, a BSTE should be organized by a relatively 'neutral' party who would have to provide a vision that can unite the participants, counter self-destructive internal pressures on the process, and frame its goals in terms of learning. The concept of sustainability, largely absent from the GMO discourse thus far, provides a powerful uniting theme for creating such a vision.

Conclusions

This chapter lays out a new framework for managing the GMO controversy. We have argued that GMOs constitute an example of a new technology with largely unknown consequences and risks, as well as high potential benefits for society. Risk assessment in its traditional form appears to be inadequate and many stakeholders perceive it as overly technocratic. Many have called for improved transparency and public participation in the GMO policy debate, but their pleas are seldom specific.

The Global Reporting Initiative (GRI) provides a model for engaging the public and other key stakeholders at the R&D stage of GMO development where the chances for influencing corporate behavior are greatest. This will not be easy, given the secrecy of companies and the high economic and social stakes, but it is necessary to alleviate the social unease with GMOs.

The GRI model offers the means for developing higher order learning among a wide variety of stakeholders, including those who have not been involved before. Such an approach could and should be part of the GMO regulatory framework so that enough resources and time can be made available for public discourse, possible course corrections, and regulations that would satisfy the majority of concerned stakeholders. When applied as BSTEs the model would offer opportunities for experimenting and learning, for discourse and dialogue, on various levels from problem definitions on specific issues to framing the issues in different ways. Although it is highly unlikely that worldviews of the participants will change during such a discourse, it is possible that a certain level of congruence on problem definitions can be reached. In other words, different parties may recognize each other's problem definitions and problem framings as legitimate and engage in finding solutions that accommodate each parties' interests and beliefs. Mutual respect and trust building are important features of such an endeavor. The process would also enhance the deliberative quality of GMO decision making. Given widespread unease about technological developments that are advancing too fast to allow accommodation by institutions, this may be hailed as a positive development by many stakeholders, particularly those concerned about sustainability.

Of course, there will be parties who are not interested in such a discourse. On the one hand, some multinational corporations may prefer the relatively fast introduction of new GMOs to improve their market share worldwide. However, the characteristics of an emergent institution imply that such behavior becomes increasingly unacceptable, thus damaging the reputation of such companies. On the other hand, some NGOs may continue to battle against all forms of GMOs.

Finally, the GRI model and BSTE format could be criticized as just another form of an enlightened technocratic approach. For better or for worse, emerging technologies cannot be ignored. They deserve serious attention from technologists, social scientists, policy makers, and the general public. Solutions cannot be realized without employing some technical approaches together with all nontechnical arguments. Whether this process will be branded as neo-technocratic or as truly democratic depends on the reporting system's specifics and the socio-technical experiment. GRI and BSTE could provide effective methods to integrate perspectives in democratic processes and resolve the GMO policy debate.

Acknowledgments

We want to thank Sujatha Byravan from Gene-Watch for her critical and constructive comments. The research related to the Global Reporting Initiative was supported by a grant from the National Science Foundation.

Appendix

The reputation of the mining companies, especially multinationals with operations in developing countries, was at a very low point during the 1990s, just as the Corporate Social Responsibility movement became popular. The reputation derived from the long history of environmental mismanagements and from several cases of egregious disregard for social and economic impacts on the local communities hosting these facilities in developing countries. Realizing the need to address their poor public image in a collective manner, the mining sector formed in 2001 the International Mining and Metals Council (ICMM). The first act of ICMM was to develop, collaboratively with International Institute for Sustainable Development, a Code of Conduct for Mining and Metals Industry, and to require all its members to formally adopt the Code. Furthermore, the members were required to produce annual sustainability reports as the means of demonstrating compliance with the Codes. The Council chose the GRI Guidelines (G2 version) as the reporting framework because of its requirement that both the guidelines and subsequent reports use a broadly based multi-stakeholder process. "At that time the mining industry had no choice but to engage with all their stakeholders – local communities, activists, global NGOs governments, and others – solve its many 'on the ground' problems" remarked an ICMM executive we interviewed. Furthermore, GRI had both the reputation and the experience with conducting such multi-stakeholder processes.

In 2003, ICMM went a step further by taking the initiative to develop a Sector Supplement for mining and metals, to be used by all its members. The Supplement was developed by a twenty-member international working group – co-chaired by the ICMM and GRI representatives – which included representatives from ten mining companies, Oxfam International, World Wildlife Fund, IFC/World Bank, National Union of Mineworkers of South Africa, two international socially responsible investment firms, one representative of an indigenous community in South America, and several technical experts and NGOs. This was a major step in reaching out between traditional adversaries, given that the NGOs in the group had a history of adversarial political actions directed at some of the participating companies. Over the next six months, the group produced numerous discussion papers and held three intense two-day meetings to reach consensus on the appropriate social, environmental, and economic indicators of sustainability performance. This was followed by an eleven-week public comment period, and a fourth working meeting to incorporate the comments from thirty-nine organizations. "This was emotionally and mentally an exhaustive process," noted one NGO participant, "It took us quite some time to internalize that our task was to develop the criteria for reporting performance, not the guidelines for performance itself. That was a learning experience."

As attested by several participants, on numerous occasions the coalition came close to dissolution over several contentious issues. Among those was the question of how specific to be in reporting waste (mine tailings), with opinions ranging from reporting absolute volumes to reporting policies and practices for safe handling of waste. Another contentious issue was whether companies should be required to report only on their processes for engaging indigenous communities or, at the other extreme, on the nature of the free prior informed consent from communities. The symbolism and the practical value of the latter dispute were huge because the concept of consent allowed to the host communities to stop or start mining production. Having a variety of participants appears to have been very helpful. Among the companies, the "best practice" companies cajoled and pulled forward other companies that were reluctant to adopt changes that the reporting indicators would require, or saw insurmountable difficulties in doing so. The socially responsible investors formed a natural bridge between NGOs and companies, having the trust, shared interests, and a common language with both. The World Bank brought an accumulated experience from around the globe, which could illuminate a discussion at crucial junctures. "It is possible, through conversation, to get to the point where you can move the discussion into an entirely new direction, one that was not the option when you first began," remarked the ICCM executive.

According to participant interviews, the final draft version, which was signed off by all group members late in 2004, embodies compromises from all participants. The process also exposed the structural resource-based imbalance of power in the multi-stakeholder GRI process. Because the participants are compensated only for direct expenses, but not for time, it puts NGOs and community representatives at a great disadvantage. "I had a difficult time making the case to my boss that the time I spent on this project was justified" remembered one NGO participant. And the representative of the indigenous communities dropped out midway, feeling out of place among the business-savvy westerners and their abstract concepts. However, the process of producing the Sector Supplement accomplished something very significant: it mobilized the individual participants to bring to the open, in a nonadversarial environment, those issues that were most important to them. It produced an agreement on the agenda for a social discourse about the impact of mining industry while not overstretching the capacity of the fragile coalition with a more difficult discussion about what level of performance is acceptable.

At the time of this writing, all ICMM members are required, as a membership precondition, to issue sustainability reports in accordance with G2 and the Sector Supplement. This is considered a pilot stage for the Supplement. Over the next year or so, and prior to producing the final version, GRI Secretariat will establish a Structured Feedback Process under the supervision of its Technical Advisory Council to capture the new learning that emerges through the use of the Guidelines. This process will once again engage a wide range of stakeholders, including the reporting companies and users of the GRI reports. "This is how you create a meaningful dialogue, isn't it?," noted a representative of one mining company.

9 Applying Safety Science to Genetically Modified Agriculture

Mathilde Bourrier

Introduction

Our main goal in this chapter is to determine whether decades of work in safety science and safety management have value for resolving controversies about GM agriculture. The implicit hypothesis is that there may be some commonalities between the safety issues posed by GM agriculture and other risky technologies, and potential benefits from using the toolbox of safety science that has been developed for more than thirty years in these other technological sectors. To avoid any misunderstanding, the discussion and points raised in this chapter do not cover the totality of the issues posed by genetic engineering. Our objective is to apply the safety science toolbox to the sharp end of the industry, that is, the crop growing practices on farmland.

Historically, safety science has dealt with high-risk technological enterprises (nuclear power industry, chemical industry, aviation industry) and more recently with medical practices (Vincent & De Mol, 2000; Amalberti, Auroy, & Berwick, 2005). Safety science has expanded over the years. It consists of research blending several disciplines, notably ergonomics, engineering, design, occupational health, sociology, or environmental studies. Issues like human and organizational failures, contributing factors to error production, implementation of risk/hazard mitigation strategies (such as risk analysis and modeling, event analysis, systematic incident reporting system, or safety culture and management surveys) are recurrent topics in safety science (Hale, 2006). Thus, another goal of this chapter is to further extend the reach of safety science to GM farming.

"Classical" agriculture has rarely involved safety experts except for accidental explosions of silos or batches of fertilizers on sites, or misuse of pesticides. A quick search of recent *Safety Science*'s journal abstracts from 1992 to 2008 supports this observation. A few exceptions are nevertheless worth mentioning (Morgaine, Langley, & Mc Gee, 2006; Thelin, 2002). On the contrary, food safety has always been a concern. Historians kindly and sometimes ironically warn us against the declared newness of such topics, recalling for example recurrent episodes of worries about the quality of bread throughout the past centuries (Ferrières, 2002; 2005; Kaplan, 1996). Similarly, although GM agriculture raises many concerns and fears, it has not been addressed by safety science experts. Indeed, as this volume demonstrates, GM farming adds new safety issues such as the inadvertent contamination of conventional crops, impacts on the environment, sustainability, as well as new food safety issues.

It is therefore quite remarkable that safety science has not been brought to bear upon the daily operations of GM farms, for example, as if genetic engineering, once outside the labs, were operator free. As if there were no need to study current practices of "first-line actors" as they are called in other industrial settings, namely the farmers, distributors, and food processors. Indeed, there is a need to consider said practices and their safety implications. There are some exceptions, when we turn to the economic literature for example. Economists are concerned with choices. Therefore, some papers offer an analysis of the significant variables that affect the use of GM products by specific farmers (Darr & Chern, 2002). In this volume, Menrad, Hirzinger, and Reitmeier also introduce us to the world of farmers through the lens of agricultural economists, when evaluating costs for farmers of the measures they must take to ensure coexistence between GM fields and non-GM fields (conventional or organic).

In the context of GMOs, the little we know points toward a model of farmers, knowledgeable but dependent upon the companies that develop and sell the seeds. Therefore, farmers growing GM crops are more like company employees than independent producers. In this context, the question of the management and the organizational factors involved in their daily agricultural practices should be of keen interest to safety science practitioners. This is a critical problem because the large and powerful corporations that are producing GMOs dictate the growing of GM crops, farming sites and practices, and essentially determine the fate of conventional farming and the environment.

The social science literature reflects this inclination to neglect the safety issue: it produced a vast body of studies on expertise and experts in the early days of genetic engineering, while GM crops were still a R&D issue. Some studies shed light on the intricacies of decision making within various expert committees in the beginnings of genetic engineering (Roy, 2001). Others have focused on expert discourse and misunderstanding of public perceptions (Wynne, 2001), while the organization of public debates and the level of public acceptance of GMOs have also been a recurrent topic for scholars (Joly et al., 2000). Not surprisingly, the interest in public perceptions of agricultural biotechnologies in Europe has been fuelled by the controversy over GMOs itself in Europe (PABE report, 2002; Gaskell et al., 1999).

Naturally the application and applicability of the so-called "precautionary principle" has been the meatiest part of this discussion (Godard, 1997; Bourg, 2001). The precautionary principle is a moral and political principle according to which if an action, policy, or product might cause severe or irreversible harm to the public or to the environment, in the absence of scientific consensus on the uncertainties of risks involved, the burden of proof rests on those who advocate taking the action, adopting the policy, or marketing the product. In European law, the precautionary principle has the status of a compulsory general principle, yet it is actually not as mandatory as it sounds.

The differences between Europe and the United States have also been of interest to scholars notably focusing on distinctive ways of regulating biotechnological innovations, such as GMOs across the Atlantic (See Baram's chapter in this volume [Chapter 2], Gaudillière & Joly, 2006). More recently, scholars have also explored the changing characteristics of food safety regulation in Europe (Ansell & Vogel, 2006) following food crises like BSE, beef hormones, or dioxin in poultry. Ansell and colleagues, for example, linked the GMO controversy to a long list of earlier crises, which paved the way for a strong and lasting mobilization in Europe. As Ansell puts it: " ... the mad cow crisis created an opportunity structure particularly conducive for the mobilization of anti-GMO demands" (2006:335).

However, industrial-scale agribusinesses cover vast territories in many countries; that fact calls for a different focus. It especially requires fieldwork studies at the production sites, which would enable experts to seriously discuss current farming practices, hence related quality and safety practices. There are such studies, to the extent that they address the complex evaluation of the costs of coexistence measures. Depending on the agreed-upon threshold (0.9% or 5% of traces of GM products in non-GM products), various scenarios are provided to farmers to assess the overall costs of cultivating GM products (see Chapters 2 and 6). Yet, the primary focus is not safety but economics at this stage, as it appears that costs of such measures are quite significant for European farmers.

A similar neglect for human and organizational factors and risks induced by medical practice was common only ten years ago in medicine. The report *To Err is Human: Building a Safer Health System*, published by the American Institute of Medicine in 1999, brought to light a gloomy picture that ended such a lack of interest.[1] The current catching up of the medical field and its dedication to improving both procedures (importing for example checklists from the aviation industry like Peter Pronovost's

---

[1] The report established, in particular, that more people are dying in the United States, in a given year, as a result of medical errors, than from motor vehicle accidents, breast cancer, or AIDS.

crusade, see Gawande, 2007) and the system design of health care (Gaba, 2000, Roberts, Madsen, & Van Stralen, 2005; Singer et al., 2003; Gaba, Singer, & Rosen, 2007; Singer et al., 2007) might give ideas to GM agribusiness.

Plan

In the first section of this chapter, GM crop growing is compared with more traditional industries concerned historically with safety paradigms. Is there any parallel to be drawn between GM farming and for example the nuclear industry or the chemical industry? A similar attempt had been made by Fahlbruch, Wilpert, and Vincent (2000) in their discussion of the transposition of traditional approaches to safety in the field of medicine. These authors concluded that medicine could import many safety policies and principles already in place in the nuclear industry or the aviation industry, such as event analysis, systematic reporting of near misses, comprehensive human factors training for employees of all ranks and safety culture surveys to determine the level of appropriation of safety principles by the workforce at large. In the context of GM crop growing, the implementation of safety policies of this kind could for instance prevent the contamination of conventional crops and minimize environmental impacts. Also, the design of "safety barriers" (which will be further detailed in the remainder of the chapter), a classic approach from the safety science toolbox, might help restore public trust and confidence with regard to the consumer's ability to maintain free choice. It might also be paramount in limiting liability costs in the event of contamination.

In a second section, we will present the various properties of the implicit safety model of GM crop growing. As it is clear from the various contributions in this volume, early experiments of GM crops made choices (or refrained from making choices) about safety that have strongly influenced the framing of safety issues in the context of GM crop growing.

Finally, some important principles that are at the core of safety management in high-risk industries are presented and discussed in terms
of their transferability to GM crop growing and its operating systems.
The sections will show that technological and organizational remediation
strategies have not yet been fully laid out in the context of GM crop cultivation. They could constitute part of the institutional and organizational
conditions for this production to be successful, and gain widespread
social acceptance.

Parallels that can be Drawn

Contested Technology

GMO engineering, and notably GM farming, is a *contested* technology much like the nuclear industry, or the chemical industry, which
have faced fierce opposition since their inception (Jaspers, 1988 & 1990;
Touraine et al., 1980). Despite the fact that some countries (France and
Japan) are nowadays using civil nuclear power with little opposition, the
possibility of a severe incident would be damaging to the entire industry even in countries where public acceptance is comparatively high.
Chernobyl has not been the "big one" (meaning an accident with the
potential to kill the whole industry or technology at stake) that experts
had predicted for the industry, but it surely eroded public confidence in
the industry worldwide, as is attested to by numerous polls and surveys.
(See for example the French Institut pour la Radioprotection et la Sûreté
Nucléaire yearly "Barometer of public opinion perception of risks and
safety measures," report, July 2007.)

In many respects, the management of GM farming activities is facing
the same kind of challenge. Similar to the nuclear experience, there are
parts of the world, where anti-GMO activists have destroyed GM experimental fields (French activist José Bové has earned worldwide fame for
his actions), whereas in other parts of the world there is well-established
legitimacy for such crops (for instance, Canada and the United States).

The "nuclear-free zones" of the seventies mirror the "GMO-free zones" discussed in Europe and notably in Switzerland and in Russia, where areas like the Volgograd, Kostroma, Murmansk, Ryazan, Sverdlovsk, or Ulyanovsk may possibly become "GM-free zones" (Sobolevskya, 2007). As shown in the case of Brazil developed by Farias and Allain in this volume (Chapter 5), the GMO issue may even evolve over a ten-year period from being highly controversial to innocuous, at least officially, for the benefit of a growing industry, operating under the "fight against hunger" banner.[2] According to Farias and Allain, this rapid conversion is to be interpreted in the larger context of the influence of globalization on developing countries.

As noted by Ansell and Vogel (2006) and reinforced in this volume by Vergragt and Szejnwald Brown, public controversy over GMOs has not been limited to the toxicity issue. It quickly expanded and touched upon issues such as the perceived power of strong corporations over farmers, the consequences of trade liberalization, globalization effects, the conservation of species and plants, and consumers' free choice (Bray, 2003).

As other examples of high-risk/high-hazards industries have shown (nuclear industry for example), a highly political profile implies an increase of the degree of public scrutiny and oversight. The latter in turn impact greatly on the daily operations of such an industry, in our case the management of GM crop growing. Although it may not be the case at the moment, in time it will surely become a growing concern for the management of GM agribusiness. As explained years ago by La Porte, the potentially highly publicized nature of any event or mishap is a burden, which in itself constitutes a risk for any organization (La Porte, 1996). Clearly, for such high-profile industries, tremendous efforts and substantial resources are geared to either building or restoring public trust and confidence (La Porte & Metlay, 1996, La Porte, 2001). This is with no doubt the case of the GM industry.

[2] Recently, a similar development affects civil nuclear power, operating now under the "fight against global warning" banner. After decades of suspicion, there is undoubtedly a nuclear revival worldwide including the United States.

Some experts go so far as to claim that the means devoted to these activities are in fact counterproductive: they are diverting precious resources that could actually be more fruitful to the organization, including invested in safety devices. The efforts to appear transparent and open to criticism is seen as pumping a lot of energy, at the expense of vigilant but sober safety management (Perrow, 1999: 366–368; Nichols & Wildavsky, 1987). From a different angle, Heimann (2005) is also weighing in on this issue. He suggests that the efforts a company puts into restoring safety after a big accident lead to an almost "fatal" drift toward type II risk – a waste of resources – which will "naturally" lead to safety shortcuts to be able to deliver on time as expected. Heimann describes this vicious circle as the biggest obstacle to sustained investments in safety.

Among industrial actors there is certainly a tendency to limit detailed regulation, and reluctance to address growing public anxiety. In Baram's description of the U.S. case, clearly a relaxed regulatory regime is more popular than any other. Yet, as Vergragt and Szejnwald-Brown suggest in their chapter, the growing practice of voluntary sustainability reporting by companies can serve to enhance a positive stance toward transparency by including as many stakeholders as possible. The example of the Global Reporting Initiative (GRI) could serve as a three-point framework to support the development of safety initiatives. Under the first part "Social Performance Indicators," human factors training could be offered to foster workplace safety and product safety. Under the section "Economic Performance Indicators," economic impact on non-GM crops growers could be addressed. And a third section called "Environmental Indicators" could be an adequate umbrella for worker safety and quality practices, waste management, and prevention of environmental risk. There are options worth investigating.

Uncertainty of the Hazards

It is probably not accurate to say, that like the nuclear industry or the chemical industry, GM crops have the potential to kill, cripple, or disable hundreds or thousands of people in an instant. Still, at this stage, the uncertainties[3] surrounding the toxicity issue, the dissemination issue, and the mutagenic potential are calling for close monitoring of any adverse effect. StarLink and ProdiGene are two emblematic examples of such unwanted events. They certainly both revealed a lack of "safety culture."

To a certain extent, the mutagenic potential that GM crops pose for the human body and the environment are similar to the potential of low radiation. These are hazards where the timeline question is particularly complex to evaluate, as the long-term effects might not be measurable nor visible for years or decades. In the case of GM plants, it might even been trickier: genetic mutation induced by radioactive exposure is much more documented than the potential genetic disorders induced by long-term ingestion of GMOs, or dissemination and cross-pollination of GMOs (creating super-bugs and super-plants).

In this respect, GM crop growing could be considered as a high-hazards industry, because it is bound to adopt very strict and tight regulation to prevent or deal with any unwanted consequences that at the moment are not totally envisioned nor proven (Marvier et al., 2007). In addition, failure during operations is not yet well characterized. As things stand, storage mingling between GM and non-GM products seems to qualify as failure, but such events do not prompt the same worry as a chemical spillover for example. As Armin Spök suggests in his chapter (Chapter 7), it might be different for the third generation of GMOs, the plant-made pharmaceuticals, GM crop-produced vaccines, and other pharmaceutical products. GM drug-producing crops could contaminate GM and non-GM food crops and derivative food products, as in the Prodigene incident and ultimately impact food consumers. For these

---

[3] As a recall, seven types of risk apply to GMOs, summarized by Pretty (2001): "1) Horizontal gene flows; 2) New forms of resistance and pest problems; 3) Recombination to produce new pathogens; 4) Direct and indirect effects of novel toxins; 5) Loss of biodiversity from changes to farm practices; 6) Allergenic and immune system reactions; 7) Antibiotic resistance marker genes."

special products, the dissemination issue should be approached with extra care.

Other parallels can be drawn: for instance the effects of low radiation near nuclear power plants is one of those issues, as well as the slow poisoning and health effects on human beings (especially on the fertility rate) due to the heavy use of pesticides over the long run. One needs to mention of course that in these two cases, experts disagree (which does not mean that they deny the problems, but that they do not agree on the magnitude of the consequences). Similarly experts disagree on the two main issues regarding full-scale production of GM crops: the dissemination issue and the toxicity issue (we will return to this point in the second section).

Moreover, as in more traditional high-risk industries, suspicion is so high in parts of the world that as La Porte predicted years ago those industries will in fact be subject to "never ending management." La Porte applied the term to the operations of nuclear waste facilities, where tons of toxic radioactive waste has to be stored long-term, regardless of possible policy changes over time. Society has to be robust enough to actually ensure that such products will always be monitored in terms of commitments that former generations made for future ones. Undoubtedly GMOs have the potential to require the same treatment, institutional care, and constancy (La Porte & Keller, 1996).

Complexity, Tight Coupling, and Failure

If we take the "classic" definition of a high-hazard and complex system, three characteristics emerge: high potential consequences, tight functional coupling, and potentially rapid evolution of untoward events. On these terms, by and large the production of GM crops appears to fit with this definition.

In addition, according to Perrow's theory (1984, 1999), the more complexity and tight coupling there is in a system, the more safety is in danger. In fact, it is extremely interesting to benchmark GM production processes against Perrow's classic distinction between loosely coupled systems and tightly coupled systems. GM crop growing seems to qualify for a rather tightly coupled system in the causal sense. For example, once the seeds are in the fields, there is no turning back, no exit route: burning the crops is possible, but only if the eventual safety problem has been detected in due time, that is, before the harvest. However, these processes are also loosely or semi-coupled in the social sense. GM crop growing itself is quite loosely coupled. Fields are spread all over the world. Yet, because the GMO market is in the hands of just a few corporations, one could argue that there is an element of centralization. Hence, the term semi-coupled seems preferable.

Perrow's classic idea that buffers and redundancies fortuitously available are a major requirement for safer design is of special interest for our discussion. In the case of GM crops, these buffers could probably never be fortuitous. One cannot yet picture a future where some plants will naturally and spontaneously grow to encapsulate GM plants, and become a sort of a plant-made cocoon to protect genetically modified organisms from dissemination. The whole question actually is how to put these buffers in place rigorously with respect to two stringent requirements.

The first one is economic. Buffer zones between GM crops and non-GM crops have to be kept minimal, to maximize land use and minimize GM farmers' sunk costs. In addition, because in Europe GM farmers are responsible for applying and bearing the cost of coexistence measures such as buffers, the smaller the fallow field the better, for GM farmers to make enough money. The evaluation provided by Menrad, Hirzinger, and Reitmeier in this volume (Chapter 6) gives a rather undecided picture on this issue. According to their study, two variables are of great importance: (1) the size of neighboring non-GM seed production plots; (2) the level of threshold for GM presence in non-GM seeds. Small variations of these factors impact the results quite substantially. Interestingly, Menrad and colleagues stress the fact that the cost of specific stewardship or training programs designed for farmers and aimed at helping them to implement the suggested coexistence measures in agronomic practices is not included in available studies.

The second requirement deals with safety and has to do with the prevention of any adventitious presence of GM seeds in conventional seeds. When plant-made pharmaceuticals reach their full deployment, this requirement will be critical. In this case, buffer zones have to be large and the distance between crops as big as possible. These precautions might not be enough, and other strategies detailed further next are under discussion. As we can see, such dilemma is at the core of any concrete discussion of GMOs future in Europe for example, where the coexistence requirement is applied (Beckmann, Soregaroli, & Wesseler, 2006; Coléno, Angevin, & Lécroart, 2009).

Following further upon Perrow's framing of the complexity issue, it is certainly true that there are "hidden complex interactions" in GM crop growing, notably those posed by the environmental impact of such crops. Some of these interactions are not yet foreseeable, because data collection is too limited so far. Some scientists are dissatisfied with the data currently at their disposal.[4] It will take decades to properly compare data and draw conclusions on potential negative effects of GMOs on wildlife or biodiversity.

Last, one could argue that the relative diversity of the stakeholders increases the risk that safety might not be dealt with at the required level of stewardship. The GMO industry is a rather complex network of stakeholders. First, we encounter the biotech firms (Mosanto, Bayer, Syngenta, DuPont, Dow, and so on), the operators (managers, technicians, and farmers) of large, industrial-scale agribusiness, those growing

---

[4] As Marvier et al. (2007:1465) put it: "Public debate regarding risks and benefits of genetically modified crops continues unabated. One reason for the unrelenting controversy is that disagreement about new technologies often has little to do with scientific uncertainty but instead arises from differing personal values and differing levels of trust in public institutions. However, in the case of GM crops, scientific analyses have also been deficient. In particular, many experiments used to test the environmental safety of GM crops were poorly replicated, were of short duration, and/or assessed only a few of the possible response."

GMOs and those who do not choose to grow GMOs, and expect to be protected from any dissemination incident in their fields. Secondly, consumers: Those who do not bother, and those who bother actively, more precisely anti- and pro-GMO activists; We find also independent labs, scientific experts from different disciplines (biology, toxicology, environmental sciences, agricultural economics . . .) along with regulators – at national, federal in the case of the U.S. or supranational level in the case of the EU –, and last politicians, to only name the most important ones. All these stakeholders bring different perspectives to the question of GM farming safety.

Stewardship probably would require a minimal institutional centralization. This point will later be addressed in the context of potential benefits for the GM industry from transposing existing safety managing devices. One such benefit could be the implementation of events reporting systems, thus prompting collective action in support of some kind of centralized monitoring system.

Unfolding the GM Crop Growing Safety Model: The Legacy of Early Choices

In this section, we will turn to the implicit GM crop growing safety model as grasped through the various contributions in this book. This exercise in itself entails notable difficulties. In fact, "safety" is a bit of a misnomer here, as for most experts there are no safety issues in the classic sense, regarding GM products. Yet, some of the claims that GM crops pose environmental risks and also threaten non-GM crops are increasingly supported by new scientific evidence (for example, gene flows are occurring). This situation requires the adoption of constraints on the sitting of GM crops and the implementation of and adherence to special practices for their farming, storing, and distribution to minimize risks and simultaneously minimize "contamination" costs for the GM and non-GM industry.

Despite some resistance to tackling these issues under the "safety" umbrella, two distinct problems could be of interest for a safety approach. First, the toxicity issue: will eating GM products affect our health, modify how certain organs function, now or in the future? Toxicity measures and tests are provided to assess this matter. Secondly, the dissemination issue: will growing GM crops affect the environment so much as to provoke substantial ecological changes in living species, in other categories of plants? Ecological assessment is currently being developed but more time is needed to be able to draw conclusions. Furthermore, will it reduce biodiversity?

The toxicity issue has been dealt with from the outset, in the early eighties and outcrossing, at the very end of the pre-market tests in the mid-1990s. This recent history gives us insights on choices made at the time that precluded the adoption of broader safety practices, aimed at mitigating environmental risk for example.

The Implications of a Product Safety Model Versus a Process Safety Model

At the beginning, the kind of safety assessment performed by the various institutions in charge of the food safety standards, when authorizing GM products on the market, mainly focused on the intrinsic qualities of the product. This has been (and still is) especially the case for the American philosophy toward GMOs and less so for the struggling EU philosophy, embodied by the European Food Safety Authority.

In retrospect there has been much consideration of the qualities and performance of products per se, and less so of their possible interactions in the field with other plants and species or deterioration at storage sites. Consequently, safety has mainly been dealt with in two ways: First, through the assessment of each novel GM trait. For example, the safety of a particular protein regarding toxicity is assessed using animal feeding tests; secondly, through the assessment of the unforeseen changes in plant metabolism as a result of gene transfer. Therefore, at first safety issues involved in growing, storing, or exporting the GM plants were not seen as part of the scope. They were left out.

At present, in the United States there is no obligation for farmers and growers to organize postmarket environmental monitoring. Limited attention is paid to the exact conditions under which such plants are cultivated, stored, exported, and handled. From the beginning a deliberate choice was made to treat them as any other food product (see Chapter 2). In addition, the various incidents that have been reported, concerning dissemination, cross-pollination, or commingling errors between storage facilities, have not been directly life threatening for human beings. For many experts, these events are not classified as "safety-related" problems but more as "quality-related" issues.

Nonetheless, these events received a lot of public scrutiny, especially because they exposed to the world the hidden face of the whole process: that is, the daily operations at the production sites. Human and organizational factors are suddenly in the loop, seeking a place at the table. As Armin Spök warns us in his eye-opening chapter (Chapter 7), these human and organizational issues will not be ignored for long, as they constitute challenges for further development of plant-made pharmaceuticals. These crops should not occur accidentally in the food and feed chain because unlike first-generation GM crops, plant-made pharmaceuticals are purposely designed to have a biological effect on man or animal health and well-being.

This neglect for environmental issues is less true in EU recommendations and philosophy, although interest in the subject is somewhat moderate. An excerpt of the "Opinion of the Scientific Panel on Genetically Modified Organisms on the Post Market Environmental Monitoring (PMEM), adopted on January 25, 2006," will illustrate our point. Indeed, when read carefully, ambiguity emerges. If the first sentence is quite clear "A plan for Post Market Environmental Monitoring (PMEM) of genetically modified (GM) plants is *mandatory*[5] in all applications for deliberate release submitted under EU directive 2001/18/EC and EU regulation 1829/2003," the further developments in the opinion weaken

[5] Italics added.

the point: "PMEM is composed of case-specific monitoring and general surveillance of GM plants. Case-specific monitoring is *not obligatory*[6] but may be required to verify the environmental risk assessment, whereas a general surveillance plan must be part of the application," continuing with "The GMO panel concludes that general surveillance cannot be hypothesis-driven, but *should when possible*,[7] make use of existing monitoring systems in addition to more focused monitoring systems (i.e., farm questionnaires)." The wording limits the impact of the first sentence. One can conclude from these excerpts that Post-Market Environmental Monitoring (PMEM) is not yet standard practice among growers and farmers. Safety management has not yet come to GM production at farm sites.

This original orientation, previously summarized, has been further supported by the type of safety assessment, the "substantial equivalence principle" that is currently accepted as state of the art for market authorization of GM products. It certainly led to a rather restricted safety perspective on large-scale GM production.

The Implications of the "Substantial Equivalence" Principle for a Safety Approach

The "substantial equivalence" concept explained in this book by Marianne Shauzu is paramount. Essentially, for regulators to grant market authorization, the required demonstration revolves around a systematic comparison between the properties of the GMO-derived food with existing, "natural" products used as food or food sources. As stated by Marianne Shauzu: "It is based on the idea that existing products used as foods or food sources can serve as a basis for comparison when assessing the safety and nutritional value of GMO-derived food. It implies that if the modified food is found to be substantially equivalent to an existing food

---

[6] Italics added.
[7] Italics added.

or food component with regard to phenotypic and agronomic character-istics and chemical composition, it can be treated in the same manner with respect to safety" (see Chapter 3).

Earlier in the history of GMOs, molecular biology was the core, and almost the unique science that was able to evaluate and authorize exper-iments throughout Europe (for example) in the late 1980s and early 1990s. At the time, it was argued that the safety of GM products was essentially determined by the quality of the molecular design. The better and duly described by biotech firms seeking approval for tests, the safer the design would be, according to biologists. Moreover, the conviction that the design had to be as simple and elegant as possible to be deemed safe contributed heavily to producing a type of safety assessment, based on the intrinsic qualities of the new plant itself (Roy, 2001). At this point, safety was only considered from the angle of molecular biology. There was no attempt to broaden the context of safety issues, and include mat-ters such as dissemination or commingling errors at storage sites.

The second term of reference is then a "natural" product that does not need to be assessed because it has already been cultivated for decades (or centuries) with no history of toxicity. For many experts, a GMO is after all just another plant. For most of them at the time, a GMO was structurally safer because complete design traceability could be detailed and provided. Explicitly the dominant philosophy was that GMOs were much more under control than existing plants (which have centuries of enhancement with less rigorous techniques), hence, they were deemed much safer (Kahn, 1998).

One of the implications of such a narrow vision of safety is that it focuses mainly on the plants' characteristics, and neglects the interaction of such plants with existing ecosystems. Also it fails to address compa-nies' responsibilities for growing them, or the type of organization of work needed to manage safely such crops.

This early choice had to be reevaluated when growing concerns emerged among experts who put this new technology's weak point on the table: namely, the integration of such seeds, when sown on large fields, with their environment and the necessity to address current agricultural practices. So far the safety evaluation of GM products had been conducted without consideration for farmers and growers. Moreover, producers claimed that it was their responsibility, their turf, to watch over such a safety issue, if any. Interestingly enough, a similar claim has always been made by the nuclear industry, for instance, when asked how it goes about contracting practices during maintenance outages. Even in heavily regulated industries, some domains are beyond the reach of regulators.

The Dissemination Issue, Outcrossing, Commingling Error: The Hidden Flaw in the Safety Model of GM Production

Finally, ten years ago the safety assessment of GMOs was forced to incorporate the dissemination issue. In Europe, the controversy over such problems emerged in the mid-1990s, when the Belgian firm, Plant Genetic System (GPS), sought authorization by the British authority for its rapeseed, in 1994. It was only then that biovigilance appeared as a major part of the safety assessment of GMOs.

This rather late emergence is rooted first, as we explained earlier, in the predominance of molecular biologists in the early stages of the evaluation process and second, in the type of experiments that had taken place up until that point. Furthermore, it seems traditional biomolecular experts considered that agronomic practices were outside their competency, scope, and mandate. Mostly, they were used to implementing biological containment, that is "pollen proof" tunnels, and limiting interaction with other fields, as pillars of their safety protection policy. For small-scale experiments, these protection measures seemed adequate. However, transposing these measures and techniques to large fields seemed rather unrealistic.

This narrow vision of safety, linked only to the product, with no consideration for its environment nor for the production system involved, strongly influenced the fate of GM crop growing safety management. In the early 1990s, market authorizations seemed far away for experts and their model of reference was still the lab, with its biological containment possibilities (pollen tunnel for example), and the capability to destroy small experimental crops in case of a problem. At the time, studying pollen flows had not been seen as a priority. Suddenly, market authorization had to be granted and along came biovigilance as a new and inescapable pillar in the safety assessment. Yet, "classical" safety barriers used in other high-risk industries are not at all perceived as a reference model. There is no connection between the two worlds: contamination (of radioactive materials for example) and dissemination (adventitious presence of GM seeds in conventional crops) do not compare. Be that as it may, such a far-reaching comparison is worth drawing, as the workshop that spawned this volume shown. What could serve as reasonable safety options for the production of GM crops, given the safety toolbox available?

Opening the "Classic" Safety Science Toolkit

Classic Barriers

The dissemination issue raises a well-known safety problem, revolving around buffers and system barriers. The truth is that providing for an efficient strategy against wind blowing and bees is probably much more complex than containing the activities of a high-risk technology.

In other high-risk industries where the dissemination issue is critical, being directly related to radiological contamination, chemical spills, or toxic effluents, the thinking is further advanced. Along with "safety zones" or "exclusion zones," the notion of "defense-in-depth" combines several types of barriers. At first, "defense-in-depth," historically from the nuclear industry, was almost exclusively seen as technological in nature.[8] Now it is understood as a much more complex notion,

---

[8] In the case of nuclear power plants, as a first barrier the nuclear materials are encapsulated in zirconium metallic tubes, the reactor has a stainless steel envelop, and thirdly; massive concrete walls protect the whole machine. That arrangement makes for the historical "defense-in-depth" of the nuclear industry.

blending technology, procedures, organization, communication, and individual behavior.

The "modern" defense-in-depth concept has profited from two sources at least: (1) The results of the human factors research on categories of errors and mishaps, which led to more effective error prevention and risk mitigation strategies (Reason, 1990; Reason, 1997; Amalberti, 2005); (2) The results of organizational studies attempting to better understand the social production of safety during "normal" operations (Rochlin, La Porte, & Roberts, 1987; Weick, 1987; La Porte & Consolini, 1991; Rochlin, 1998; Weick & Roberts, 1993; Bourrier, 1999, Bourrier, 2002; Perin, 2005), along with important work done on major accidents (Vaughan, 1996; Starbuck & Farjoun, 2005), which revealed the mechanisms of what Vaughan has labeled "the normalization of deviance," or Snook, "the drift into failure" (Snook, 2000).

Of course, the idea that barriers have to be diverse has been heavily influenced by the findings that numerous accident investigation commissions brought to light: Big accidents are rarely triggered by a unique, isolated human error, as often claimed in the past. Nor are they only caused by faulty technology. On the contrary, organizational factors play a crucial role in the fatal development of catastrophes, such as Chernobyl (Reason, 1987), Bhopal (Shrivastava, 1987), the two losses of the NASA shuttles (*Challenger*, 1986, *Columbia*, 2003), or the contaminated blood scandal in Europe in the late 1980s (Setbon, 1993), to name only a few. For most safety experts, the organizational factors are the next frontier to be explored so as to see continuing progress in safety in high-risk industries. This hard-to-achieve progress will guarantee that the central role of these systems in the functioning of our societies, despite the risks and hazards involved, still meet with broad public support. To illustrate our point: airplanes are considered as safe as possible, safer than any other means of transportation (even if new technical improvements are always possible, probably not much progress can be obtained there), yet the current civil aviation safety problems point toward problems in air traffic management and airport infrastructure, which are complex organizational problems and serious contributing factors to near-misses, incidents, and accidents.

Briefly, the first barrier is *physical or technological,* essentially owing to the design of the technology itself. Typically, massive concrete walls, fire- and explosion-proof structures, earthquake-proof structures, flooding-proof levees, or spill receptacles are technological in nature. *Administrative barriers* constitute a second line of defense, through detailed procedures, that describe the exact functioning and limitations of each safety agency. They also provide preventive maintenance and routine surveillance to limit exposure to potential problems and to check potential degradation of passive barriers. *Organizational barriers* are a third defense. They describe the exact responsibilities of each category of employee and a description of key processes along with a predetermined division of labor covering various situations for all stages, from the routine production mode to the emergency mode. Formal communication flows and standardized language are also provided, as well as the emphasis on formal and informal debriefing and opportunities to exchange freely on surprises and unwanted events. Finally, adequate training, personnel selection, and specific licensing can be considered *individual barriers.* In addition, these industries have put in place access limitations and diverse devices (alarms, red flags, and signature checkpoints on procedures) to avoid breaches in the defenses or to warn employees about possible breaches. The key point is to provide the first-line actors with an updated view of the state of the system at all times.

It is of interest to note in passing that the medical field is also interested in this line of thinking, and is struggling to put in place system barriers capable of reducing preventable errors (Amalberti et al., 2005; Carroll & Rudolph, 2006).

This description is not aimed at suggesting that those barriers are sufficient to guarantee operational safety. Of course they are not. The whole debate after Chernobyl led to the recognition that much more was needed to operate such complex systems and ensure reliability and safety (Schulman, 1993; Bourrier, 2001; Weick & Sutcliffe, 2001; Perin, 2005). The idea here is to envision plausible parallel efforts to tackle the dissemination issue for GM crop growing. What could be a sensible "defense-in-depth" for large-scale GM production?

Defense-in-depth for GM Crop Growing: A Snapshot?

The design of "defense-in-depth" for this kind of production should certainly not be envisioned in the same way as the more traditional "defense-in-depth" already in place in high-risk industries. Building fences against gene flows and winds is a daunting challenge. However, the difficulty should not and have not discouraged the various stakeholders from finding acceptable precautions, which could contribute to building a modern hazard-mitigation strategy. Several ideas have been brought in, as this volume illustrates. They could be interpreted as an embryonic model of "defense-in-depth," whose development is more pressing in the context of Plant-Made Pharmaceuticals. Vaccines, monoclonal antibodies, therapeutic enzymes, hormones, or interferon are among the substances that could be obtained from GM plants such as maize, tobacco, soybean, or barley. Some examples of possible barriers are explored next.

Technological and Physical Barriers

Biological containment could be envisioned as a technological barrier. It includes measures aimed at preventing genetically modified organisms and their transgenes from disseminating into the environment. So far three major technical strategies are under consideration: cleistogamous plants; male-sterile plants, and transplastomic plants. In cleistogamous plants, flowers do not open, hence no pollen is released. In male-sterile plants, no pollen is produced and in transplastomic plants, the new genes have not been inserted in the nuclear DNA but in the DNA of the chloroplasts, hence pollen is not a transmitter, which prevents gene flow from the genetically modified plant to other plants. So far this third option has only been proven reliable for tobacco. As an example of a so-called technological barrier, operating like a "natural" molecular confinement mechanism, there is a provision under discussion to the effect that plant-made pharmaceuticals will only be hosted by nonfood/nonfeed crops (like tobacco), hence reducing the risk of contaminating the food/feed chain. These strategies relate to "safety by design" strategies.

In addition, the setup of a closed system for production (contained conditions and no chance of open pollination) using airtight greenhouses, and covering inflorescence, qualifies as a physical barrier. Crop destruction after extraction of protein is also a physical barrier to prevent any unwanted mutation. Of course fences and "no entry" signs, as in any high-risk plant, are also considered.

A fourth element, included in the first barrier type, uses agronomic techniques: coexistence measures like crop rotation, cultivation in remote areas, buffer zones, staggered planting of GMOs versus neighboring food and feed crops, or distinct visual markers exist already and could serve as an interesting addition to a more complete arsenal.

Administrative Barriers

In Chapter 7, Armin Spök gives examples of several Standard Operating Procedures currently discussed or proposed by the U.S. Department of Agriculture. They are geared to plant-made pharmaceuticals, but could well apply to first-generation GM crops. Relying on Spök's information, Standard Operating Procedures will be developed for seeding, transplanting, harvesting, cleaning, storing, dying, and processing of biomass. They will also control the use of machinery, and promote dedicated use of machinery to minimize contacts between GM and non-GM products. Incidentally, this list of concrete activities carried out on farm sites gives us a perspective on the broad safety aspects involved.

Organizational Barriers

The different provisions under the label organizational barrier in tradi-tional high-risk industries do not seem to have been laid out yet in the context of large-scale GM production. We have no information on the way agronomic activities at set up on farm sites. Who are the "first-line operators," how are they organized? Who is in charge of monitoring sur-prises, dissemination issues, commingling, storage errors, safe disposal, destruction or recycling of biomass, and surveillance of interaction with the environment? What is the nature of the division of labor and what is its role in the safe production and delivery of the end products? What kind of contingency planning is there in the event of adventitious pres-ence of GM seeds in conventional seeds?

There is no doubt that these organizational factors will come under public scrutiny in the case of a severe contamination incident, with poten-tially negative health effects. Yet so far, as in early periods of "classic" high-risk industries development, emphasis on these issues has not been a priority.

Human Barriers

In line with our comment on organizational factors, there is no informa-tion on the characteristics of the operators handling GM production. No information on the requirements that corporations or agricultural firms have put in place for the recruitment and the specific safety and qual-ity training of their employees. No doubt such issues could potentially become important in the case of unwanted errors and mishaps.

As Menrad, Hirzinger, and Reitmeier (Chapter 6) and also Spök (Chapter 7) observed in their respective chapters, so far the adoption of coexistence measures on one hand and the adoption of good safety and quality practices to avoid dissemination and contamination incidents on the other, are not top priorities. Even so, both should have a great impact on the social organization of crop coexistence. Moreover, it appears that coexisting measures and safety and quality practices are kept separately.

Interim Conclusion

Despite some elements that are already envisioned in the field, a systematic hazard-mitigation response combining technological, physical, organizational, and individual barriers on a par with what exists in other high-risk industries has not been fully deployed. To appreciate this situation, one has to recall that most experts do not see the dissemination issue in safety terms. The dissemination problem is rather presented as a consequence of consumers' free choice, mainly in Europe. Therefore buffers or rotation zones are not seen as a risk-mitigation measure to contain/prevent/reduce the possible adverse effects of products, as their interaction with the rest of the environment is yet to be understood. These measures are only tolerated and promoted as a market requirement. This might explain why a comprehensive response has not yet emerged. However, this attitude might change drastically in the context of plant-made pharmaceutical development.

Conclusions: Propositions

The Standard Operations Procedures (SOPs) emerging in the context of molecular farming could also be applicable to more traditional GM cultivation. SOPs could constitute a first response to the growing public demand for more systematic quality and safety traceability. This effort could foster a keen interest in agricultural and agronomic practices and a necessary consideration of organizational and human factors that have been so far neglected throughout the process.

However, the march toward SOPs should not become an alibi and be the sole response to safety and quality alarms. As the examples of other industries have taught a vast community of experts, one can only achieve part of the goals by designing procedures. There should also be a consideration of the various factors that play a role in fostering safety culture on sites and throughout the marketing process. Special attention given to organizational issues at industrial-scale agribusiness and sites and a better understanding of the sociology and economy of GM crop growing, including its institutional and political environment, are two key aspects of a possible step toward this goal. It is also one way to start building an emergency-preparedness response in case of an adverse event.

So far, the public has little knowledge of the organizational and institutional policies already put in place by this industry to recover promptly from a problematic event. Studies on the day-to-day operations at farm sites could also contribute to a new perspective on this technology, too often considered only as laboratory "magic," or a potentially harmful technology.

The other tool that could be put in place addresses the systematic reporting of unwanted and adverse events (such as contamination of non-GM crops, commingling at storage sites, and gene flows). Clearly, this kind of effort would require the industry and/or the regulators to don a stewardship role that seems lacking at the moment.

The nuclear industry as well as civil aviation has now developed institutional links across countries and companies (even imperfectly) that assume this stewardship role.[9] The chemical industry is struggling to put in place a formal exchange of information, as transparent as possible. Industry patents and trade secrets are serious obstacles to such initiatives. The same sort of obstacles is certainly at the core of the wariness one can perceive from the GM firms. However, such efforts have gradually been considered as mandatory after severe accidents struck not only

---

[9] For the nuclear industry, several institutions are taking on this stewardship role: IAEA, the International Atomic Energy Agency, a United Nations agency based in Vienna, INPO, the Institute of Nuclear Power Operators in the United States, WANO, the World Association of Nuclear Operators, WENRA, the World Association of Nuclear Regulators. In the case of the civil aviation, the International Civil Aviation Organization is a strong equivalent.

a single company, operating the site or plant responsible, but the industry as a whole. As if the perspective of having to suffer from bad operators prompted each of these high-risk industries to organize their own vigilance (Rees, 1994).

The fact that NGOs and anti-GMO activists have websites collecting data on various incidents regarding the production of GM crops (the Greenpeace contamination index for example) could also be a strong motivation for the industry to organize at a more macro level to set up its own forum of exchange and data collection, notably on unwanted and adverse events. The growing practice of voluntary sustainability reporting by companies, described in this volume by Vergragt and Brown (Chapter 8) could be an adequate vector for such cultural change.

Finally, comparing the situation of GM crop growing with "classic" high-risk industries on one hand and the medical field on the other hand according to the various dimensions discussed in the chapter, sheds light on the merits of such a comparison (see Table 1).

To sum up, compared to classic high-risk industries and hospitals, there is scant maturity regarding the human and organizational factors issues involved in the safe and reliable management of GM agricultural sites. Interestingly, the medical field, where failure is accepted (less and less so) and death always possible, as opposed to the production of GM crops, where failure would not be tolerated, is far more advanced in taking into account the crucial contribution of teamwork, communication, and organizational dimensions in the delivery of safe care, than the GM industry.

Hence, there is much room for improvement in the management of hazards and risks at agricultural production sites. It could certainly benefit from programs developed for other high-hazards industries. For one thing, political pressure and public opinion will probably force corporations to initiate some actions in this direction. However, more importantly, the requirements in term of quality and safety of the end-products (GM, as well as non-GM), and those of the plant-made pharmaceuticals will probably compel companies to attend to these issues, because they

Table 1. *Summary of Properties Across Industries*

"Classic" High-Risk Industry	Hospital	GM Crop Growing
Contested Technology	Consensual Technology	Contested Technology
High public scrutiny	Growing public scrutiny	Growing public scrutiny
Risks are well documented	Partial uncertainty remains	Uncertainty of the hazards and risks
Some uncertainties remain		
Operational errors can be characterized	Operational errors exist They are sometimes difficult to trace	What is an operational error?
Failure is unacceptable	Failure is acceptable (less and less so)	Failure is unacceptable
Death is not expected	Death is possible	Death is not expected
Rather centralized	Rather decentralized	Rather decentralized
Highly regulated	Mildly regulated	Mildly regulated (national differences)
Safety in design	Some safety in design	Some safety in plant design
Systematic defense-in-depth	No defense-in-depth	No defense-in-depth (some is appearing for molecular farming)
Physical containment	Not really applicable	Some physical containment
No fortuitous buffers	Informal recovery of errors	No fortuitous buffers
Incident Reporting Systems exist	Incident Reporting Systems exist more and more	Absence of Incident Reporting System
Standard Operating Procedures for every thing	Some Standard Operating Procedures	Standard Operating Procedures under discussion
Safety centered	Duty of care centered	Safety is not an issue
Organizational and Human Factors important for safety	Organizational and Human Factors important for a safe care	Organizational and Human Factors so far absent from the picture
Safety culture a key issue	Safety culture becoming a key issue	No safety culture

are at the core of any safe production. Probably equally important for safe GM production are the intrinsic biological traits of the GM product *and* the social conditions in its production.

Acknowledgments

I thank Claudine Burton-Jeangros and Todd La Porte for their important help with this chapter.

REFERENCES

Amalberti, R., Y. Auroy, D. Berwick, P. Barach, Five System Barriers to Achieving Ultrasafe Health Care, *Annals of Internal Medicine*, Vol. 142, N° 9, 756–765, 2005.

Ansell, C. & D. Vogel, *What's the beef? The contested Governance of European Food Safety*, The MIT Press, 2006.

"Opinion of the Scientific Panel on Genetically Modified Organisms on the Post Market Environmental Monitoring (PMEM), adopted on January, the 25th, 2006," *The EFSA Journal*, N° 319, 1–27, 2006.

Beckmann, V., Soregaroli, C., & Wesseler, J., Coexistence rules and regulations in the European Union, *American Journal of Agricultural Economics*, Vol. 88, N° 5, 1193–1199, 2006.

Bourg, D., *Parer aux risques de demain: Le principe de précaution*, Paris, Seuil, 2001.

Bourrier, M., *Le nucléaire à l'épreuve de l'organisation*, Paris, Presses Universitaires de France, 1999.

Bourrier, M., Constructing Organizational Reliability: the Problem of Embeddedness and Duality, in Misumi, J; Wilpert, B.; Miller, R. (Eds.), *Nuclear Safety: A Human Factors Perspective*, London: Taylor & Francis, 25–48, 1999.

Bourrier, M., *Organiser la fiabilité*, Paris: L'Harmattan, 2001.

Bourrier, M., Bridging Research & Practice: The Challenge of Normal Operations Studies, *Journal of Contingencies and Crisis Management*, Vol. 10, N° 4, 173–180, 2002.

Bray, F., Genetically Modified Foods: Shared Risk and Global Action, in Barbara Herr Harthorn and Laury Oaks (Eds.), *Risk, Culture, and Inequality*, Westport, CT: Praeger, 185–207, 2003.

Carroll, J. & J. W. Rudolph, Design of High Reliability Organizations in Health Care, *Quality and Safety in Health Care*, Vol. 15, N° 4–9, 2006.

Darr, D. & W. Chern, Analysis of Genetically Modified Organism Adoption by Ohio Grain Farmers, Paper presented at the 6th International conference on "*Agricultural Biotechnology: New Avenues for Production, Consumption, and Technology Transfer*," Ravello, Italy, 11–14/07, 2002.

Fahlbruch, B., B. Wilpert, & C. Vincent, Approaches to Safety, in Vincent, C. & B. de Mol (eds.), *Safety in Medicine*, Oxford: Pergamon, Elsevier, 9–30, 2000.

Ferrières, M., *Histoire des peurs alimentaires, du Moyen Âge à l'aube du XXème siècle*, Paris, Seuil, 2002.

Ferrières, M., Risque alimentaire et conférence du consensus: l'expérience de 1669, in Cécile Lahellec (Ed.), *Risques et crises alimentaires*, Paris, Lavoisier, 3–20, 2005.

Gaba, D. M., Structural and Organizational Issues in Patient Safety: A Comparison of Health Care to Other High-Hazard Industries, *California Management Review*, Vol. 43, N° 1, 83–102, 2000.

Gaba, D. M.; S. J. Singer, & A. Rosen, Safety Culture: Is the Unit the Right Unit of Analysis? *Critical Care Medicine*, Vol. 35, N° 1, 314–316, 2007.

Gaskell, G., Bauer, M., Durant, J., & Allum, N., Worlds apart–The reception of genetically modified foods in Europe and the US, *Science*, 285 (16 July), 384–387, 1999.

Gaudillière, J.-P. & P.-B. Joly, Appropriation et régulation des innovations biotechnologiques: Pour une comparaison transatlantique, *Sociologie du travail*, 48, 330–349, 2006.

Gawande, A. The Checklist, If something so simple can transform intensive care, what else can it do?. *New Yorker Magazine*: p. 86, Dec. 10, 2007.

Godard, O. (Ed), *Le principe de précaution dans la conduite des affaires humaines*, Paris, MSH/INRA, 1997.

Hale, A. Method in your madness: System in your Safety, Afscheidsrede, Technische Universiteit Delft, Sept. 15., 2006.

Heimann, L. C., Repeated Failures in the Management of High Risk Technologies, *European Management Journal*, Vol. 23, N° 1, 105–117, 2005.

Institute of Medicine, *To Err is Human: Building a Safer Health System*, Washington, DC: National Academy Press, 1999.

Jaspers, J. *Nuclear Politics: Energy and the State in the United States, Sweden, and France*, Princeton, NJ: Princeton University Press, 1990.

Jaspers, J. The Political Life Cycle of Technological Controversies, *Social Forces*, 67, 357–377, 1988.

Joly, P.-B, Assouline, G., Kréziak, D., Lemarié, J., & Marris, C., L'innovation controversée: Le débat public sur les OGM en France, INRA, Grenoble (http://www.inra.fr/Internet/Direction/SED/Science-gouvernance, 2000).

Joly, P.-B., Les OGM entre la science et le public? Quatre modèles pour la gouvernance de l'innovation et des risques, *Economie Rurale* 266, 11–29, 2001.

Kahn, A., Génie génétique, agriculture et alimentation: entre peurs et savoirs, in M. Apfelbaum (ed.), *Risques et peurs alimentaires*, Paris, Odile Jacob, 57–70, 1998.

Morgaine, K., J. D. Langley, & R. O. Mc Gee, The farmsafe Programme in New Zealand : Process Evaluation of year One (2003), *Safety Science*, Vol. 44, N° 4, 359–371, 2006.

Kaplan, S., L. *The Bakers of Paris and the Bread Question, 1700–1775*, Durham: Duke University Press, 1996.

La Porte, T. R. & P. Consolini, Working in Practice But Not in Theory: Theoretical Challenges of "High-Reliability Organizations," *Journal of Public Administration Research and Theory*, 1, 19–47, 1991.

La Porte, T. R. & A. Keller, Assuring Institutional Constancy: Requisite for Managing Long-Lived Hazards, *Public Administration Review*, Vol. 56, N° 6, 535–544, 1996.

La Porte, T. R. & D. Metlay, Hazards and Institutional Trustworthiness: Facing a Deficit of Trust, *Public Administration Review*, Vol. 56, N° 4, 341–347, 1996.

La Porte, T. R., High Reliability Organizations: Unlikely, Demanding at At Risk, *Journal of Contingencies and Crisis Management*, Vol. 4, N° 2, 60–72, 1996.

La Porte, T. R. Fiabilité et Légitimité soutenable, in M. Bourrier (ed), *Organiser la fiabilité*, Paris, L'harmattan, 71–105, 2001.

Marvier, M., C. McCreedy, J. Regetz, & P. Kareiva, A Meta-Analysis of Effects of Bt Cotton and Maize on Nontarget Invertebrates, *Science*, 316, 1475, 2007.

Nichols, E. & A.Wildavsky, Nuclear Power Regulation: Seeking Safety, Doing Harm, *Regulation*, 45–53, 1987.

"Opinion of the Scientific Panel on Genetically Modified Organisms on the Post Market Environmental Monitoring (PMEM), adopted on January, the 25th, 2006," *The EFSA Journal*, N° 319, 1–27, 2006.

Perin, C., *Shouldering Risks, The Culture of Control in the Nuclear Industry*, Princeton University Press, 2005.

Perrow, C., *Normal Accidents, Leaving with High Risk Technologies*, New York, Basic Books, 1984 (2nd edition, 1999).

Pretty, J., The rapid emergence of genetic modification in world agriculture: contested risks and benefits, *Environmental Conservation*, Vol. 28, N° 3, 248–262, 2001.

Public Perceptions of Agricultural Biotechnologies in Europe, Final Report of the PABE research project (http://www.pabe.net), 2002.

Reason, J., The Chernobyl errors. *Bulletin of the British Psychological Society*, 40, 201–206, 1987.

Reason, J., *Human Error*, Cambridge University Press, 1990.

Reason, J., *Managing the Risks of Organizational Accidents*, Aldershot: Ashgate, 1997.

Rees, J. V., *Hostages of Each Other: The Transformation of Nuclear Safety Since Three Mile Island*, Chicago, IL: The University of Chicago Press, 1994.

Roberts, K., P. Madsen, & D. Van Stralen, A Case of the Birth and Death of a High Reliability Healthcare Organization, *Quality and Safety in Health Care*, Vol. 14, N° 3, 216–220, 2005.

Rochlin, G. I, The Social Construction of Safety, in J. Misumi, B. Wilpert & R. Miller (Eds.), *Nuclear Safety: A Human Factors Perspective*, London, Taylor & Francis, 5–23, 1998.

Rochlin, G. I., La Porte T. R., & K. Roberts, The Self-Designing High Reliability Organization: Aircraft Carrier Flight Operations at Sea, *Naval War College Review*, 40, 76–91, 1987.

Rochlin, G. I., Defining High Reliability Organizations in Practice: A Taxonomic Prologue, in *New Challenges to Understanding Organizations*, K. Roberts (Ed.), Macmillan, New York, 11–31, 1993.

Roy, A., *Les experts face au risque: Le cas des plantes transgéniques*, Paris, La découverte, 2001.

Schulman, P., The Negociated Order of Organizational Reliability, *Administration & Society*, 25, 353–372, 1993.

Setbon, M., *Pouvoirs contre Sida*, Paris, Seuil, 1993.

Shrivastava, P., *Bhopal: Anatomy of a Crisis*. Cambridge, MA: Ballinger, 1987.

Singer, S. J., D. M. Gaba, J. Jeffrey, A. Geppert, A. D Sinaiko, S. K. Howard, & K. C. Park, The Culture of Safety in California Hospitals, in *Quality and Safety in Health Care*, Vol. 12, N° 2, 112–118, 2003.

Singer, S. J., M. Meterko, L. Baker, D. M. Gaba, A. Falwell, & A. Rosen, Workforce Perceptions of Hospital Safety Culture: Development and Validation of the Patient Safety Climate in Healthcare Organizations Survey, *Health Research and Educational Trust, forthcoming. Health Serv Res.* October; *42(5)*: 1999–2021, 2007.

Snook, S. A, *Friendly Fire: The Accidental Shootdown of US Black Hawks over Northern Iraq*, Princeton, NJ: Princeton University Press, 2000.

Sobolevskaya, O., Food for thought: Russia joins the battle over GM products, *Organisation of Asia-Pacific News Agency*, March 7, 2007.

Starbuck, W. H. & M. Farjoun, *Organization at the Limit, Lessons from the Columbia Disaster*, Blackwell Publishing, 2005.

Thelin, A., Fatal Accidents in Swedish Farming and Forestry, 1988–1997, *Safety Science*, Vol. 40, N° 6, 501–517, 2002.

Touraine, A. et al., *La prophétie anti-nucléaire*, Paris, Seuil, 1980.

Vaughan, D., *The Challenger Launch Decision*, Chicago, IL, The University of Chicago Press, 1996.

Vincent, C. & B. de Mol (eds.), *Safety in Medicine*, Oxford, Pergamon, Elsevier, 2000.

Wynne, B., Expert discourses of risk and ethics on genetically manipulated organisms: the weaving of public alienation, *Politea*, N° 62, 51–76, 2001.

Weick, K. E., Organizational Culture as a Source of High Reliability, *California Management Review*, 2, 112–117, 1987.

Weick, K. E., & Roberts, K. H., Collective Mind in Organizations Heedful Interrelating on Flight Decks, *Administrative Science Quarterly*, Vol. 38, 357–381, 1993.

Weick, K. E., & K. Sutcliffe, *Managing the Unexpected, Assuring High Performance in an Age of Complexity*, University of Michigan Business School Management Series, Jossey-Bass, San Francisco, CA, Wiley & Sons, 2001.

Index